Harvard East Asian Studies

1. China's Early Industrialization: Sheng Hsuan-huai (1844–1916) and Mandarin Enterprise. *By Albert Feuerwerker.*

2. Intellectual Trends in the Ch'ing Period. *By Liang Ch'i-ch'ao. Translation by Immanuel C. Y. Hsü.*

3. Reform in Sung China: Wang An-shih (1021–1086) and his New Policies. *By James T. C. Liu.*

4. Studies on the Population of China, 1368–1953. *By Ping-ti Ho.*

5. China's Entrance into the Family of Nations: The Diplomatic Phase, 1858–1880. *By Immanuel C. Y. Hsü.*

HARVARD EAST ASIAN STUDIES 5

The Center for East Asian Studies at Harvard University administers postgraduate training programs and research projects designed to further scholarly understanding of China, Korea, Japan and adjacent areas.

CHINA'S ENTRANCE INTO THE FAMILY OF NATIONS

THE DIPLOMATIC PHASE, 1858–1880

CHINA'S ENTRANCE

INTO THE

FAMILY OF NATIONS

THE DIPLOMATIC PHASE
1858–1880

Immanuel C. Y. Hsü

Foreword by
William L. Langer

HARVARD UNIVERSITY PRESS

Cambridge, Massachusetts

1 9 6 0

© Copyright 1960 by the President and Fellows of Harvard College

Distributed in Great Britain by Oxford University Press, London

This volume was prepared in part under a grant from the Carnegie Corporation of New York. That Corporation is not, however, the author, owner, publisher, or proprietor of this publication and is not to be understood as approving by virtue of its grant any of the statements made or views expressed therein.

Publication of this book has been aided by a grant from the Ford Foundation.

Library of Congress Catalog Card Number 60–5738

Printed in the United States of America

TO
MY PARENTS

Foreword

The study of diplomatic history has been much deepened in the course of the past generation. In the days of the "new history" it was both attacked and ridiculed as shallow, not to say insignificant. To the extent that much writing of diplomatic history at that time consisted of little more than the digest or at most the analysis of official correspondence, the charges leveled against it were certainly justified. But in recent years much more attention has been given not only to the forces influencing foreign policy and the mechanisms by which international relations are conducted under various forms of government, but also to the particular conditions — strategic, economic, cultural — underlying the problems with which diplomacy was obliged, in any particular instance, to concern itself. The best current writing in this field cuts so deeply into sociological and psychological factors as to leave the official diplomatic correspondence merely the expression of the forces inherent in any specific issue, which is as it should be.

At the same time, diplomatic history has vastly expanded its field of interest. Originally it dealt almost exclusively with the relationships of the European states with each other, with rather slighting reference to colonial disputes and imperialist rivalries as they bore on the basic European alignments. Although the Ottoman Empire had, in 1856, been officially admitted to the "family of nations," it continued for a long period to be an object of European policies. It was really only at about the dawn of the present century that the United States and Japan began to play a continuing and important role as great powers, as conclusively demonstrated in the course of the first world war. Thereafter the area of international affairs has expanded at an almost dizzying pace, till now we live in a world of sovereign states. It has long since become impossible to deal with international affairs as though they were the concern merely of a few "great powers." We must now take into account not only the huge combinations of the western and communist blocs, but also the vast uncommitted areas of the Middle East, Africa, and Asia.

This deepening and broadening of the scope of diplomatic history has inevitably increased the difficulties of working in the field. The student has had to devote himself to the problems of areas and cultures far different from his own and has had to secure a competence in languages and disciplines which formerly lay outside the area of diplomacy. There is, obviously, a limit to what any one scholar may hope to achieve along these lines. He finds himself increasingly dependent on the work of others — specialists in one subject or another relevant to the field of his study. Indeed, the requirements are so varied that, for the most part, scholars are now obliged to limit themselves to areas and problems for which they either have or may hope to achieve a sufficient equipment.

The problems are naturally greatest in the case of countries or areas of old and well-established cultures, which themselves have had effective governmental systems and extensive records. The Ottoman Empire is a case in point, and the Chinese Empire another. Both conducted their affairs with the outside world according to certain concepts and principles, and both kept elaborate documentary records. In the case of the Turks, however, these materials were kept altogether secret. The Ottoman archives have only recently been opened, and consequently work on the Turkish side of the so-called "Eastern Question" has only just begun. The Chinese, on the other hand, have published many of their records *in extenso*, in one form or another, and it has been chiefly the formidable language problem that has kept scholars from tapping these rich sources. Now that Chinese students have, in increasing numbers, received training in western methods of historical research, they have come to grips with this problem. They have already published a number of valuable monographs dealing with Far Eastern diplomatic issues in the light of the Chinese or Japanese materials as well as of the western records, and I am sure that we can look forward with confidence to the early rectification of what heretofore has been a serious imbalance.

Dr. Hsü's present volume is a particularly welcome contribution, for he has concerned himself with a period of some twenty years during which the Chinese government was more or less forced to abandon its traditional isolation and accept membership in the society of equal states. The British played the leading role in bringing about this revolutionary change. Dr. Hsü provides a succinct account of the gunboat diplomacy of Lord Elgin and on occasion adverts to the differing attitudes of the British government, of British officials in China, and of the old China hands. But his chief concern is with the Chinese side — the traditional Chinese methods of dealing with the "barbarians," the Chinese conception of the universal character of the Middle Kingdom, the hatred and distrust of the "foreign devils," the resentment at the disturbance of the accepted attitudes and the great reluctance to accept the need for change and adjustment. Exploiting the Chinese sources to the full, he has provided a vivid and fascinating picture of the internal conflicts within Chinese society, the opposition of the traditionalists and those who recognized that there was no hope for the future except by adjusting to the new conditions, however repulsive they might be. His analysis of the last-ditch opposition to the establishment of foreign legations in Peking and the utter unwillingness of the Chinese to send diplomatic representatives abroad will give the reader an entirely new conception of the deeper factors in the Far Eastern situation in the late nineteenth century, and will help to explain the easy acceptance by the Chinese of extraterritoriality, customs control, and kindred arrangements which later were to create such serious tensions. Dr. Hsü's work is in every way exemplary and constitutes a splendid addition to the literature of international relations.

WILLIAM L. LANGER
August 12, 1959   Coolidge Professor of History
Harvard University

ACKNOWLEDGMENTS

I am extremely grateful to Professor William L. Langer for his kindness in writing the Foreword. My deep thanks also go to Professor John King Fairbank for commenting on and improving the whole manuscript and to Professors Lien-sheng Yang and Benjamin I. Schwartz for reading parts of it. Professor Banno Masataka of Tokyo Metropolitan University benefited me with his insight into modern Chinese history during his sojourn at Harvard in 1956–57. Professors Joseph R. Levenson and Armin Rappaport of the University of California at Berkeley made a number of suggestions which materially improved my manuscript. I am also indebted to Mrs. Elizabeth Matheson for numerous editorial and stylistic improvements. Thanks are due Mrs. Susan Parsons Cramer and Mrs. Nien-ling Leung for typing the manuscript.

Immanuel C. Y. Hsü

Harvard University
June, 1959

CONTENTS

Foreword by William L. Langer   ix

1. *Prologue: The Meeting of the Western and Eastern*
   Families of Nations   3
   a. *The East Asian Family of Nations*   3
   b. *The Universal Chinese State and Its Relation with the Barbarians* 6
   c. *Chinese Institutions of "Foreign" Intercourse*   13
   d. *The Issue of Diplomatic Representation*   16

PART I. THE ESTABLISHMENT OF FOREIGN LEGATIONS IN CHINA, 1858–1861

2. *The Resident Minister Issue: The Diplomatic Prelude*   21
   a. *The Western Aims in 1858*   24
   b. *Difficulties Preceding the Tientsin Negotiations*   31

3. *The Tientsin Negotiations*   46
   a. *Elgin and Lay vs. Kuei-liang and Hua-sha-na*   50
   b. *Court Politics*   55

4. *The Shanghai Tariff Conference*   71
   a. *The Secret Plan*   71
   b. *Kuei-liang Resumes Negotiations*   75
   c. *The New Imperial Commissioner in Shanghai*   79

5. *Personality and Diplomacy: A Study in Leadership*   83

6. *The Resident Minister Issue after Taku*   92
   a. *The British Response*   94
   b. *Elgin's Second Mission*   98
   c. *The Legations and the Tsungli Yamen*   105

7. *The Ideological Issue: Diplomatic Representation vs. T'i-chih* 109

PART II. THE INTRODUCTION OF INTERNATIONAL LAW, 1862–1874

8. *The Translation of International Law into Chinese*   121
   a. *Lin Tse-hsü's Attempt to Translate Vattel*   123
   b. *Martin's Translation of Wheaton*   125
   c. *A Textual Criticism of Martin's Translation*   129

9. *Success and Failure: China's Limited Application of International Law*   132

    a. *Reactions to Martin's Translation*   132
    b. *The Failure to Make Positive Use of International Law*   138

PART III. THE ESTABLISHMENT OF PERMANENT CHINESE LEGATIONS ABROAD

10. *Early Approaches to the Problem*   149

    a. *China's Traditional View of Foreign Missions*   150
    b. *Early British Proposals, 1858–1866*   152
    c. *The Court's Response*   158

11. *The Envoy Question as a National Issue, 1867–1876*   163

    a. *Treaty Revision, 1867–1868*   163
    b. *The First Missions to the West, 1868–1870*   167
    c. *The Japanese Treaty of 1871 and the Formosa Incident of 1874*   172
    d. *The Margary Incident, 1875–1876*   176

12. *Legations Abroad as Permanent Institutions*   180

    a. *The Apology Mission and the First Legation, 1876–1877*   181
    b. *Other Legations, 1875–1880*   185
    c. *The Plight of Kuo Sung-t'ao*   186
    d. *Organization and Finance*   190

13. *Epilogue: The Imperial Chinese Tradition in the Modern World*   199

    a. *The Ideological Opposition to Legations Abroad*   199
    b. *Tradition within Change: China among the Nations*   206

Appendix A: Major Foreign Diplomatic Representatives in China during the Nineteenth Century   212

Appendix B: Chinese Diplomatic Representatives in Major Foreign Countries during the Nineteenth Century   216

Appendix C: Funds Supplied to Chinese Legations in Major Foreign Countries   218

Appendix D: Expenditures of Chinese Legations in Major Foreign Countries   219

Notes   223

Index   249

REFERENCE MATTER

Bibliography   i
Glossary   xxxiii

CHINA'S ENTRANCE INTO THE FAMILY OF NATIONS

THE DIPLOMATIC PHASE
1858–1880

CHAPTER 1

Prologue: The Meeting of the Western and Eastern Families of Nations

The term "family of nations" is a figurative description of the community of states in the world. While it is now almost identical in scope with the whole of international society, it originally applied only to a group of Western European Christian states which were signatories to the Treaty of Westphalia in 1648. Characteristic of this family of nations has been its continual expansion from Western Europe; notable early examples of this process were the inclusion of the Muscovite Empire of Russia in 1721 and of the United States in 1783. The nineteenth century saw its intrusion into non-Christian areas of the world with the admission of Turkey into this fellowship by express sanction of the Treaty of Paris in 1856. When the Western family of nations reached into the Far Eastern world, it found itself confronting another family of nations under the leadership of China. Clashes arose between these two mutually exclusive systems and in the end the advancing Western one eclipsed the other. It is within this conceptual framework that the present study is undertaken.

a. The East Asian Family of Nations

Relations between the states in the Far East were much like those between members of a family, far more so than the relations between the Western nations. It is literally correct to describe them as constituting their own family of nations in East Asia. China, as the Middle Kingdom, took the position of family head, and the smaller states on her periphery — Korea, Annam, Siam, Burma, and Japan for a time — assumed the position of junior members, paying homage to her in the form of periodic tribute. This was an extension to the interstate level of the Confucian idea of the proper relation between individuals. Just as every person in a Confucian society had an assigned status as the basis of his relations with others, so the state in an "international" society must have a properly defined status. By virtue of her cultural, political, economic and military preeminence, China unhesitatingly assumed the role of family head, while others acknowledged her leadership by willingly accepting their junior status as tribute-paying members. In Korean records, relations with China were described as *sadae*, or serving the senior, whereas those with Japan were known as *kyorin*, or relations with a neighbor.[1] This distinction illustrates well the basic spirit of the East Asian family of nations.

Tributary relations involved both rights and duties. China had the responsibility of maintaining proper order in this family. She recognized the junior members by sending special emissaries to officiate at the investiture of new tributary kings and to confer on them the imperial patent of appointment. China also went to their aid in time of trouble; one of the causes for the downfall of the Ming dynasty was said to be its extensive military aid to Korea in her defense against the Japanese invasion under Hideyoshi at the end of the sixteenth century. Relief missions from China, with messages of sympathy and commiseration from the emperor, were often sent to the tributary states in the wake of such natural calamities as famines, floods, droughts, and typhoons.

Tributary states, as junior members of the family, accepted China's calendar as theirs and paid homage to the head by sending periodic *ad hoc* tribute-bearers to Peking via an assigned route under Chinese escort. The closer the relation between the tributary state and China, the more frequent the tribute. In the Ch'ing period, Korea paid tribute four times a year, presented all at once at the end of each year. Liu-ch'iu and Annam paid tribute every two years, Siam every three years, and Burma every ten years.[2] The size of each tributary mission was fixed by the Chinese, who also underwrote all the expenses of the mission while in China. The tributary envoy was lodged in the official hostel in the Chinese capital and presented his credentials *(piao)* and tribute to the emperor through the Board of Ceremonies. A felicitous day was then selected for the Son of Heaven to receive him and, in the full assemblage of the Chinese court, the envoy performed the celebrated three kneelings and nine knockings of the head on the ground — the *kowtow*. In return, the emperor showed his appreciation of the homage and his benevolence toward men from afar by bestowing on the envoy, his suite, and the tributary king liberal gifts, which usually far exceeded the tribute in value. Following the audience, the tributary mission was allowed to open a market at the hostel for three to five days to sell the local products of its country, which had been brought in tax-free. The mission was then feted several times by the Board of Ceremonies before departing from Peking over the same assigned route and under the same escort until it left Chinese territory. This system of "international relations" was known as the tributary system; its basis was not the recognition of equality among sovereign states as in the West, but a father-son or senior-junior relationship. In contrast with the relations between Western imperialist nations and their colonies, the tributary relations were primarily ceremonial and ritualistic, rather than exploitative.[3] Economically, the tributary practice was a loss to China, yet its prestige value could not be overlooked. The Chinese emperor may be said to have been not so much an "economic man" as a "political animal" in the Aristotelian sense.

It was this system that the Western family of nations encountered when it intruded into the Far East in the early and middle nineteenth century. Conflict arose when neither the Western nor the Eastern system could accommodate the other without radical sacrifice. The Western nations could not accept the Chinese tributary system without sacrificing valued principles of state sovereignty and diplomatic intercourse based on international law. The Chinese empire could not accept the Western idea of equality of states without changing radically its traditional thinking and the age-old institutions of "foreign" relations as recorded in the *Collected Statutes of the Great Ch'ing Empire*.[4] Hence the arrival of each Western mission in China invariably marked an occasion for quarrel because the Chinese insisted that such missions be treated as tributary missions. Unsupported by military forces and anxious to achieve trade benefits, early Western envoys usually yielded grudgingly to the Chinese practice. Of the seventeen missions between 1655 and 1795 — six from Russia, four from Portugal, three from Holland, three from the Papacy, and one from Britain — all but the last, under Lord Macartney, performed the *kowtow*.[5] It was not until after the Napoleonic Wars that Western nations, notably Britain, with vastly increased surplus energies resulting from the Industrial Revolution, resolved to alter this situation by force.

Needless to say, the Chinese attitude on "foreign" affairs was the product of traditions and a political philosophy that had been in effect since time immemorial. It is therefore imperative to study the nature of the Chinese state and the traditional Chinese views on and approaches to "foreign" affairs, in order to understand the seemingly strange mentality and baffling behavior of Ch'ing officials in their dealings with the West.

b. *The Universal Chinese State and Its Relations with the Barbarians*

The unique political philosophy of the Chinese considered the ultimate objective of government to be the setting in order of the whole known world, rather than the state. The emperor claimed to be the Son of Heaven, who ruled supreme over all mankind with the Mandate of Heaven. The *Book of Odes* expressed this sentiment in the following words: "Under the wide heaven, there is no land that is not the Emperor's, and within the sea-boundaries of the land, there is none who is not a subject of the Emperor." [6] The emperor's ministers considered world statesmanship *(p'ing t'ien-hsia)* their highest objective, and *The Great Learning* held that only by first rectifying his mind, cultivating his person, regulating his family, and governing his state could a man reach the goal of setting the world in order. Confucius envisaged a "Universal Commonwealth" *(Ta-t'ung)* as the ultimate stage of human development.

The world as known to the Chinese in earliest times was the Yellow River valley in what is now North China. By the time of the Chou dynasty (1122 B.C.–255 B.C.) it had expanded southward to include the Yangtze River area. The Ch'in unification (221 B.C.) and the subsequent expansions in the Han (206 B.C.–220 A.D.) and T'ang (618 A.D.–907 A.D.) periods virtually pushed the Chinese frontiers to the edge of the Far East, and China became in fact a world in itself, with a group of tributary states clustered on its borders.[7]

Since the emperor claimed to rule over all under heaven, his domain naturally included the barbarian tribes, whose existence was early recognized in ancient records. The test of barbarity was not so much race or religion or national origin as it was cultural achievement; this suggests the Greek standard of regarding a foreign tongue as a sign of barbarity. He was barbarian who did not accept Chinese civilization and who knew not the refinement of ceremony, music, and culture. In their utter ignorance of the beauty of the Chinese way of life and in their lack of sufficient intellect to appreciate reason and ethics, the barbarians were considered no different from the lower animals. Nothing expresses these sentiments so well as the ideographic Chinese characters used to designate the barbarians. The designation for southern barbarians, *Man*, is written with an "insect" *(ch'ung)* radical, and that for the northern barbarians, *Ti*, is written with a "dog" *(ch'üan)* radical. Ch'iang, a Western tribe, is written with the "sheep" *(yang)* radical. Not only the Chinese language, but the Chinese people in their attitude toward the barbarians, often compared them to animals. Pan Ku, author of the *History of Han*, described the Huns *(Hsiung-nu)* in the following terms: "The Sage-King [of China] treated them as animals, not entering into oaths with them or fighting or chastising them. Their land cannot be used for the cultivation of food, and their people cannot be treated as subjects." [8] Su Shih, a famous poet and statesman of the Sung, made a statement which has since become famous: "The barbarians cannot be governed in the same way as China is governed. That is to say, to seek good government among animals will inevitably lead to great confusion." [9] The Ch'ing officials, therefore, did not lack historical foundation when they described Western barbarians as having the disposition of "dogs and sheep."

Barbarians, in a strict sense, were not foreigners, for they were not outside the domain of the universal Chinese empire. They were but "uncivilized and outlandish" peoples awaiting assimilation into the Chinese orbit through a cultural transformation. It was indeed the duty of the emperor, as mediator between Heaven and Man, to effect such a transformation and confer the boon of civilization upon those who had unfortunately been born barbarian. The *Book of History* is replete with advice to the emperor on the importance of winning the hearts of the barbarians through a virtuous rule. The "Canon of Shun" in the Book of Yu states:

Be kind to the distant, and cultivate the ability of the near. Give honor to the virtuous and your confidence to the good, while you discountenance the artful: — so shall the barbarous tribes lead on one another to make their submission. [10]

"The Counsels of the Great Yü" enjoins:

Do not fail in due attention to the laws and ordinances. . . . Do not oppose the people to follow your own desires. Attend to these things without idleness or omission, and from the four quarters the barbarous tribes will come and acknowledge your sovereignty.[11]

Furthermore, the "Hounds of Leu [Lu]" of the Book of Chou observes that:

The intelligent kings have paid careful attention to their virtues, and the wild tribes on every side have willingly acknowledged subjection to them. The nearer and the more remote have all made offerings of the productions of their countries.[12]

From these quotations one gathers the inevitable impression that the wise emperor was one who won the admiration of barbarians by his irresistible virtue, and in return the barbarians expressed their gratitude by offering their local products to the Son of Heaven. Herein lay the basic spirit of the tributary system.

Since the test of barbarity was primarily one of cultural standards, barbarians could become Chinese when they advanced to the Chinese level of civilization and conformed to the higher Chinese standards of living. Conversely, the Chinese became barbarians when they debased themselves through uncivil practices. In other words, elevated barbarians could be superior to debased Chinese.[13] Confucius once said: "The rude tribes of the East and North have their princes, and are not like the states of our great land which are without them." [14]

However, if the barbarians refused to accept the benefits of civilization and continued to disturb China, then, and only then, a policy of chastisement must be followed. The *Book of Odes* states: "Our prince's chariots are a thousand . . . . His footmen are thirty thousand . . . . to deal with the tribes of the West and North, and to punish [those of] King and Shoo [Ching and Shu] so that none of them will dare to withstand us." [15]

It is these ideas and admonitions in the classical canons, which every scholar-statesman studied, that became in time the cornerstone of Chinese policy toward outlandish peoples. The basic tenet of such a policy was that the Chinese emperor should be virtuous and benevolent so that the barbarians, through spontaneous admiration, might voluntarily seek assimilation. It was not an active and aggressive policy of going out to convert the outlandish tribes, but rather a passive, "laissez-faire" policy of expecting them to come to obtain transformation of their own accord.

Exceptions, of course, may be found in especially ambitious emperors or powerful ministers. For instance, Chang Ch'ien and Pan Ch'ao of the Han period were sent by Emperor Wu in 138 B.C. and Emperor Ming in 73 A.D., respectively, to the Western Region, which included the Indoscythians in Central Asia, and the Hsiung-nu and Scythians in Eastern Turkestan. Through their efforts these areas came under Chinese control or influence. There was also the case of the powerful Ming eunuch Cheng Ho, who led a large fleet to the South Seas seven times between 1405 and 1430, bringing Cambodia, Siam, Java, Burma, and other countries into the Chinese tributary system. But these were exceptions to the general Chinese approach to the outside tribes. By and large, the Chinese believed that if the barbarians did not aspire to a higher life, there was no need to force them to do so. The fundamental spirit of the traditional approach to the barbarian problem, therefore, was nongoverning and nonintervening. As Ho Hsiu (129–182 A.D.), the great Han scholar of the Modern Text school of classical learning, expressed it: "The Emperor does not govern the barbarians. Those who come will not be rejected, and those who leave will not be pursued." [16] The lack of a tradition of positive policy toward the barbarians predisposed China to a state of unpreparedness in case of emergency, new challenge, or new trouble. This may have been one of the basic causes of China's unreadiness to meet the new Western "barbarians" in the nineteenth century.

A corollary of the philosophy of nonintervention was the doctrine of nonexploitation of the barbarians. The Confucianists advocated China's not wearing herself out in endless warfare with the outer tribes, but winning their submission through a benevolent concern for their welfare. During the reign of Emperor Hsüan-tsung (73–49 B.C.) of the Han dynasty, disorder arose in the Hsiung-nu (Huns) tribe. The emperor, tempted to exploit the situation to China's favor, was advised by his minister Hsiao Wang-chih to avoid such opportunistic inclinations and instead to send a mission of commiseration to the Huns tendering his sympathy, so that the barbarians might be moved to gratitude and so to transformation.[17]

On the other hand, barbarians, not being Chinese until assimilation was complete, were watched with vigilance. Meticulous care was taken to prevent their infiltration into the heartland of China and their mixing with the Chinese populace, acts which threatened to adulterate the established way of life.[18] The great Sung states- man and poet Su Shih emphatically pointed out that one of Con- fucius' purposes in writing the *Spring and Autumn Annals* was to guard against the mixing of barbarians and Chinese. This policy of separate existence stemmed from the fear that barbarians residing in China would breed mischief and intrigue, or learn the ingenious methods of the Chinese whereby they might make trouble with China when they returned home. Thus Empress Wu (reign: 684– 704 A.D.) of the T'ang was advised by her ministers against letting barbarian tributary envoys tarry long in the Chinese capital or allow- ing barbarian princes to serve in the Chinese court.[19] During the Yung-lo (1403–1424) and Hsüan-te (1426–1435) periods of the Ming, Li Hsien, a secretary of the Board of Civil Office, expressed alarm at the increasing migration into the capital area of Tartars, toward whom the court was kindly disposed. He urged the court to expel them, on the ground that treatment of men must be based on degrees of intimacy:

I have heard the Way of the Kings is [to treat Chinese] people as in- fants, and barbarians as animals. To treat people as infants means to endear them; to treat barbarians as animals means to keep them distant. While the sages looked upon all with equal benevolence, their favor nevertheless started from the near [and proceeded] to the far. There should not be anything like giving favor to the animals before giving the infants their just share. Furthermore, could the sages bear to feed animals with the food of the infants? [20]

The mistrust with which the barbarians were viewed crystallized into a policy of segregation and of constant watchfulness and pre- caution when they had to be admitted into China. Thus the tribu- tary envoys were escorted by Chinese guards over an assigned route to and from Peking and were not allowed to purchase Chinese guns or books while in the capital, lest they make trouble or become too wise. They were not allowed to roam about freely in the streets with- out first securing permission from the proper Chinese authority, who would then specially guard the streets they were to pass through. Westerners who came to China for trade were carefully quarantined in Macao and in the thirteen factories outside the city of Canton.

Certainly at the bottom of all these precautions was the traditional policy of segregation, which also explains the unusually strong Chinese opposition to the Western demands for diplomatic residence in Peking and free travel in the interior.

The policy of benevolent nonintervention and its corollary, the policy of dissociation, were possible only when China was strong enough to maintain its control over the barbarians. When the barbarians became too powerful and could no longer be controlled, China had to devise new methods to deal with them. Such methods often took the form of appeasement, through the creation of some new personal relationship between the emperor and the chieftain of the trouble-making barbarian tribe, by marriage or some other form of personal diplomacy. For instance, when the Han Emperor Kao-tsu (reign years: 206–193 B.C.) lost the battle to the Huns at Pai-teng, he adopted the suggestion of a minister, Liu Ching, that peace be bought at the price of marrying a Chinese princess to the chieftain of the Huns. The future chieftains of the Huns would thus be his grandson and great grandson and hence less likely to be rebellious. This policy of diplomacy by marriage placed the Huns on a more or less equal footing with China. Emperor Wu of the Han dynasty made an even more deft use of the marriage policy by marrying a Chinese princess to the chieftain of the Wu-sun tribe, who were enemies of the Huns, thereby effecting an alliance against the Huns. The celebrated policy of using one barbarian to check another barbarian *(i-i chih-i)* was born.[21]

A more remarkable example of equal and "personal" relationship existed between the Sung dynasty and the Liao nation. After twenty-five years of futile warfare with the Liao, the Sung Emperor Chen-tsung (reign years: 993–1022) made an agreement with the Liao king at Shan-yüan (in modern Hopei Province) by which he consented to treat the Liao Empress Dowager as "an aunt," and the Liao king agreed to treat the Sung Emperor as an "elder brother." The Sung was also to subsidize the Liao with 100,000 taels and 200,000 rolls of silk annually. For 160 years *ad hoc* envoys were exchanged between the two on an equal footing on such occasions as New Year's Day, royal birthdays and deaths, and the ascension to the throne of new emperors and kings. The functions of the envoys were primarily ceremonial and ritualistic, rather than diplomatic, and they all performed the *kowtow* before their accredited rulers.[22]

The policy of diplomacy by marriage in the Han dynasty, and the brotherly relations between the Sung and the Liao reflected the Confucian emphasis on the importance of human relations in solving problems. Such precedents throw light on the diplomatic behavior of Ch'i-ying, the famous barbarian manager in the 1840's. His eagerness to befriend Sir Henry Pottinger and his insistence on adopting the latter's son as his godson, if viewed in a historic light, were but latter-day variations of the traditional "personal diplomacy" with the barbarians.

In passing, mention must also be made of the interstate intercourse in the Warring States period of the late Chou dynasty. Numerous *ad hoc* envoys were exchanged between the states, the most famous being Su Ch'in and Chang I. The relations here were not strictly "diplomatic," however, for theoretically all these "states" were feudal principalities still under the nominal rule of the Chou emperor. Because of the decline of the Chou power, they had become independent states in all but theory. Since such interstate intercourse was conducted among the Chinese themselves within the universal empire, rather than between the Chinese and the outlandish barbarian tribes, it is beyond the scope of this study.

Cursory as is the above account, it nevertheless indicates some of the stereotyped Chinese thinking and practices vis-à-vis the barbarians. It is from this heritage that Ch'ing officials of the nineteenth century drew their guidance and inspiration in dealing with the advancing Western states. Needless to say, the lack of a traditional positive approach to the barbarian problem predisposed the Ch'ing government to a state of unpreparedness in meeting the new challenge. The Ch'ing officials' description of foreigners as unreasonable, fickle, unfathomable, and violent, like dogs and sheep, and their stubborn resistance to foreigners' mixing with the Chinese through diplomatic residence in the capital and trade and travel in the interior, all manifested the influence of the past. Yet the past was a poor guide, for the industrial West was as different from the traditional ephemeral barbarian tribes as day is from night. China blundered time and again in her foreign transactions largely because she had no better sources to draw guidance from. Knowledge of history had not been flexibly used to China's advantage; in fact it had limited her response.

c. *Chinese Institutions of "Foreign" Intercourse*

The existence of a foreign office in a state presupposes an awareness of the necessity for relations with other more or less equal states. Such an awareness was lacking in the universal Chinese state, where there was recognition only of barbarian, and not foreign, affairs. Hence a foreign office did not exist. Parallel to the absence of a foreign office was the absence of any national sentiment; there was no national flag in Imperial China; there were only dynastic or royal banners. It is amusingly reported that before the Opium War in 1839 the British Superintendent of Trade in China, Charles Elliot, urged the Viceroy of Canton, Teng T'ing-tseng, to settle the differences between the "two nations" peacefully. Teng is said to have been puzzled by the term "two nations," which he mistook for England and the United States.[23] A bold sinologist has asserted that China of old was not so much a state as a cultural entity.[24] Doubtless, Imperial China was not a nation-state.[25]

The absence of a foreign office, however, need not imply the absence of institutions and officials in charge of "foreign" affairs. During the Warring States period in Ancient China, the feudal principalities of the Chou dynasty appointed Directors of State Ceremonies and Emissary Affairs (*Ta-hsing-jen, Hsiao-hsing-jen*) to take charge of the reception of envoys from other princely kingdoms. The Ch'in unification saw the creation of the Commissioner of Guests, known as *Tien-k'o*, which office later metamorphosed into the Court of State Ceremonial *(Ta-hung-lu)* under the Han Emperor Wu. The Commissioner of Guests was assisted by an interpreter and reception-secretary known as *I-kuan lin-ch'en*, the forefather of the *Hui-t'ung-kuan* (Common Residence for Envoys) of the Yüan and Ming periods. The Ming dynasty created in addition the *Ssu-i-kuan*, or Residence for Barbarian Envoys, under the Court of Sacrificial Worship.

The early Ch'ing emperors, having inherited the *Hui-t'ung-kuan* and *Ssu-i-kuan* from the Ming, placed the former under the Hanlin Academy to take charge of receptions, and the latter under the Board of Ceremonies to specialize in translation. In 1748 the Emperor Ch'ien-lung combined these two *kuan* into a single organization known as *Hui-t'ung ssu-i kuan*, or Common Residence for Tributary Envoys, superintended by a senior secretary of the Board of Ceremonies. The main functions of this combined organization were reception and lodging of tributary envoys, while leaving matters of ceremony to the Court of State Ceremonial (*Hung-lu Ssu*). There was, in addition, a third organ, the *Li-fan-yüan*, or Court of Colonial Affairs, in charge of Mongolian, Mohammedan, and Russian affairs. Presumably Russia was included because it was an Asiatic state bordering on Mongolia and had trade relations with Mongolia and Manchuria.[26]

Sino-Russian relations rested on a somewhat peculiar ground. China's first equal treaty with a foreign power, the Treaty of Nerchinsk, was signed with Russia in 1689, and after the Treaty of Kiakhta of 1727 the Russians were allowed to maintain a religious mission in Peking, with a language school attached to it. On the other hand, Russian envoys to China accepted the tributary practices and performed the *kowtow* to the Son of Heaven, while the Chinese envoys to Russia in 1729 and 1731 also performed the *kowtow* to the Russian ruler. The relations were thus more or less equal, although on the Chinese side it was the Court of Colonial Affairs that was responsible for the conduct of relations with Russia.

Western maritime nations actually did not fit into the Chinese pattern of "foreign" relations. They were neither regular tributary states, nor like Russia located in Asia, with an overland border trade relationship. But the Ch'ing dynasty insisted that if Western nations came to China on their own, they must come as tributaries. The various editions of the *Collected Statutes* from K'ang-hsi (1662–1722) to Chia-ch'ing (1796–1820) proudly listed Western nations alongside other regular tributaries, with an explanatory note that these Western nations were too distant from China to fix definite tribute periods. The Chinese were remarkably successful in inducing the Westerners to accept the Chinese practice when they did come to China. As has already been noted, of the seventeen early Western missions to China from 1655 to 1795, sixteen yielded to the Chinese demand for the *kowtow*. While the Ch'ing court was uncompromising in its relations with Western officials, it was far less adamant with private Western traders, who were allowed to reside in Macao and Canton as a special imperial favor toward men from afar, in contravention of the tributary system, which allowed no tributary personnel to dwell permanently in China. But they were allowed no direct communication with Chinese officials; they could only "petition" through the Chinese monopolistic merchants and the Customs Superintendent, known as the Hoppo.

The Ch'ing government appears early to have realized the importance of Western barbarian affairs. They were reported directly to the court in great detail by local officials and received careful examination by the emperor in conjunction with members of the all-important Grand Council. A brilliant and resourceful emperor was practically his own "foreign" minister. For instance, Emperor K'ang-hsi, in sending T'u-li-shen on a special mission to the Turgut khan, Ayuki, in southern Russia, in 1712, personally gave such detailed instructions that he practically told his envoy: "Should they ask you such and such a question, you should answer in such and such a way. . . . " [27] A less resourceful emperor was more likely to follow the advice of his Grand Councillors. Emperor Tao-kuang accepted the Treaty of Nanking and supported Ch'i-ying's conciliatory policy in the 1840's largely on the recommendation of the powerful councillor, Mu-chang-a.

When the barbarian problem grew to unusual proportions in a province, the emperor's confidence in the ability of the local officials to manage it was sometimes diminished, and he would appoint a specially deputed Imperial Commissioner to investigate the situation. In 1838 Lin Tse-hsü, viceroy of Hu-Kuang, was dispatched to Canton as imperial commissioner specifically to investigate the opium problem. This novel practice of appointing an imperial commissioner to take charge of barbarian affairs continued after the Opium War and became part of the institutions of "foreign" intercourse. During the Opium War, viceroys and governors in coastal provinces were authorized to receive foreign communications, and the old practice of limiting such authority to the viceroy of Canton was ended. Ch'i-shan, viceroy of Chihli, could thus receive and negotiate with Captain Elliot. In 1844 Ch'i-ying, signer of China's first treaties with the West, was appointed viceroy of Canton and imperial commissioner in charge of trade in the ports and of other affairs relative to foreign nations. Since the imperial commissioner had his office in the yamen of the viceroy of Canton and deposited his files there, the Canton viceroyalty became a modified foreign office in all but name during the Opium War-Arrow War period of 1842–1856. This was a makeshift arrangement in deference to the new demands of the time. Viewed historically and institutionally, it was an intermediary development in the transition from the tributary system to the creation of a more modern foreign service. The device of using Canton as China's center for foreign affairs is known as the Canton Viceroy System.[28]

This system worked rather well in the years immediately after the Opium War when Ch'i-ying was the imperial commissioner. But foreigners became increasingly discontented over the fact that Peking was still inaccessible. Neither foreign diplomats nor private individuals were allowed to go to the Chinese capital, and their representations were either sidetracked or sent back to the viceroy of Canton. Foreigners entertained misgivings that the Chinese had no intention of fulfilling Article Eleven of the Treaty of Nanking, which authorized foreign diplomats to have direct correspondence, on an equal footing, with high Chinese officials in the capital.

The conviction grew that Peking was using the Canton viceroy as a breakwater to keep foreigners from direct contact with the court and that the Canton system was a subtle device to slight the Westerners. This the Westerners could not endure. They were convinced that the diplomatic opening of China must be the logical consequence of the commercial opening that had been brought about by the Opium War and the Treaty of Nanking.

d. *The Issue of Diplomatic Representation*

From what has been said above, it is not surprising that diplomatic representation, a common practice among Western states since the Renaissance, was unknown in the East Asian family of nations. No resident envoys were ever exchanged between China and her tributaries. Even in her dealings with Western nations since the late Ming, China had received only temporary emissaries, like Thome Pires from Portugal in 1517 and Ivashko Pettlin from Russia in 1618. Of the handful of Europeans allowed to reside in Peking, none enjoyed diplomatic status. The Jesuit fathers serving in the court as astronomers, and the Russian language students attached to the religious mission were required to wear Chinese attire. In fact, as "transformed barbarians" and members of the Chinese bureaucracy, the Jesuits were not allowed to leave the country. The lack of a precedent for resident ministers in China and the absence of the concept of modern diplomacy predisposed the mandarins of the eighteenth and nineteenth centuries to antipathy to any foreign demand for diplomatic accreditation.

Western nations, on the other hand, had tried ceaselessly to gain access to the Chinese court. The eastward expansion of the Russian empire since Peter the Great in its search for a "window," and the Industrial Revolution in the West since the eighteenth century had brought Russia and Western Europe much closer to China and had made greater contact with the Middle Kingdom a foregone conclusions. The Russians developed border trade with China in Manchuria and Mongolia, and the Western nations maintained maritime trade with her in Macao and Canton. From increased contact arose the Western desire to regularize relations with China through the establishment of formal diplomatic missions. As early as 1727, during the negotiations of the Treaty of Kiakhta, the Russians had tried to secure the right of consulate in Peking, but had succeeded only in obtaining permission to establish a religious mission. Three decades later, in 1759, interpreter James Flint of the British East India Company tried to go to Peking to present the company's grievances directly to the emperor. He reached Tientsin, where his representation was received by the local *taotai* and transmitted to the court. This abortive private attempt was followed years later by an official British demand for diplomatic representation in 1793, when Lord Macartney was sent to China. Emperor Ch'ien-lung rejected the request on the ground that it was incompatible with all Chinese usages and institutions of foreign intercourse. After this failure the British government took no new steps until 1816, when peace was restored in Europe after the Napoleonic Wars and Lord Amherst was sent to China to renew requests for trade expansion and diplomatic representation. His refusal to *kowtow* before the Chinese emperor doomed the project from the start, and nothing came of his mission. Undaunted by this fiasco, the British traders in China petitioned their soverign in 1834 to send another mission to Peking, but they failed to elicit a favorable response.[29]

The Treaty of Nanking in 1842 did not solve the problem of diplomatic representation. It opened five Chinese ports to Western commerce and consulates, but made no provision for diplomatic accreditation. A concerted attempt to reach Peking for treaty revision was made in 1854 by the representatives of the three maritime nations: Sir John Bowring of Britain, Robert MacLane of the

United States, and M. de Bourboulon of France. They were summarily told in Tientsin that the imperial sanctuary in Peking was closed to outer barbarians; the mission was thus nipped in the bud.[30] It was not until 1858, a century after Flint's initial trial, that Lord Elgin, with powerful military support, finally succeeded in exacting the right of legation in the Chinese capital, and China became diplomatically open to the West.

The first theme of this study is the resident-minister issue in the Sino-Western relations of 1858–1861. More particularly, it deals with Lord Elgin's acquisition of the right of legation during the negotiations of the Treaty of Tientsin in June 1858, his promise at the Shanghai Tariff Conference in November 1858 that he would not exercise this right for a while, and his final reassertion of the right in 1860. But before embarking on this complex subject, a glimpse at the general events leading to the Tientsin negotiations in June 1858 is necessary.

PART I

THE ESTABLISHMENT OF FOREIGN LEGATIONS IN CHINA

1858–1861

The Resident Minister Issue: The Diplomatic Prelude

The negotiations of 1858 came as the climax of a number of new problems which had arisen in Sino-Western relations after the Opium War. These included the entry of foreigners into the city of Canton, the contumaciousness of the successive Canton viceroys, the legalization of the opium trade, the coastwise commerce, and the *likin* exaction. Sino-Western relations became increasingly strained and as the 1850's wore on, it was clear that a breaking point was approaching. After the failure of the attempt to obtain treaty revisions in 1854 the Western governments, newly freed from the Crimean War, were ready for action in Asia. Fear of the Russian advance in the Far East after her defeat in the Near East increased British determination to move in China.[1] The *Arrow* incident of 1856 and the murder of the French Catholic priest, Abbé Auguste Chapdelaine, in Kwangsi province in February of that year provided the British and French governments with much needed pretexts for making demands on China.

The *Arrow* was a Chinese-owned lorcha registered with the British authority in Hongkong. While lying at anchor in Pearl River in Canton with a British flag on its mast, it was boarded by Chinese police on October 8, 1856. Twelve Chinese crew members were arrested on a charge of piracy and the British flag was hauled down during the turmoil. Harry Parkes, British consul in Canton, with the support of Sir John Bowring, British plenipotentiary and chief superintendent of trade in China, protested to Viceroy Yeh Ming-ch'en of Canton against the insult to the flag and demanded an apology as well as release of the sailors. The sailors were eventually turned over to the British but Viceroy Yeh refused to apologize. Parkes thereby called in the British navy to bombard the city of Canton; the Chinese retaliated by burning the foreign factories. A grave incident was thus created.

To be sure, the *Arrow* incident was not popular in England. In Parliament strong sentiments against another China war were expressed, and Her Majesty's Loyal Opposition exploited the situation to its full advantage. In both the House of Lords and House of Commons, Sir John Bowring and Harry Parkes were scathingly criticized for involving Britain in trouble.[2] Parkes was disparagingly described by Cobden as a "young man, without experience, and without having gone through the gradations of civil employment calculated to give him that moderation, prudence, and discretion which he one day may possess."[3] An impression was successfully created by the Opposition that the great English nation was being dragged into war by her petty overseas servants.[4] "You have turned a consul into a diplomatist," Gladstone grandiloquently declared on March 3, "and that metamorphosed consul is forsooth to be at liberty to direct the whole might of England against the lives of a defenceless people."[5]

The Opposition succeeded in unseating the government by a vote of 263 to 247 in the House of Commons, and a new election was called for March 21, 1857. In his campaign speeches, Palmerston appealed to voters to uphold British honor and pride and overseas interests. The election returned him a majority in Parliament, and his China policy was saved. But his confidence in Sir John Bowring was shaken beyond repair by the strong sentiments in Parliament. Even before the election, Palmerston had decided to send a new plenipotentiary to China to settle the differences between the two countries.[6] His first choice for the position was the Duke of Newcastle, who, however, declined the honor. The appointment then went to Lord Elgin (1811–1863), who had been governor of Jamaica in 1842 and governor-general of Canada in 1846.[7] The selection of Elgin, who "preferred measures of conciliation to aggression or even coercion," represented a "concession to the public sentiment of a formidable popular minority."[8]

To concert measures with Britain and to match a man of Lord Elgin's stature, the French government chose a veteran diplomat of thirty years' experience, Baron Gros, who was considerably older than Elgin and had previously served in Portugal, Spain, Egypt, Mexico, Argentina, and Greece. Russia sent Admiral Putiatin of the Russian Navy and the United States sent William B. Reed of Philadelphia to cooperate with the Anglo-French representatives, but not to participate in their military operations.

Lord Elgin arrived in Hongkong on July 2, 1857, only to find that the Sepoy Mutiny had necessitated the diversion of his troops to India. For a while he toyed with the idea of proceeding to the Peiho to negotiate with the Chinese without a military force. When he realized that he could not counter a Chinese rebuff without an army, he went instead to India in the *H.M.S. Shannon* to give the appearance that large English reinforcements were coming to suppress the mutiny.[9] He returned from India in September and on October 4 received authorization from Clarendon to take Canton by force.[10] The arrival of Baron Gros and the French troops in October called for a detailed arrangement for the joint attack, and a whole month elapsed before anything definite was worked out, the English being very reluctant to let the French in on their quarrel with the Chinese. After long delay, a joint Anglo-French ultimatum was sent to Viceroy Yeh Ming-ch'en of Canton; when it was not properly answered, Lord Elgin declared that the "season for remonstrances" had ended and that punitive action must follow.[11] The Allies stormed the city of Canton on December 28, 1857, captured Yeh as a prisoner of war, and set up what was probably the first puppet government of modern times in Canton. This done, Elgin and Gros proceeded north to demand of Peking "reparation for past, and security for future, wrongs." [12]

Elgin was hopeful of a quick settlement in Shanghai.[13] He had prepared a message to Yü-ch'ien, the leading Grand Secretary at the court in Peking, requesting the appointment of a high-ranking plenipotentiary to meet him in Shanghai.[14] This message and identical French, American and Russian notes were delivered personally to the governor of Kiangsu, Chou Te-tse, in Soochow by Lawrence Oliphant, Elgin's private secretary, in the company of the British and French consuls in Shanghai and the American vice-consul. In line with the old practice, the Russian note, attached to the American one, was addressed to the Grand Council.[15]

Yü-ch'ien did not answer Elgin directly since no Chinese subjects or officials were allowed foreign intercourse *(jen-ch'en wu wai-chiao)*. He instructed Ho Kuei-ch'ing, viceroy of Nanking, to inform Elgin that his request to meet with an imperial commissioner at Shanghai could not be met for want of precedent; that the proper place for such a meeting was Canton, where a new viceroy, Huang Tsung-han, had been sent to examine the state of affairs impartially.

Elgin was advised to repair there.[16] Putiatin was told that the *Li-fan-yüan*, in accordance with established practice, would take up the various subjects of his note with the Russian Senate.[17]

Elgin felt insulted at not being answered directly. He believed that the stipulation in the Treaty of Nanking that Her Britannic Majesty's High Officer in China had the right to correspond with high Chinese officials in the capital or in the provinces had been violated. Determined to establish the principle of direct communication with the court once and for all, he refused to accept Ho Kuei-ch'ing's communication transmitting Yü-ch'ien's note. On April 1, 1858 he tersely announced to Peking that he would "at once proceed to the north, in order that he may place himself in more immediate communication with the High Officers of the Imperial Government at the capital." [18] His hope for a quick settlement in Shanghai thus evaporated; so did Yü-ch'ien's plan to persuade him to go back to Canton. The refusal of the Chinese to negotiate with Elgin at this point was a fatal mistake, for which they were to pay dearly at Tientsin. On April 14, Elgin arrived at the Gulf of Pechili off the Peiho, and on April 24, he asked Peking to send a duly authorized plenipotentiary to meet him at Taku within six days, after which he would resort to military action to effect what he had failed to achieve by this peaceful overture.[19] The request was granted by the Chinese and the stage for negotiations was set. In order to attain a proper perspective on the importance of the resident minister issue, it is necessary to review the instructions of the Western representatives.

a. *The Western Aims in 1858*

The Earl of Clarendon, Foreign Secretary, issued a set of detailed instructions to Lord Elgin on April 20, 1857, giving him complete authority to determine where negotiation with the Chinese was "to be carried on; how long it is to be continued; and when, if unsuccessful, it is to be broken off." [20] He was to proceed "to the mouth of the Peiho river with as considerable a naval force as can be spared from the neighborhood of Canton," but the exact place of negotiation "should not be fixed on, where you would be in the power of the Chinese, or so far removed from Pekin as to deprive the Chinese Plenipotentiary of easy and quick communication with the Chinese government." [21] His objectives in negotiation were specified by Clarendon as follows:

1. For reparations of injuries to British subjects, and, if the French officers should cooperate with you, for those to the French subjects also.

2. For the complete execution at Canton, as well as at the other ports, of the stipulations of the several Treaties.

3. Compensation to British subjects and persons entitled to British protection for losses incurred in consequence of the late disturbances.

4. The assent of the Chinese government to the residence at Pekin, or to the occasional visit to that capital, at the option of the British government, of a Minister duly accredited by the Queen to the Emperor of China, and the recognition of the right of the British Plenipotentiary and Chief Superintendent of Trade to communicate directly in writing with the high officers at the Chinese capital, and to send his communications by messengers of his own selection: such arrangements affording the best means of ensuring the due execution of the existing Treaties, and of preventing future misunderstandings.

5. A revision of the Treaties with China with a view to obtaining increased facilities for commerce, such as access to cities on the great rivers, as well as to Chapoo and to other ports in the west, and also permission for Chinese vessels to resort to Hongkong for purpose of trade, from all ports of the Chinese Empire without distinction.[22]

As to the method of realizing these five objectives, Lord Elgin was authorized to use coercive measures for the first three and negotiation alone for the remaining two. Should the employment of force lead to an outbreak of war, "a new state of things" would arise; he was then to insist on the fulfillment of all five demands and, in addition, seek an indemnity, which Her Majesty's government would not "absolutely insist" on if "satisfactory terms were agreed to as regards opening the ports of China and the improvement of the commercial intercourse with that country." [23] The official emphasis was obviously on trade. Making this unmistakably clear, Lord Clarendon issued another message on the same day reminding Elgin that the chief object of his mission was to liberate "the trade with China" from existing restrictions.[24] There seemed to be little stress on the cooperative aspect of the Anglo-French alliance.

That the issue of diplomatic representation stood fourth among the five objectives and was to be achieved only by peaceful negotiation indicated its relative unimportance to the British official mind. The primary concern of the British government appeared to be the widening of trade facilities and the settlement of differences arising from the existing treaties rather than the establishment of diplomatic relations with China. Treaty rights and trade interests were concrete and solid things, the protection of which, in the eyes of the rising commercial elements in the government, warranted the use of military power. Diplomatic representation, on the other hand, was only a means to safeguard the commercial interests; it was something good to have but not worth a war. Nevertheless, a resident British minister in Peking would be in Britain's interest. A note from the Foreign Office to the Admiralty, dated January 24, 1857 stated: "It is impossible for H.M.'s government to form an opinion whether the conduct of the Imperial Commissioner at Canton is grounded only on his own views of local policy, and is adopted solely on his own responsibility, or whether it is known to, and pursued in obedience to orders from the Imperial government at Pekin." [25] In other words, London felt that if the Canton viceroy was not representing Peking policy, it would be necessary to demand direct contact with the court. On February 9, 1857 Sir John Bowring was instructed by Clarendon that in any new treaty with China the "first matter to be provided for" should be the right of a resident minister in Peking, because "without such a guarantee for ready access to the supreme government, all other concessions will be more or less precarious." [26] Clarendon had serious doubts that the local authorities duly transmitted foreign complaints and representations to the imperial government in Peking.

Moreover, since the Crimean War, the British Government had been increasingly inclined to view China as a second Ottoman Empire, in which a British resident minister would undoubtedly serve useful purposes.[27] Yet it did not consider the issue in itself important enough to justify a war and a costly expedition. Should hostilities break out on other accounts, the British government would make full use of the occasion to include this right in its total demands. But this issue alone was not to be the *casus belli*. Hence Lord Elgin's orders to procure this right only by peaceful negotiation. It is a matter of interest to see how faithfully Elgin carried out his instructions.

Unlike Britain, France had little commercial interest in China. Her ruler, Emperor Napoleon III, in his hunger for glory, wished to propitiate the Catholic element at home by posing as the propagator of the faith abroad. In 1856 he ordered his representative in China, M. de Bourboulon, to turn his chief attention toward acquiring the right of permanent residence in Peking: "Notre propre dignité, les besoins du commerce, la nécessité de prévenir des éventualités re-grettables, tout enfin, nous commande aujourd'hui par conséquent, de placer nos relations avec la Cour de Pe-king dans des conditions régulières et pour atteindre ce résultat, il importe que la résidence des agents diplomatique soit transférée dans la capitale de l'Empire. C'est vers cet but, Monsieur, que vous devrez, avant tout, diriger vos efforts, c'est la concession à laquelle nous devons attacher le plus grand prix et vous ne négligerez rien pour l'obtenir." [28]

On the other hand, Napoleon III was not anxious to have Chinese representation in the Western world, since his chief concern was to establish French influence in Peking.[29] The French attitude toward diplomatic representation in the Chinese capital, however, changed somewhat when France joined England in the expedition to China, knowing that this demand was only the fourth of Elgin's five ob-jectives and that if necessary, Britain would settle for only occasional visits to the capital. Baron Gros was therefore ordered by Napoleon III on May 9, 1857 to obtain the right of occasional visits to Peking, if not of permanent residence: "Nous pensons, avec le Gouverne-ment anglais, que le moment est venu d'obtenir pour nos Ministres accrédités en Chine le droit de résider à Pe-king, sinon d'une mani-ère permanente, du moins toutes les fois qu'ils croiront ou que nous-mêmes nous croirons leur présence dans la capitale utile au soin des affaires." [30]

Baron Gros was given wide powers to determine the place, time, and duration of his negotiations with the Chinese, but he was to avoid unnecessary bloodshed and to push the "progress of civiliza-tion" along with French interests in China. An indemnity was to be demanded but not at the expense of such more fundamental issues as diplomatic representation and trade extension. His instructions stressed the cooperative aspect of the expedition more than El-gin's.[31]

The United States was considered a very likely ally by both Britain and France, but Washington saw no point in involving itself in the China imbroglio. On February 2, 1857 Secretary of State W. L. Marcy informed the American agent in China, Dr. Peter Parker, "the British government evidently have objects beyond those contemplated by the United States, and we ought not to be drawn along [with] it." [32] Lord Napier, British Minister in Washington, requested of the Department of State on March 14 that the United

States "grant Great Britain that concurrence and active cooperation which the Government of France has already accorded, and that they will authorize their naval and political authorities to act heartily in concert with the agents of the allied powers." [33] Lewis Cass, successor to Marcy as Secretary of State, replied that since most Chinese injuries to American citizens had been redressed, he could find no justification for starting a war with China. He reminded the British diplomat that in the United States, Congress, and not the executive branch of the government, held the authority to make war; consequently President Buchanan could not by himself grant "that concurrence and active cooperation" or order the Navy "to act heartily in concert with the agents of the allied powers." [34] A similar French request for American participation in opening a way to Peking by force was likewise declined by the President, who ventured to add that in his opinion the Chinese, having already promised treaty revision, had no obligation to carry it out in Peking.[35]

While the United States rejected an alliance with Britain and France, she consented to send an envoy extraordinary and minister plenipotentiary to cooperate with the Allied representatives in a peaceful demonstration. Selected for this assignment was William Bradford Reed of Philadelphia, who had previously held state offices in Pennsylvania and had taught American history at the University of Pennsylvania. He was instructed to aid in the accomplishment of Anglo-French objectives only "by peaceful cooperation," since the United States was not at war with China. He was to inform the Chinese that the United States, not a party to the war, had no "intention to interfere in their political concerns or to gain a foothold in their country"; that she did not seek "territorial aggrandizement or the acquisition of political power" in China but only "protection of the lives and property of its citizens." [36] Nevertheless, Reed was escorted by an impressive force, to show the Chinese that it was not "the want of means which compels the United States to abstain from measures of hostility." [37]

The President considered it "just and expedient" for Reed to pursue the following objectives for the United States: (1) a resident minister in Peking, (2) new ports, (3) reduction of domestic tariff, (4) religious freedom for all foreigners in China, (5) suppression of piracy, and (6) extension of treaty benefits to all civilized nations. A copy of Clarendon's instructions to Elgin, which had been transmitted to the Department of State by Lord Napier, was forwarded to Reed for reference.[38] He was further authorized to "communicate frankly" with the British and French agents on all matters of common interest, and he was also told that Russian cooperation might be "highly advantageous." [39]

When the Russian government learned of the Anglo-French expedition from Count Putiatin, its naval agent in London, it saw in this move a threat to Russian interests in the Far East. Grand Duke Constantin Nicholaivich quickly arranged the appointment of Putiatin as ambassador plenipotentiary to China in February 1857 to safeguard Russian interests in Manchuria and to obtain whatever rights China might grant to the maritime nations.[40] When asked the nature of Putiatin's mission by the British ambassador, the Russian Foreign Minister, Prince Gorchakov, replied that it was entirely peaceful, and that Russia was quite willing to cooperate with Britain.[41] Gorchakov also advised the Russian minister in Washington, Eduard Stoeckel, on February 12, 1857, that "Count Putiatin, whose mission is of an entirely peaceful character, is commissioned only to come to an agreement with the Chinese government on secondary points (*vtorosterennykh punktev*) connected with the question (of the Amur)." [42]

Major General Kovolevsky, a Far Eastern expert, appears to have played an important role in the formulation of Russian policy in China. He submitted a memorandum to Prince Gorchakov on January 22, 1857, which was later presented to the Tsar, stating: "Our interests [in China] are quite different from those of other European powers . . . . To join the enemies of China, at a time when we have no reason for enmity, would be, even in a political sense, incompatible with our relations with China. It remains, therefore, for us to resolve our pending problems by peaceful negotiations." [43]

Putiatin was instructed to dissociate himself, before the Chinese, from the European interventionists and to emphasize the age-old Sino-Russian friendship; he was not to accept diplomatic assistance from Elgin except in case of extreme Chinese intransigence. Nor was he to press China too hard, for fear of losing the privilege of maintaining a Russian religious mission in Peking and the rather lucrative China trade.[44]

Putiatin was to play the role of mediator (*posrednik*), in cooperation with the other neutral-ally, the American minister. He was to keep a watchful eye on the maritime countries and to use his influence to prevent the extension of the war to the point of endangering the Manchu dynasty, with which the Russians had concluded all the existing treaties. If the Manchus were to fall from power and be replaced by the Chinese, these treaties might be nullified and the center of political gravity in China would also shift from the north to the south, in which case the maritime nations, especially Britain, would enjoy a more advantageous position than Russia.[45] Such an eventuality had to be prevented by all means, but Russia reserved the right to obtain from China any special concessions in addition to those that she might share in common with the maritime countries. Furthermore, the Russians had no enthusiasm for the establishment of foreign legations in Peking, because this would destroy the monopolistic position of the Russian religious mission there.[46] Putiatin informed Elgin on March 29, 1858 that he would lend his *appui moral* to the common cause but not military assistance: "The Imperial Ministry . . . directs me to lend my moral support to all demands of common interests which may be made by the Plenipotentiaries of other Powers to the Court of Pekin . . . and enjoins me to abstain from all coercive measures against the Chinese Government." [47]

There is evidence that Putiatin's appearance in China did not particularly please Governor Muraviev in Siberia. Muraviev, regarding the Far East as his own sphere of activity, wrote to Prince Gorchakov on June 7, 1857 that Putiatin should not concern himself with the Amur question.[48] Putiatin traveled overland to China, announcing his mission to the *Li-fan-yüan* as one of "discussing confidential affairs, in view of England's sinister designs." [49] Refused entry at Kiakhta, he descended the Amur and reached the Peiho by August 1857, whence he journeyed to Nagasaki and Shanghai. Irked by Peking's consistent refusal to receive him, he suggested to St. Petersburg on December 19, 1857 that the Peiho be bombarded. The disgruntled Muraviev, then in the Russian capital, seized the opportunity to oppose this plan as too serious and violent, and succeeded in persuading the Tsar to take the Amur question out of Putiatin's hands. Putiatin was left with the power to deal with commercial matters only.[50] With the removal of the sensitive Amur issue, he was better able to play the role of "mediator."

In summary, the four Western nations were operating at cross purposes in China. The British government considered diplomatic residence in Peking an important but not absolutely indispensable objective, to be achieved by peaceful negotiation with the Chinese unless war broke out on other accounts. The French government was willing to accept occasional diplomatic visits to Peking, if not permanent residence there. The United States found herself in the strange and awkward position of neutral-ally; she refused to join the Anglo-French alliance but cooperated with it in a peaceful demonstration. Russia posed as mediator between China and the West, with the dual purpose of thwarting the objective of the British and French of establishing themselves in the Chinese capital while achieving for herself maximum profits from the troubled waters of China. The lack of singleness of purpose among the four nations was compensated for by their common desire for gain. This unity in difference resulted in a highly complex chapter in the history of Chinese foreign relations.

b. *Difficulties Preceding the Tientsin Negotiations*

Although the court at Peking had acceded to Lord Elgin's demand of April 24 that high plenipotentiaries meet with him at Taku, two obstacles stood in the way of negotiations: the problem of full powers and the unexpected appearance of the veteran barbarian expert, Ch'i-ying.

Two imperial commissioners — Ch'ung-lun, superintendent of the government granaries, who had dealt with Sir John Bowring and Robert M. McLane in 1854, and Wu-erh-kun-t'ai, subchancellor of the Grand Secretariat — were sent by the emperor on April 25 to inquire into the barbarian demands.[51] The appearance of a granary official as a diplomat astonished the European allies.[52] Although T'an T'ing-hsiang, viceroy of Chihli, was added as the third commissioner on April 30, giving an appearance of seriousness on the part of the Chinese, Lord Elgin refused to see them on the ground that they lacked full powers to negotiate a treaty. He demanded of T'an an imperial authorization of full powers, such as Ch'i-ying had had when negotiating with Pottinger in 1842, and a copy of the latter was given to T'an as a reminder. Six days were allowed him to procure a like document from the court.[53]

T'an disputed the authenticity of Ch'i-ying's full powers of 1842, claiming that since it had never been China's practice to issue such documents, Ch'i-ying's must have been false. He wrote to Elgin on May 10, 1858: "There being no such title in China as 'tsinen kinen' [*sic;* complete authority] when the former Commissioners, Kiying and Ilipoo, negotiated the Treaty of Peace, the things done by them 'as occasion required' were from time to time submitted to the Throne. They had no independent [or absolute] authority whatsoever to act." [54] T'an insisted that he was as competent a negotiator as Ch'i-ying, and proved this by quoting to Elgin the imperial edict on his appointment: "Ch'ung-lun and his colleague, being high officers commissioned by us, are, properly speaking, competent to conduct discussions to an issue. As T'an T'ing-hsiang is, by virtue of the post he fills, an officer of great responsibility, we command him to associate himself with them in their deliberations. Respect this!" [55]

Elgin took this answer as circumlocutory and evasive, a sign of the emperor's refusal to accede to his demand for full powers. His use of military force was averted only at the last moment by the mediating efforts of Putiatin, who, counseling forbearance in expectation of new imperial instructions for T'an, argued that it was "not possible to get the Chinese yet to adopt all those forms which Western nations had agreed upon in such matters, but it was better to take the spirit of their acts rather than reject them for informality." [56] Putiatin himself believed that the Chinese government had acceded to the allied demands for proper persons for negotiation at the appointed place and time.[57] He deviated from the Anglo-French course and received T'an for an interview, at which time he warned that China must make concessions in order to avoid hostilities.[58]

Also in disagreement with Elgin over this diplomatic technicality was the American minister, William B. Reed, who saw no reason why the possession of full powers should be a prerequisite for an interview with a representative formally sent by the emperor. He could not understand why the British received Ch'i-shan and others as commissioners in 1841 and not T'an in 1858, since all of them had the same powers to negotiate but not to make decisions without reference to the court.[59] He further observed: "It would have been a mischievous punctilio that prevented me from at least meeting him [T'an], and then ascertaining the precise extent of his functions . . . . Besides, I could not persuade myself that the technical rules of Western diplomacy should be asserted against this strange people." [60] Reed, therefore, proceeded to receive T'an at the Taku forts on May 3, but nothing came of it except T'an's assurance of his competence to negotiate and his guarantee to refer the whole treaty, and not each article, to the throne for approval.[61] To defend his isolated action, Reed wrote to Elgin on May 4 that "peace is too important to the relations subsisting between China and the United States to be imperilled by my adherence, in a preliminary correspondence, to the strict rules of Western diplomacy." He persuaded Elgin not to start hostilities prematurely. His sentiment on this occasion can best be seen in his May 4th report to Lewis Cass, Secretary of State: "I have seen enough already of war in China to make me think of it with disgust. It is the bloody warfare of the strong and the weak . . . and the idea of forcing access to Pekin by the exertion of military power is to me utterly repulsive." [62]

The court of Peking, understanding neither the concept of full powers nor the seriousness of the situation, was entirely unconcerned about the argument. If the barbarians did not want to meet with the imperial commissioners in the north, they should go back to Canton. Why should they be persuaded to meet with T'an? On May 8, 1858 T'an was instructed to inform Elgin that Ch'i-ying had been granted great discretionary powers in 1842 because the place of negotiation, Canton or Nanking, was far away from Peking; even then he had never acted dogmatically but had memorialized to the court for guidance on every detail. There had never been any title like plenipotentiary, or authorization for anything like full powers, in China. If the Canton commissioners could deal with the foreigners without such a title or authorization in the past, and if Ch'ung-lun likewise could deal with Bowring and McLane in 1854, why should Elgin now act differently? [63]

The negotiations were deadlocked. On May 20, Elgin ordered the forceful occupation of the Taku Forts and then pushed on to Tientsin, "to place himself in more immediate communication with the High Officers of the Imperial Government at the capital." [64] This advance shocked Peking, and the court immediately dispatched to Tientsin Grand Secretary Kuei-liang and Hua-sha-na, President of the Board of Civil Office, as the new imperial commissioners to negotiate with Elgin. Full powers were given them in deference to foreign prejudices, so as "to dispel their suspicion first and talk sense later." [65] On June 3, the two new commissioners presented their cards to Elgin bearing the titles "Ministers with full authority to act as the occasion shall demand" in addition to a long list of other titles.[66] On the following day a meeting was arranged. When shown Elgin's full authorization to negotiate treaties without the necessity of further instructions from home, Kuei-liang was startled and stated that China never issued "any special document of the nature of his Lordship's full powers to any officer holding, as he and his colleague did, a temporary appointment." [67] He and Hua-sha-na then produced their documents of authorization:

> Because the different nations have made requests previously, and T'an T'ing-hsiang and his colleagues had not done well in their management, Kuei-liang and Hua-sha-na were specially commissioned to proceed to Tientsin to devise means for discussions and management [of affairs]. Judging from the communications of the various nations, which still doubt that Kuei-liang and his colleague could decide independently, we command Kuei-liang and Hua-sha-na to set the right before them affectionately and earnestly. If the matters in question are within reason, and the desire for the cessation of hostilities truly sincere, *whatever is not injurious to China* will certainly be granted; there should be no further doubts or hesitation. Kuei-liang and his colleague having been specially chosen by ME must needs carefully uphold the national dignity and watch the human feelings in silence. Excepting those provisions which tamper with propriety, they should act as the circumstances may require. Let them manage according to discretion. Be zealous! [68]

Thomas Wade, Chinese secretary in Elgin's mission, remarked that these instructions, while similar to Ch'i-ying's in phraseology, were nevertheless somewhat vague, like Ch'ung-lun's in 1854, in such wording as "whatever is not injurious to China." According to Wade, the emperor's abstention from an explicit pronouncement of what should and what should not be granted was dictated by his fear of prompting the British to ask for something new and different from what had already been demanded. The powers of Kuei-liang could thus be as full as those of Ch'i-ying in 1842 or as restricted as those of Ch'ung-lun in 1854.[69] H. B. Morse, writing half a century later, was of the opinion that this document was even more liberal in its phrasing than Ch'i-ying's.[70] Elgin was satisfied with the new Chinese document but intentionally left the impression that the powers granted in the decree were still not sufficient.[71]

Kuei-liang was instructed to inform Elgin orally that the granting of full powers and the title of plenipotentiary did not imply unquestioning acceptance of all foreign demands. It would be within his discretionary power to reject without reference to the court whatever was unreasonable and difficult to grant.[72] But these ideas were not borne out by Kuei-liang in his June 4th meeting with Elgin; he merely said that he could only accede to "what was practicable."[73]

The question of full powers having been settled, Lord Elgin next demanded that official seals be issued to the Chinese commissioners, to which the court in Peking could not but accede even though it was not the Chinese practice to issue seals for temporary appointments. Special seals were cast and arrived in Tientsin on June 13.[74] Lord Elgin had won every point in his battle over diplomatic technicalities. One wonders why he insisted on these minute points in dealing with a people he knew to be unfamiliar with Western practices. The reason was that he wanted to show the Chinese that he was not to be trifled with as were Bowring and McLane in 1854, who were met by Ch'ung-lun with only enough powers "to get rid of the barbarians as soon as possible."[75] From the captured Chinese documents in Canton he had learned that the Chinese officials attached great importance to manners; so he was determined to impress them with his stern, unyielding manners.[76] While confident that he could coerce the Chinese delegates into accepting his demands, Elgin was less sure of the throne's approval of their acts. If the imperial commissioners were given in advance unlimited powers to negotiate a treaty, then their acceptance of his demands would bind the emperor to approve the treaty.[77] He was acting under the concept then prevailing in European international law that the approval of a treaty should not be refused unless the representatives had exceeded their powers or violated their secret instructions, in which case the treaty was called a *sponsio*.[78]

Since treaty negotiations in the eighteenth and nineteenth centuries were often conducted in secret, the sovereign's ratification was considered a legal obligation, being but a confirmation of an authority duly exercised. This idea had its root in the private law concept *ratihabitio retrotrahitur ad initium*. Ratification in those days meant the ratification of the act of the man signing a treaty, whereas today it means the ratification of the substance of the treaty.[79] Hence a state nowadays reserves complete freedom to ratify or reject a treaty signed by its authorized representatives. The

American process of treaty-making is different from the European practice: a treaty negotiated by a plenipotentiary must be approved by the Senate and ratified by the President. Partly because of this difference, Reed disagreed with Elgin.

The Chinese way of negotiating a treaty was in a sense quite close to the American way and to the general practice of most nations today. The imperial commissioner negotiated the treaty, which was then submitted in the aggregate to the emperor for approval or disapproval. Originally, the Chinese had no concept of plenipotentiary or full powers. These terms, when rendered into Chinese, literally meant "all-powerful" and "almighty," [80] which could be applied only to the emperor. As the mediator between man and nature, the Son of Heaven could not be represented in the same way as a Western monarch, by his ambassador. The emperor alone was responsible for all issues under heaven. He might invest powers in a chosen commissioner for the discharge of a certain duty, but he still retained the right to make the final decision. The imperial commissioner, *ch'in-ch'ai ta-ch'en*, literally an "imperially sent great minister," was an *ad hoc* royal emissary in the European sense or an imperial "trouble-shooter" in American parlance. His fate depended upon the result of his mission rather than the observance of a prescribed set of instructions as in the West. [81] His assignment was temporary, terminating with the completion of each mission, but during the period between the Opium War and the Arrow War, 1842–1856, the imperial commissioner in charge of foreign affairs, who was concurrently the viceroy of Canton, became a sort of semi-permanent official. [82]

The powers of an imperial commissioner depended upon the nature of his mission. In negotiating a foreign treaty within China, due to the proximity of the scene of negotiations to the seat of the government, he did not enjoy as extensive powers as those of the European plenipotentiaries of the eighteenth and nineteenth centuries, who had gone overseas. These European plenipotentiaries' powers really allowed great discretionary authority within the framework of their instructions.

The Chinese, however, could understand Lord Elgin's position as plenipotentiary, for there was an old Chinese saying that when a general is out on the battlefield he may ignore orders from the emperor. [83] T'an T'ing-hsiang frankly admitted to the American minister that he could see the need for great discretionary powers on the part of foreign ministers who had come from afar for a long and uncertain period of time, but he could not see why the Chinese should imitate them since the place of negotiation was so near the capital, from which fresh instructions could easily be obtained.[84] In point of fact, Elgin's instructions also stressed that the locale for negotiation "should not be . . . so far removed from Pekin as to deprive the Chinese plenipotentiaries of easy and quick communication with the government." [85]

Although the Chinese ultimately acceded to Elgin's demand for full powers, they did it in deference to foreign guns and not out of understanding. The true character of the imperial commissioner remained unchanged and the emperor did not seem to feel more bound to approve the treaty. The issuance of full powers was merely a device to dispel the suspicion of the barbarians before talking sense to them.[86] The Chinese idea of a plenipotentiary was explicitly stated in an imperial edict of 1860 in response to a similar demand from Elgin during his second mission: "The imperial commissioner appointed by China is in fact the so-called plenipotentiary of your country. The name is different but the reality is the same. If the things in question are possible, they may be granted first and memorialized later; if the things are impossible they may not be granted at all. Our earlier statement that there was nothing that could not be discussed originally referred to deliberations between the two countries as to what could be done away with and what could be retained. It did not mean complete compliance with the one-sided view of your country. This is what we mean by plenipotentiary." [87]

When the problem of full powers was finally solved and the negotiations were about to enter the main phase, the Allies were surprised by the sudden appearance of Ch'i-ying, the deposed viceroy of Canton and famed barbarian expert, as a new imperial commissioner. The Allies suspected that he had come to re-establish himself in the court's favor by skillful management of the barbarians as he had in Canton in the 1840's. The British claimed to notice a sudden change in attitude among the Tientsin inhabitants after his arrival and were convinced that the old Canton game was being repeated. Baron Gros remarked that "there could be no doubt that he was making mischief underhand." [88] Lord Elgin, intuitively feeling that

Ch'i-ying's intentions were malicious, resolved to use strong measures to remove him from the scene.[89]

Ch'i-ying, signer of China's first treaties with the West and virtually her foreign minister from 1842 to 1848, had been in a political eclipse for eight years before his appearance in Tientsin in 1858.[90] His policy of conciliation, adjustment, and friendliness with foreigners had won him a reputation for being "pusillanimous"; and when the violently anti-foreign Emperor Hsien-feng ascended the throne in 1850, he demoted Ch'i-ying from the important positions of viceroy of Canton and imperial commissioner in charge of barbarian affairs to the humble post of fifth-grade mandarin in disgrace. With the reopening of the difficult barbarian problem in 1858, his name, anathema for many years, once again came to the fore. Upon the joint recommendation of Prince Hui, Mien-yü, Imperial Clansman Tuan-hua, and Grand Secretary Peng Yün-chang, the emperor summoned him out of disgrace; Ch'i-ying once again walked in the political limelight.[91]

That the emperor expected much of him is seen in the speed of the court activities surrounding his reappointment. On June 2, 1858 he was given the title of vice-president of a board and on June 3 an edict was issued to the Grand Councillors explaining his appointment: "Since he has managed all the affairs relative to the signing of peace treaties with the English and other barbarians during the Tao-kuang period, I have again ordered him to proceed forward to manage them." [92] On the same day Ch'i-ying was authorized to use the seal of the viceroy of Chihli and to transfer anyone in the Chihli area to his service. "All affairs relative to appeasement will henceforth be managed *exclusively* by Ch'i-ying" the edict stated; "T'an T'ing-hsiang need no longer participate in the management." [93] The emperor now showed a higher confidence in Ch'i-ying than in Kuei-liang and Hua-sha-na, who were ordered on June 4 to wait for his arrival to deliberate countermeasures against the British demands.[94]

Prince Kung, intensely anti-foreign at this moment, warned the throne on June 6 of the danger of reposing too much confidence in Ch'i-ying, who he feared would not dare to face Elgin firmly. A soft policy of offering concessions to the barbarians, the prince argued, could be easily executed by anyone; there was no need to call upon Ch'i-ying to do it. On the contrary, Ch'i-ying should be instructed to take an aggressive stand against the barbarians first and to reprimand them for violating the peace treaties, so as to put them on the defensive. Only after he had seized the initiative in this way should he be allowed to make a few concessions. Even then, his intercession on behalf of the barbarians should not be lightly granted by the throne. Prince Kung further urged that the dikes be broken to make the rivers unnavigable for the barbarians' large ships, thus forcing them to fight on land. He expected that the barbarians, totaling less than 10,000 men, would surely be annihilated by General Seng-ko-lin-ch'in.[95]

Prince Kung's memorial, which the emperor commented was not without some useful points, called forth an edict from the throne on June 6, 1858: "The Peace Treaty of a Myriad Years [i.e., the Treaty of Nanking of 1842] that was fixed upon formerly has unexpectedly become such as it is today. Since Ch'i-ying was the original manager, he naturally can talk sense to (the barbarians) in a formal tone, frustrate their arrogant and scornful spirit and devise means to bridle them gently, so that the dignity of our national polity may be kept and their hostile intentions suppressed. If Ch'i-ying has a conscience he should not beg favors for the barbarians on those issues that definitely cannot be granted, as someone has predicted he would. Having once again trusted Ch'i-ying with an important assignment, I feel called upon to point this out in earnest, hoping that he may understand my inner thought. Be fearful! Be careful!" [96]

The emperor, assuming personal direction of the negotiations, formulated with pride a dualistic strategy: Ch'i-ying was to frustrate the barbarians first, then Kuei-liang was to follow up by bargaining with Elgin. If Kuei-liang's concessions did not satisfy him, Ch'i-ying should step in to patch the situation up with a few more concessions. The positions of the two commissioners would be different, yet complementary. On June 7 the emperor ordered: "At present Kuei-liang and his colleague should make the first rejection, keeping Ch'i-ying in the background as the man to complete the business." [97]

Confident of his ability to manage the barbarians, Ch'i-ying, during a confidential audience with the emperor before his departure for Tientsin, boldly expressed his desire to tackle the barbarian problem alone and requested independent power of negotiation.[98] The emperor was lulled by him into the belief that the pressing barbarian problem could be easily solved and that greater confidence should be placed in him.[99] On June 10 the emperor empowered him to act independently of the other two commissioners: "On matters that require discretionary power, Ch'i-ying need not be punctiliously bound to consultation with Kuei-liang and his colleague, but may at once personally open the way to the barbarian in question [i.e., Elgin]. With respect to the various articles under demand, he may consider the granting of a few more [than have already been granted] . . . so as to prevent a rupture. . . . Ch'i-ying should know well what can be done and what cannot be done; I shall not check from afar." [100] So much did the emperor expect of Ch'i-ying that it almost portended the tragedy when Ch'i-ying failed him.

Ch'i-ying's physical appearance had deteriorated considerably during the unhappy years of his eclipse. When he reappeared on the political stage in 1858, he was described as bearing the "marks of extreme decrepitude" both bodily and intellectually, as "much broken" and "very blind." [101] He arrived in Tientsin on June 9 and requested an interview with Elgin, who declined to see him. William B. Reed sarcastically commented in his diary: "The English may be very anxious to introduce Western civilization into China; they certainly are not introducing Western courtesy — I think this is a very gross thing." [102] Reed himself received Ch'i-ying, who he said was known in the United States as an "eminent man," with "such honors as my limited means enabled me to pay him." [103]

On June 11, Ch'i-ying formally notified Elgin of his status as new minister plenipotentiary with authority to use the official seal *(kuan-fang)* alongside the other two commissioners. Elgin still refused to see him, but sent his two youthful assistants, Horatio Lay and Thomas Wade, to remove him from the conference table by tactics which included bullying, threatening, embarrassing, and ridiculing. Ch'i-ying, who had no knowledge of their mission, upon their arrival immediately tried to win control over them by personal charm and gentle restraint, as he did over Pottinger in 1842. Looking at Lay, he burst into tears, saying that the recollection of his friendship with Lay's father, George Tradescant Lay, had deeply moved him. He called his servant to see Lay's great likeness to his father and introduced his son and Lay as friends of the second generation. According to Lay and Wade, "His conversation was a perfect clatter of compliments and moral sentiments, delivered with that mixed air of patronage and conciliation which, it may be observed, was considered by the mandarins earlier in contact with us as the true means of 'soothing and bridling the barbarians.' " [104]

The two youthful Britons watched his performance with patience until he reached the height of eulogy of the foreigners. Then suddenly Lay produced a document from his pocket and made Hua-sha-na read it aloud. It was Ch'i-ying's famous memorial of 1844 on the management of barbarians in which he described the foreigners disparagingly and apologized to the throne for maintaining social intercourse with them as a means of gentle control. [105] As Hua-sha-na reached the following passages in his reading, the atmosphere became unbearable:

> Certainly we have to curb them by sincerity, but it has been even more necessary to control them by skillful methods. There are times when it is possible to have them follow our directions but not let them understand the reasons. Sometimes we expose everything so that they will not be suspicious, whereupon we can dissipate their rebellious restlessness. Sometimes we have given them receptions and entertainment, after which they have had a feeling of appreciation. . . .
>
> With this type of people from outside the bounds of civilization, who are blind and unawakened in styles of address and forms of ceremony, if we adhered to the proper forms in official documents and let them be weighed according to the status of superior and inferior, even though our tongues were dry and our throats parched [from urging them to follow our way], still they could not avoid closing their ears and acting as if deaf. Not only would there be no way to bring them to their senses, but also it would immediately cause friction. [106]

In this embarrassing situation, Ch'i-ying could only respond with tears; Kuei-liang looked abashed, but the two foreigners left highly elated. [107]

The three imperial commissioners were dumbfounded and completely lost. In desperation they turned to Putiatin for help. Putiatin was "really disturbed" by Lay's abuse and went to see Baron Gros, who disclaimed any knowledge of it. [108] The Russian then related the story to Reed, who thereupon wrote Elgin a letter of protest against Horatio Lay's offensive conduct. [109] Reed himself felt that the "odd phraseology" in the 1844 memorial should "excite a smile rather than a frown" and that it was "very irrational" to attribute all evils to Ch'i-ying. [110] He wrote to the Secretary of State that the conduct of Lay and Wade was "almost incredible and could only be accounted for, if authorized, by a new determination on the part of the English to trample on this defenceless people and seek a pretext for new hostilities. I was very loath to credit it." [111]

Lord Elgin pointedly replied to Reed that Lay's "language was entirely conformable to the instructions which he received from me for his guidance." He reminded Reed that the Americans surely intended to share whatever advantages the British were exacting from the Chinese.[112] Putiatin was more tactful; he did not himself approach Elgin but sent his secretary, von der Ostenon Sacken, to register his dissatisfaction with Lay's bludgeoning tactics. Baron Gros discreetly kept quiet.[113]

After the tempestuous meeting of June 11, the three imperial commissioners helplessly reported to the court: "After we lost Canton, our old files on barbarian affairs in Yeh Ming-ch'en's office were looted by the English barbarians, and the traditional methods [of management] have all been seen through. Our techniques of control are lost, and our intelligence and courage exhausted." [114] Weighing the exigencies of the situation, they came to the conclusion on June 12 that in the interest of peace Ch'i-ying had better leave the negotiations. If the barbarians inquired about his whereabouts, they should be told that he had been recalled by the emperor since Elgin refused to see him; if the merchants and people inquired, the answer should be that he had gone on an official mission and would be back in a few days.[115] Kuei-liang and Hua-sha-na then memorialized requesting the recall of Ch'i-ying, stating that the English barbarians, who felt deceived by him in former days, were intent upon revenge, and that his continued presence might impair the peace talks. Ch'i-ying himself did not join in the memorial for fear of arousing the court's suspicion.[116]

There may have been a grain of jealousy on Kuei-liang's part in requesting Ch'i-ying's removal. It has been suggested that Kuei-liang was not particularly pleased by the appearance of Ch'i-ying, who overshadowed him and reduced his power in the negotiations. After Lay's abuse of Ch'i-ying, Kuei-liang was said to have made Lay a gift of a saddle.[117]

Lay's offensive conduct, considered by the imperial commissioners as a national insult, was not reported in detail to the court, which remained unaware of the exact situation in Tientsin.[118] Puzzled by the request of Kuei-liang and Hua-sha-na, the court hastily inquired why they wanted to dispose of the better qualified barbarian expert and why Ch'i-ying himself did not attach his name to the memorial.[119] Before this edict arrived in Tientsin, however, Ch'i-ying had already left without authorization. The angry emperor thereby ordered his arrest, and Ch'i-ying was put in chains by General Seng-ko-lin-ch'in in Tungchow. The veteran diplomat, who had only recently boasted of his skill in soothing the barbarians, was taken as a prisoner to Peking.[120]

For the trial of Ch'i-ying, a grand tribunal of the Imperial Clan Court was set up, composed of five princes (Hui, I, Cheng, Kung, and Tun) and four Grand Councillors (P'eng Yün-chang, Po-chun, Mu-yin, and Tu Han). In self defense Ch'i-ying presented a report that he had prepared earlier in Tungchow en route to Peking and three depositions, all dated June 21, 1858. In the report he stressed the English malice toward him as a result of their discovery of his old files in Canton, and justified his departure from Tientsin on the ground that the other two commissioners considered it best to "remove the object of their [English] venom to safeguard the general situation." [121] His first deposition stated that he risked his life to leave the negotiations, in order to avoid a split and to make to the throne, in person, a report on national security and the barbarian situation which he feared was unsafe to put in writing because of the ubiquitous traitors and spies. His second deposition stressed the importance of getting personal guidance from the emperor in devising secret means of blocking the barbarian demands on inland trade and travel, and his third deposition attacked the treacherous and fickle nature of the barbarians in a rather unintelligible style, revealing the confused mental state of a terrified and exhausted old man.[122]

Prince Hui, who had recommended him earlier, now demanded his head. Prince Kung, who had previously suggested a strong stand, now pleaded leniency for him on the ground that his departure, though unauthorized, was different from military desertion; and also, in view of the fact that Kuei-liang and Hua-sha-na had memorialized for him, this was not a case of evasion of duty. He called attention to the fact that nothing in the penal code demanded punishment for the unauthorized leave of a civilian official from his post.[123] Possibly Prince Kung was concerned about the future of his father-in-law, Kuei-liang, who might end up in the same way.[124]

The tribunal reached a verdict on June 26, recommending that Ch'i-ying be confined to the prison of the Imperial Clan Court to await death by strangulation. Su-shun, president of the Court of Colonial Affairs, protested against the lightness of the sentence, advocating a summary execution of Ch'i-ying in order to maintain the law and admonish "official depravity." [125] On June 29 the princes and ministers gathered in the Summer Palace to receive the emperor's personal edict, which reviewed the case in detail and ordered Ch'i-ying's suicide in the Death Chamber of the Imperial Clan Court.[126]

Why was the emperor so angry with Ch'i-ying, whose real crime was only leaving his post without authorization? The emperor had stated that the offense of leaving was slight, but that the offense of disclaiming guilt and of evading responsibility was serious.[127] In view of Prince Kung's defense that the crime was not one of evasion of duty, one is tempted to search for the hidden reasons behind the emperor's wrath.

The emperor was conscious of his responsibility; he felt guilty for having appointed the wrong man. His edict to the Nei-ko (Secretariat) on June 15 stated: "I reappointed Ch'i-ying this time with great reluctance, hoping that he could accomplish [the task of solving the barbarian problem]. Although he was recommended in a memorial by Prince Hui, I myself made the final decision. I am deeply ashamed of my lack of foresight." [128] In punishing Ch'i-ying the emperor was actually punishing himself. Moreover, he felt he had been cheated by Ch'i-ying, whose boastful assurance had lulled him into a false complacency and whose unauthorized leave had slighted his dignity. In leaving the negotiations Ch'i-ying had rendered unworkable the emperor's proud dualistic approach to the barbarian problem. No doubt he had deeply disappointed the emperor, and the offense of deceiving the Son of Heaven was unforgivable.[129] The emperor's hatred in the end was even stronger than his hope in the beginning; his desire for revenge was not unnatural.

Elgin appears to have completely misjudged the nature of Ch'i-ying's mission, which was to find peace in the darkness rather than to destroy the chances for a settlement. The emperor truly wanted peace when he sent Ch'i-ying to Tientsin.[130] Elgin's rash action precipitated the tragic death of a half-blind old man.

Ch'i-ying, from first to last a product of the force of circumstances, walked into the international limelight in 1842 because of his skill in managing the barbarians, and walked out of it in 1858 when his usefulness was outlived. He was never a great man, but perhaps he died a greater man than he had lived. He had lived as a buffer between the conflicting forces of East and West, but he died in the interests of peace. While his absence from Tientsin did not spare his country trouble, his presence would undoubtedly have complicated the situation. He was said to be ahead of his time.[131] Perhaps in his last act he was ahead of his usual self.

CHAPTER 3

The Tientsin Negotiations

The negotiations at Tientsin focused on four major issues: the resident minister in Peking, new ports along the Yangtze, inland travel, and indemnity. Of the four the resident minister issue was central to both the British and the Chinese. Lord Elgin pushed this demand with a dynamism and persistence seldom seen in the other phases of his negotiations, and Kuei-liang fought against it to the very last minute. London actually had not expected Elgin to go so far in his demands. The Indian mutiny and the subsequent diversion of the greater part of Elgin's troops, as well as the deterioration of Anglo-French relations in Europe,[1] had reconciled the mild and moderate Foreign Secretary, Malmesbury, to the prospect of a partial failure in China. He was quite willing to settle for much less than Palmerston's original bold China program, and on March 25, 1858, he ordered Elgin to arrange an early cessation of hostilities.[2] But Elgin disregarded the order and was determined to go ahead with his original plan. Why?

Lord Elgin had come to China with the understanding that the right of a resident minister in, or an occasional visit to, Peking was the fourth objective of his mission, to be achieved by negotiation only unless war broke out on other accounts. His experience in China, however, convinced him of the necessity of giving this issue top priority. He was led to the belief that "the obstinate refusal of the Court of Pekin to place itself on a footing of equality with other Powers lies at the root of our difficulties with that country. Hence, the impossibility of making the Emperor and his Government acquainted with the true state of the facts in any case of misunderstanding that may chance to arise, and of urging upon them those friendly remonstrances which, in the dealings of nation with nation, not infrequently nip in the bud the germs of more serious controversy. Hence, again, the latitude enjoyed by the Court of Pekin in promoting, through subordinate agencies, the violations of its own Treaty obligations, without, as it fondly imagines, exposing itself to the penalty which justly attaches to such proceedings." Therefore he decided that his first step should be to make direct contact with the court of Peking.[3]

Through the capture of the old Chinese files on barbarian affairs in the Canton viceroy's yamen in late December of 1857, he had gained access to various secret memorials, in which the foreigner was usually disparagingly represented as inferior in civilization, violent, crafty, and unreasonble.[4] There was no recognition of such fundamental rights of states as equality, good name, and reputation.[5] Elgin said: "In all earnestness, how is it possible international relations can subsist under such a system?"[6] Convinced that pacific relations with China could only be achieved by abolishing the viceroy of Canton as her foreign representative, Elgin was determined to force Peking to deal with foreign matters itself. This would spare the local officials the dilemma of whether or not to report unwelcome truths to the throne.[7] His conviction was strengthened by Peking's failure to be impressed by the occupation of Canton and the exile of its viceroy to India. Yü-ch'ien still refused to communicate with him. Elgin realized that it was impossible "to influence the Court of Peking by coercion at remote parts of the Empire, still more hopeless was it to effect this object by diplomacy exercised at a distance from the seat of the Government." Influence must be exerted at the heart in order to affect the extremities and not at the extremities to affect the heart.[8]

On the other hand, Elgin's sojourn in China and his visits to the treaty ports evoked in him "a sympathy for the Chinese, a sense of the deep wrongs they receive at the hands of reckless foreigners." He was determined to stress the importance of political intercourse between China and the West and to reduce the importance of increased commercial facilities. From this evolved his strong conviction that the "sovereign cure" for existing evil was the establishment of permanent diplomatic relations at Peking.[9] Of his dislike for his countrymen's activities in China he wrote pointedly: "Certainly I have seen more to disgust me with my fellow-countrymen than I saw during the whole course of my previous life."[10] He was led to believe that a good British minister in Peking could help the Chinese government regulate the foreign merchants and offer necessary advice. The embroilments of foreign merchants could thus be reduced, and the minister could prove to the Chinese that the British government, having no sinister designs against the Chinese empire, did not shield British outlaws from due punishment. Gradually, Elgin hoped, the Chinese prejudices against foreigners would be mitigated.[11]

Elgin may even have thought of diplomatic representation in Peking in the larger terms of world politics. Reed, the American minister, remarked that Elgin wanted to use it as a measure to invigorate the disorganized imperial authorities as England had done in Turkey. The Taiping Rebellion, to Elgin, was a "mischievous" convulsion that ought to come to an end and the presence of a British envoy in the capital would serve to sustain the ruling dynasty as a "diplomatic protectorate." By contacts with intelligent Western diplomats, he hoped, the Chinese would come to realize their own power and the "duty to exercise it." [12] Reed was confident that "if the choice were presented between a resident diplomatic corps at Peking, and the opening to foreign commerce, through all their branches, of the great rivers in the center and in the South of China, Lord Elgin's decision would be for the former. This is the result of his year in China." [13]

Elgin's views were doubtless influenced by his energetic aide, Horatio N. Lay, who urged unremittingly that the resident minister issue be a *sine qua non* in the proposed treaty.[14] Lay wrote in recollection: "I had urged upon Lord Elgin that the Resident Minister clause was in my humble judgment vital, that without it the treaty would not be worth the paper it was written upon. The old 'Canton Viceroy' system, the direct cause of all past misunderstandings, would be restored, and the work would have to be done over again, for in dealing with an Oriental Power, safety for the future is measured only by the completeness with which changes found imperative are pushed home." [15]

More than anyone else, Lay was determined to declare war against the Canton Viceroy system, which he held responsible for foreigners' being "tossed to and fro like a shuttle between Imperial and Provincial authorities." To prevent past and future treaties from degenerating into dead letters, the British government must gain direct access to the source of Chinese authority.[16] The buffer cleverly set up by the court in the person of the Canton imperial commissioner must be destroyed in order to deprive the court of excuses for ignoring barbarians altogether or for relegating issues to local officials.[17] The primary function of a British minister in Peking, then, would be to use his influence in pressing for the execution of the treaties and for trade expansion. In 1864 Lay criticized Minister Frederick Bruce: "The object of the Resident Minister Clause was overlooked and misunderstood. Treated as an end in itself, instead of a means to an end, it was not, and has never been, turned to proper account."[18] Here we see the difference in motivation between Lay and Elgin, and these statements of Lay's certainly lend no credence to the view that he insisted on diplomatic representation out of a desire to draw China into the family of nations.[19]

Uncertain whether diplomatic representation would invigorate the "mysterious connection between the political center and the extremities of the Empire," Reed was opposed to having Peking "converted into a new Constantinople or made the seat and scene of diplomatic squabbles and European intrigues."[20] He did not want to see a De Redcliff in Peking "control, direct, advise, and improve" China.[21] Nor did he think it fitting for an American minister, as the representative of a "much less disinterested" commercial nation, to play the role of sustaining Chinese authorities and institutions in a vortex of international entanglements.[22] Reed therefore decided that it would be "very wrong to persevere in the demand" for a resident minister in Peking.[23] He took a flexible position: "If the residence of a Minister at Pekin be denied, the effort will be to secure a right of visit and sojourn. That failing, it will still be a great result [and one to which I look much more hopefully] to break up the system of driving the foreign ministers to remote regions such as Canton, to establish the legation or a responsible Consulate General at Shanghai and to allow the Yangtze Kiang to be freely navigated and the great cities and markets on its banks to be open."[24]

Reed's position was shared by Baron Gros and Admiral Putiatin. In a meeting with Elgin on April 3, 1858, Gros made no secret of his opposition to the British insistence on the resident minister issue and suggested occasional business visits to the capital instead. The Russians all along were known to favor the extension of Western influence in China but not the establishment of permanent foreign legations in Peking.[25] Elgin therefore had to proceed alone.

a. *Elgin and Lay versus Kuei-liang and Hua-sha-na*

Elgin's demand for a resident minister in Peking was first implied in his ultimatum to Viceroy Yeh Ming-ch'en of Canton in December 1857, in which he warned that if his demands for the redress of wrongs in Canton were not met, he would take military action and reserve "to himself the right to make . . . such additional demands on the Government of China as this altered condition of affairs might seem in his eyes to justify." [26] He was of course following his instructions, which stated that the outbreak of hostilities would justify the inclusion of his fourth objective in the total demands. His first explicit mention of a resident minister was blandly made in his letter to Yü-ch'ien when he stated that had Peking been accessible to foreign ministers, the calamities in Canton could have been avoided.[27] After his arrival at the Peiho in the north, he renewed this demand. The Chinese considered it preposterous. The American minister took pains to explain to the mandarins that the exchange of envoys was a common practice among Western nations, and that relations between states, like friendship between men, could be cultivated only through direct contact. Diplomatic representation would enable both China and foreign nations to discuss their differences rather than fight them out.[28] Putiatin wittily asked T'an T'ing-hsiang, viceroy of Chihli, why a big country like China should be afraid of a handful of foreigners in the capital.[29]

T'an T'ing-hsiang apparently accepted the American and the Russian arguments. His memorials, reaching the court on May 15 and 17, stated that since Ferdinandus Verbiest and other foreigners had formerly worked in the capital, the foreign demand for residence in Peking was not totally unprecedented. It might even prove advantageous to China, because by controlling the barbarian chieftains in the capital China could also control the barbarians in the provinces and nip trouble in the bud. If, on the other hand, the barbarian chieftains showed signs of disrespect or obstinacy, the court could easily order their arrest or stop the trade. It was far better to face this issue at once in Tientsin, when the barbarians were still some distance from Peking, than later when they would have advanced further north.[30]

The emperor reprimanded T'an for seeing only part of the picture. Foreigners in the past, the emperor reminded him, had been cooperative and submissive mathematicians, whereas the foreigners of the present were unruly traders and adventurers, coming and going at will without heeding the orders of the Chinese government. Their demand for residence in Peking must be denied, not because China feared them, but because it was incompatible with the established institutions, the *t'i-chih*.[31] The barbarians were basically profit-minded traders; their demand for residence was only a bargaining tactic. Hence China must be firm in her refusal. If their demand was the result of mismanagement in Canton, let them send their petitions through the viceroys of Nanking and Fuchow.[32]

T'an warned the court of the arrival of more barbarian ships and his inability to cope with the situation if hostilities broke out. On May 20, 1858, while the emperor was still instructing T'an to defend the Chinese *t'i-chih*, Lord Elgin ordered his troops to storm the Taku forts and advance to Tientsin. On May 26, Lay warned that unless two high officials of the first rank were sent from Peking to negotiate with Elgin, English troops would march right to the Chinese capital. T'an pleaded with the court that such a request must be met to avert an immediate disaster, and that the two officials should be sent to Tientsin before June 1, 1858.[33] The loss of Taku shocked the court into realizing the gravity of the situation, and on May 28, as we have seen, Kuei-liang and Hua-sha-na were appointed imperial commissioners to meet with Elgin at Tientsin. Meanwhile, General Seng-ko-lin-ch'in was sent to Tungchow to strengthen the defense, and Princes Hui, I, and Cheng were charged with the defense of Peking.[34]

Kuei-liang (1785–1862), a seventy-three-year-old Grand Secretary at the time, was a Manchu of the Gualgiya clan and a member of the Plain Red Banner, who rose in his early years by purchasing ranks. He was president of the Board of War in 1852 and governor-general of Chihli in the following year. Hua-sha-na (1806–1859), the fifty-two-year-old president of the Board of Civil Office, was a Mongol Plain Yellow Bannerman, who attained his *chin-shih* degree in 1832 and was the chief historiographer of the Tao-kuang period (1821–1850).[35] Reed spoke of them both as "very intelligent and in all respects self-possessed." [36] Well-intentioned people hoped that the combination of their first names, Kuei-Hua, meaning Cassia flower, was a good omen.[37]

The two commissioners left Peking on May 31, and arrived in

Tientsin on June 2. They presented their cards to Elgin and Gros on the following day and met with them on June 4, at the Hai-kuang Temple (Temple of the sea of light), three *li* south of Tientsin. Elgin came with a civilian retinue of about ten men, escorted by a military band and a fully armed squadron of 200 soldiers. Greeting him were Kuei-liang and Hua-sha-na with an entourage of about twenty men, while T'an T'ing-hsiang, viceroy of Chihli, for security reason, secretly deployed 400 soldiers around the site.[38]

After preliminary exchange of courtesies, the negotiations on the British side were conducted largely by Lay because of his familiarity with the situation and also with the Chinese language. Born in London in 1832, he had gone to China in 1846 on the death of his father, George T. Lay, first British consul in Canton, to study Chinese under Dr. Gutzlaff. He became vice-consul in Shanghai in 1854.[39] His proficiency in Chinese was so remarkable that the mandarins suspected him of being an overseas Chinese whose native place was Chia-ying county, Kuangtung province.[40] At twenty-six, bursting with energy and impatience, Lay was entrusted by Elgin with the major burden of the negotiation with Kuei-liang, who was old enough to be his grandfather, and high enough in rank to be the counterpart of his prime minister.

During their meeting on June 6, Lay insisted that the Tientsin negotiations must be preceded by Chinese acceptance of the British demand for a resident minister in Peking. Kuei-liang, mindful of the emperor's reprimand of T'an, replied that the emperor would rather risk war than accede to such a demand. Lay coldly invited the Chinese to try it, assuring Kuei-liang that the only possible outcome would be an Allied advance on Peking.[41] The desperate old Manchu diplomat, resorting to tactics of *ad misericordiam*, pleaded that Lay's insistence would cost him his head at the grand old age of seventy-three.[42] Lay replied: "The provision will be for your good as well as ours, as you will surely see. The medicine may be unpleasant but the after-effects will be grand. As to your chance of losing your head, the best way of saving it is to accept the clause, and the more I make it appear that you act under compulsion, and in order to prevent an advance on the capital, the more sure will be your personal immunity. The more stern my attitude, the greater the service I render to you." [43]

Kuei-liang requested the court to approve the entry of a limited number of barbarians into Peking after the conclusion of peace and the withdrawal of the barbarian ships from Tientsin. He reminded Peking of the exposed position of Tientsin, which made it impossible to avoid barbarian gunfire once hostilities broke out. The possible rise of local banditry outside Peking was an added concern.[44] The court in its turn stressed the necessity of solving the question of ceremony in China's favor before the admission of the barbarians into the capital, and it suspected that Russian instigation was behind the actions of the British and French barbarians, who were said to be basically trade-minded and nonpolitical.[45]

Negotiations between Lay and Kuei-liang went on for days, with the former bullying, threatening, and insulting the latter in every imaginable way. Kuei-liang informed the court that it was impossible to prevent a rupture in the negotiations and a subsequent barbarian advance on Peking without accepting the resident minister article.[46] On the other hand, he believed that if this point was settled, more favorable arrangements might be worked out with respect to inland trade and travel.[47]

On June 9, Lay forcefully told Kuei-liang that, having already exhausted the subject of the resident minister, he must return to Elgin with a "yes" or "no" from the Chinese. He kept indicating that his troops were ready for action, while Kuei-liang pleaded for a little more time to consult his colleagues. The Manchu retired to a neighboring room for a quarter of an hour and returned with an affirmative answer for Lay, who demanded that it be put in writing. Kuei-liang asked him to come back on the next day for the written answer. Lay agreed and reappeared on the following morning. He was assured by Kuei-liang that the document would be ready by three o'clock in the afternoon, but at the appointed time Hua-sha-na and Ch'i-ying appeared to say that for a variety of reasons it would not be ready that day. Lay lost his temper, and raising his voice, charged them with subterfuge and keeping him in suspense for seven hours. He shouted that the result would be a British march on Peking.[48]

Early next morning, while still in bed, Reed received a letter from the Chinese commissioners complaining of Lay's overbearing conduct and requesting him to intercede with Elgin on their behalf. By the time Reed was half-dressed, Putiatin appeared, visibly disturbed by Lay's offensive conduct, and expressed his view that

Lay was "virtually making a new India out of China," and that "his Government would resist to the utmost." Reed agreed to write Elgin a "guarded but correct" note about the Chinese complaint.[49] Lay later spoke of Kuei-liang's appeal to the Allies as "an extremely wily stratagem, at once to test Lord Elgin's firmness, and the measure of my hold upon him." [50] Elgin himself could not help feeling some sympathy for the Manchu negotiators, whose heads might be cut off by the emperor if they acceded to his demand. But he refused to alter his stand, explaining: "I resolved to disregard it, and to act on the hypothesis that, being in the vicinity of Peking with an armed force, I might so demean myself as to make the Emperor think that he was under an obligation to his Plenipotentiaries for having made peace with me even on the terms objected to." [51]

In desperation Kuei-liang resorted to intimidation. A mob riot was staged in Tientsin and a man was hired to jolt Lay's sedan chair while en route to the negotiations. Lay refused to be cowed and continued to press the Chinese negotiators for a definite commitment. The negotiations were on the verge of collapse, when Kuei-liang conceded that he did not oppose the admission of a British minister to Peking, but feared that other foreign ministers might follow suit, creating a great turmoil in the capital.[52] On June 11, Lay and Wade warned that unless an agreement was reached that day, the march to Peking was unavoidable. Kuei-liang had no alternative but to draw up the following note to Lord Elgin:

> To the permanent residence of a Plenipotentiary Minister of the Britannic Majesty there is properly no objection. Unfortunately a collision has occurred with the vessels of war of your Excellency's Government, and as our dignity would be outraged by [the Minister's] proceeding at once [to Peking], his visit, we think, might best be postponed. Her Majesty's Plenipotentiary might live in Tientsin, and an official residence could be appointed him in the capital.
>
> Should your Excellency not incline to believe in the good faith [of this proposal], we request that you send an officer beforehand to make the necessary arrangements. Should he have business, [the Minister] can come and go as occasion may require, and a high [Chinese] officer of corresponding rank will be appointed to transact business with him by correspondence and personal interviews. A British officer and students with him could always reside in the building. This, we think, would be the best arrangement.[53]

The note was given by Kuei-liang and Hua-sha-na to Lay and Wade to save the negotiations from a breakdown, without the previous consent of the court. They had yet to explain their action to the emperor.

b. *Court Politics*

Kuei-liang informed the court, "the barbarian Lay attempted in a most insolent manner to force us to give in. But we put him off temporarily with adroit words." [54] He stressed the necessity of humoring the barbarians in order to avoid a break. A policy of compromise was imperative, he felt, until the Taipings were defeated. He also reported that the demands for inland travel and trade after the cessation of military activities could not be dismissed.[55] The emperor, having earlier authorized the opening of two small and two large ports in the Fukien-Canton area but not on the Yangtze, reprimanded Kuei-liang for his myopic, piecemeal solution of the problems and his failure to consider its long-range ill effects. "If all the barbarian demands must be agreed to," the court asked, "what is the use of sending high officials to negotiate?" [56] Kuei-liang pleaded that his promise to the enemy was the only alternative to a rupture of relations. The evils of breaking off the talks were far greater than those of a vague communication of general concessions. Moreover, "it did not mean that after the concession nothing could be retrieved." [57]

To isolate Britain, Kuei-liang signed treaties on June 13 with Russia and on June 18 with the United States, both countries agreeing to only occasional visits of their ministers to the capital. Baron Gros also indicated his willingness to accept the same arrangement, although, out of deference to Lord Elgin, he did not sign his treaty until June 27, one day after the British treaty was concluded. Kuei-liang now requested the Russian and French ministers to mediate. Mindful of his instructions to preserve the Manchu dynasty, Putiatin readily assented to the Chinese request and asked Lord Elgin to soften his stand on the resident minister issue, cautioning him about the possible downfall of the dynasty. His key words were "C'est la repos qui est nécessaire à la Chine." [58] Reed and Gros also advised Elgin to the same effect but were not heeded.[59] Elgin was determined to go ahead even though he knew London was reconciled to not having a resident minister in Peking.[60]

On June 17 the court received news from Kuei-liang that he had secured a barbarian promise not to come to Peking until a year after the exchange of the treaty ratifications. Only a petty barbarian officer would be sent to Peking to look for future legation quarters, but a house in Tientsin would have to be provided for their officials and students during the interval. The future British envoy would come with a small retinue of twenty or thirty men, at British expense. They would not roam about in the Forbidden City and the palaces, but would stay at their own residence and move about in the streets only. The envoy's communications would be sent to the Grand Secretaries on a footing of equality.[61] Kuei-liang now practically begged the emperor to approve his concessions lest a break occur: "Your slaves deliberated again and again. In view of the fickle and inconsistent barbarian nature, any delay may breed further trouble. If gentle restraint could be properly applied [to them], even though there are some tens of them in the capital, it is yet easy to take guard. Furthermore, at present there will be no proceeding [to Peking]. Getting rid of the [barbarian] warships will afford us a temporary breathing space to plan for [future] arrangements. . . . The barbarians, with the disposition of dogs and sheep, were most bitter when slighted by China. Therefore, they desire to station themselves in the capital in order to gain respectability and prestige. If officials are assigned to look after [them], their gratitude will turn to remorse, and their old suspicion can thus be dispelled. Even if they do not keep their proper status, their personnel, not being numerous, are still manageable." [62] After the treaty settlement and the evacuation of the barbarian ships, China must consolidate the defense of Tientsin and other treaty ports to guard against future barbarian trouble.[63]

The emperor commented that since other countries had agreed on occasional business visits to the capital, why should the English barbarians be treated differently? Elgin's assumption of the title "imperial commissioner" was considered "obnoxious and repulsive beyond the description of words." [64] With the Russian religious mission in mind, the emperor announced that if the English barbarians must come to live in Peking, they should send only students and not their would-be "imperial commissioner." These students should take an assigned land route from Shanghai northward under the escort of Chinese officials, with all their expenses paid by the Chinese government, which reserved the right of control over them. While in

Peking, they must wear Chinese attire, learn Chinese arts and crafts, and never meddle in politics. The barbarian minister himself need not come to the capital annually, but once every three or five years on business visits.[65]

When it became known in Peking that Kuei-liang was urging the court to accept a barbarian envoy there, the literati were in an uproar. Numerous memorials of protest flooded the court and war was advocated as the only means to remove this national stigma. The majority of the memorialists were censors and Hanlin scholars, who considered themselves faithful guardians of the Chinese way of life against foreign infiltration. They fought to keep intact the existing social and political order, which offered them the most comfort and the best chances for advancement, and they formed the hard core of xenophobia. Without access to the secret reports on barbarian affairs, which were considered confidential (*i-wu chi-mi*), they really did not know the gravity of the situation, and without the actual responsibility for formulating governmental policy, it was easy for them to speak out in a high-sounding tone. A typical representative of this group was Yin Keng-yün, censor for the Hu-kuang circuit, who repeatedly remonstrated with the throne against diplomatic representation in Peking.[66] In a memorial received at the court on June 12, after denouncing the Tientsin negotiations as appeasement, he asked: "The capital today is like a man whose spirit is already weak; how can we still allow foreign evils to enter?" Sarcastically he questioned the throne: "I am unaware of any ceremony with which your Imperial Highness will receive him [the barbarian envoy] after his arrival, and if he refuses to leave the capital, by what method can he be ejected?" [67]

Yin Ch'ao-yung, subexpositor of the Hanlin Academy, memorialized that if friendly and submissive tributary envoys were allowed to come to Peking only for a short duration under Chinese supervision, how could an enemy envoy be permitted to reside in the capital permanently at the peril of disrupting the Chinese way of life? Advocates of peace were denounced as defeatists who had forgotten that the Taipings under Li K'ai-fang and Lin Feng-hsiang, several times stronger than the present barbarian forces, had been defeated a few years ago simply because the imperial troops fought with a singleness of purpose. If the powerful army of General Seng-ko-lin-ch'in were to attack the barbarians from the front and the

Tientsin militia hit from behind, together with the deadly tactic of flooding the dikes and thus miring the barbarian ships in the river bed, there was no reason why the Chinese should not win. Appeasers were afraid of losing the fight, not knowing that war was a gamble in which the outcome could never be predicted. Victory might come from fighting, but never from appeasing.[68]

Suggestions of "effective" methods of warfare against the barbarians came unsparingly from various sources. Wang Mao-ying, vice-president of the Board of War, suggested drawing the barbarians away from their ships into land fighting; their "stiff waists and straight legs," he believed, made it hard for them to fight without horses and ships. Their firing power, admittedly strong, could be avoided by sending Chinese and Manchu foot soldiers in front, reinforced by horsemen in the rear. When the barbarians opened fire, the foot soldiers, prostrated on the ground, would be too low to be hit, and the horsemen too far away to be killed. Pressing forward up and down in a wavelike manner would insure victory.[69] Another memorialist suggested night fighting or close-range fighting to avoid the barbarians' big guns, and sending divers to set fire to the barbarian ships.[70] These suggestions read like tactics mentioned some 1600 years before in the *Romance of Three Kingdoms*, revealing a limited mental horizon and ignorance of the rudiments of modern warfare.[71]

June 23 was a historic day. Numerous memorials poured into the court urging the cancellation of diplomatic representation. A strongly worded memorial came from Prince Kung, proposing an all-out war against the insatiable barbarians and the arrest of Lay.[72] Tuan Ching-chuan, subchancellor of the Grand Secretariat, suspected the barbarians of ulterior motives in demanding residence, since there was no trade in the capital.[73] Hsü P'eng-shou, subexpositor of the Hanlin Academy, compared the concession on the resident minister issue to "keeping wolves at one's bedside and throwing fish bones into one's throat."[74] Ch'en Su, censor for the Shantung circuit, ascribed China's basic weakness to the fear of barbarians, against whom, he believed, China could actually win in a war because of her familiarity with the terrain and her superiority in numbers.[75]

More important than all these was the joint memorial of twenty-three high officials headed by Chou Tsu-p'ei, president of the Board of Ceremonies. It warned of the eightfold "evils" of diplomatic representation: (1) the barbarians will detect every move in the capital; (2) they will construct high buildings to look into the forbidden imperial palaces with binoculars; (3) they will select good grounds on which to build their quarters, demolishing the old houses already there; (4) they cannot be barred from seeing the emperor when he makes court offerings; (5) they will propagate Catholicism to pollute the civilized atmosphere of the capital; (6) they may engage in intrigue with rascals and lend them refuge in trouble; (7) they may shield merchants from taxes at the capital gates; (8) their arrogance will cause tributaries like Korea and Liu-ch'iu to slight China. The memorial closed with a warning that the entry of barbarians into the capital would doubtless ignite a mob-rising with disastrous consequences.[76] Another memorialist feared that the barbarians might conceal firearms in their establishments to blow up the city.[77] A publicist blamed the court for sanctioning the Russian religious mission in Peking and setting a bad example for the British to follow. He asked: "Can one tolerate another man snoring at his bedside?"[78]

Ch'ien Pao-ching, vice-director of the Imperial Clan Court, went furthest of all, demanding the recall of Kuei-liang and Hua-sha-na. He charged them with the crime of making concessions to Elgin without the court's permission, and attacked them for interceding for the barbarians:

From my examination of the various concessions that have been requested [by Kuei-liang], I found that those not granted [by the throne] on his first request were usually granted on the second. The barbarians know that Kuei-liang and his associate cannot but plead for them, and Kuei-liang and his associate know that your Imperial Highness cannot ultimately reject [their requests]. Therefore, they act without restraint and fear. What has been granted, regrettably cannot be revoked. Should the subject of residence in the capital be requested repeatedly, in the hope of obliging your Imperial Highness to accede to it, the calamitous [fate] of the Liu-ch'ius would instantly be duplicated in our Celestial Empire. . . . I humbly beg that when Kuei-liang and his associate make requests again, your Imperial Highness issue a special edict stating categorically that, with respect to those barbarian demands that have already been met at a great cost, the Imperial Highness, whose disposition is generous, will not reopen the case; but if the barbarians still insist upon residence in the capital, it shows that Kuei-liang and his associate have failed in their management of the general situation. They should at once be dismissed and recalled to the capital, no longer allowed to argue with the barbarians, and all the official communications [i.e., concessions] previously given [to the barbarians] should be nullified once for all.[79]

The court was caught between advocacy of war by this large number of officials on the one hand, and Kuei-liang's warning of a barbarian march on the other. The futility of fighting was apparent to the court, if not to the memorialists, yet the views of such a large group of high officials could not be ignored. An edict was therefore issued on June 23 calling the Manchu princes, grand councillors, and the twenty-three memorialists to a grand debate on the course of war and peace from the long-range standpoint. In this edict the emperor said:

> In my opinion, it is easy to fight but difficult to guard against complications after the fighting. Appeasement may stabilize the situation [for the present], yet it is difficult to prevent complications after the appeasement. Then, does that mean we have no alternative but to fight? Certainly not! The evil consequences of [barbarian] inland [navigation] are gradual; we still have plenty of time to work out precautionary measures while bridling them gently for the time being. [From this standpoint], appeasement is better. If we allow the would-be "imperial commissioner" of the barbarian chieftain to stay in the capital, every move of ours will be under his observation. War and appeasement are equally difficult; either course brings with it unending troubles. Must we fight then? Between the two evils, we shall choose the lesser one. By carefully considering the [elements of] time and circumstances, we will fight when we must fight. But at present, the time has not yet come when we must fight.[80]

The last sentence implied the court's inclination toward appeasement, which it knew, if the courtiers did not, was the only alternative to destruction. Therefore the purpose in calling this grand meeting may not have been to deliberate the policy of war or peace as the edict said, but to mollify the belligerence of Chinese officials through the mediation of the Manchu princes, so as to prepare the way for peace. This was the more likely in view of the fact that the emperor summoned Princes Hui, I, and Cheng for a secret audience before the scheduled grand meeting, at which time he may possibly have left them some special, last-minute instructions to be followed vis-à-vis the recalcitrant Chinese officials.[81] Not invited to this secret audience was Prince Kung, who on that very day had advocated war and the arrest of Lay.

Princes Hui, I, and Cheng, close advisors to the emperor, were men of great prestige. It will be recalled that Prince Hui [Mien-yü] was the brother of the late Emperor Tao-kuang and the uncle of the reigning Emperor Hsien-feng. Prince I [Tsai-yüan] and Prince Cheng [Tuan-hua] were entrusted, at the deathbed of Emperor Tao-kuang, with the coveted assignment of assisting the new emperor. All three enjoyed the full confidence of Emperor Hsien-feng. Since early June 1858, they had been charged with the important task of defending the capital, and had not been very vocal about the policy of war or peace.[82] Not so quiet among the royal blood was Prince Kung, and he was not asked to participate in this secret audience. This may be further evidence of the emperor's intention to restrain the belligerent Chinese officials by using these three Manchu princes.

Among the twenty-three Chinese memorialists present at the conference were three board presidents, two vice-presidents, and eighteen censors. A record of the meeting was kept by Censor Yin Keng-yün:

After the reading [of the edict quoted above], I stood with my hands folded, and the princes and great ministers were all standing too.

Prince Cheng angrily asked me: "What great ideas do you have?"

I answered: "I have no great ideas, but as recipients of imperial grace and favors for over two hundred years, we cannot bear the sight of offering [the barbarians] the imperial shrine and the dynasty."

Prince Cheng: "Why do you say we are offering them to the barbarians?"

I said: "If we allow the barbarians to establish a legation in the capital with a would-be imperial commissioner stationed in it, intrigues will arise within one day. If this is not offering [the imperial shrine and the dynasty] to the barbarians, what is it?"

Prince Hui asked, "How dare you call the barbarian envoy an imperial commissioner?"

I answered: "This is stated in the vermilion edict; it is not my own term."

Prince Hui said: "We will not let them establish a barbarian legation, but only something like the vice-director of the Imperial Board of Astronomy in the Western Hall [Hsi-yang t'ang] of the K'ang-hsi period, or like the official students of the Russian language school. They cut their hair, wear our clothes, and are only a few men."

I replied: "How can we compare the present with the early days of the dynasty? The barbarians certainly will not be so respectful and submissive now. Even if they are cooperative outwardly, they are in reality barbarian soldiers in disguise. The trouble is unpredictable. We had better fight."

Prince Cheng said: "To fight is easy. I need only to send a few scouts to defeat the barbarians. But after the victory, what shall we do about the evil aftermath?"

I answered: "The trouble with fighting is losing. If we fight and win, where is the trouble?"

Prince Cheng: "I am worried about the coastal area."

I answered: "Fighting has broken out in Canton and Tientsin successively; we could exterminate [the barbarians'] best troops in one place, and uproot their base in the other. How many barbarian troops are left to disturb our coastal area?"

Prince Cheng: "I worry about Shanghai, which yields military revenue south of the Yangtze."

I answered: "This is Ho Kuei-ch'ing's [viceroy of Nanking] bad advice to the nation. He says we should never fight the barbarians if we bear in mind the issues of sea transportation and military revenue [to fight the Taipings]. But how much sea transportation is there today? . . . What we receive from foreign taxes is but 10–20 per cent [of the total]; if military revenue is to come entirely from foreign taxes, I can't imagine how much more unruly the barbarians will become. Besides, if the barbarians take Shanghai, the capital is still there and we can plan for its recovery. If they take the capital first, will there still be Shanghai?"

Prince Cheng said: "The Emperor does not see as you see. Four seas are one family; how can we disregard Shanghai?"

I answered: "We may as well leave out the saying that the world is one family. Even if we say that the world is one body, the capital is the head and the outer provinces are limbs. It is nonsense to disregard the head in favor of the limbs."

Prince Cheng said: "What shall we do if the barbarians attack the Yangtze River directly?"

I answered: "The Yangtze River is not possessed by our dynasty today [i.e., in Taiping occupation]. We need not worry too much about it."

Prince Cheng said: "No. If [the barbarians] take Chinkiang, occupy Nanking and then say: 'We took Nanking from the Long Hair [i.e., the Taipings] and not from the Great Ch'ing,' what shall we do about it?"

I answered: "There is a way."

Prince Cheng asked: "What way?"

I answered: "We can use the fighters of the Taipings to fight the barbarians. General Chang Kuo-liang and others will do."

Prince Cheng said: "If the barbarians hook up with the Taipings, what shall we do?"

I answered: "If you offer them Chinkiang, are you sure that they will not hook up with the Taipings?"

Prince Cheng asked: "Now that Kirin, Heilungkiang and Kiakhta have already been given to the [Russian] barbarians, if [the Russians] invaded us from behind over the land, and the [English barbarians] flared up in the coastal area, what should we do?"

I answered: "I-shan and others are mediocre, feeble and incompetent. Because of the Russian chieftain Muraviev's imposing power, they have given away five thousand *li* of territory. The loss is such that there is no other way but to fight if we want independence."

Prince Cheng asked: "Why don't you go to fight?"

I answered: "If the Emperor asks me to lead troops, I will go without hesitation."

Prince Cheng became more angry and asked: "If you fight and win, the nation will have no maritime trouble for ten thousand years. Can you vouch for that?"

I answered: "Since ancient times, in deliberating state affairs and discussing the principles and the force of circumstance, there has never been the precedent of asking for an assurance of ten thousand years. Moreover, existence and extinction are pre-ordained. [We can only] do the human part and wait for Nature's disposition."

Prince Cheng chided: "What's the use of talking about the human part and Nature's disposition!"

Wang Mao-yin, vice-president of the Board of War, interposed for me: "This is the principle that Mencius told to Duke Teng-wen."

Wan Ch'ing-li, vice-president of the Board of Punishments, also interposed: "Chu-ku Liang said: 'Success or failure, luck or no luck, cannot be foreseen.' This is what [that phrase] meant."

Ch'ien Pao-ching, vice-president of the Imperial Clan Court further argued [for me].

Prince Cheng became extremely angry, saying: "I merely ask whether or not there is assurance for ten thousand years!"

I answered: "If in advocating appeasement the Prince has such an assurance, then in advocating war we have even more assurance. The Emperor has called this meeting to consider the advantages and disadvantages of war and peace, and the vermilion edict speaks of choosing the lesser of the two evils. Today, competent men are few, the treasury reserve is depleted, and military strength is inadequate. We cannot discuss the way of profiting the nation, but only of choosing the lesser evil for our Emperor and forefathers. Only so can we be considered loyal ministers and filial sons."

Prince Cheng became more angry and said: "The Emperor does not want you to mind his business."

I was also very angry.

Prince Hui mediated: "Don't get impatient!"

I said: "It is not surprising that we officials get impatient. The imperial door is far beyond our reach [lit., ten thousand *li* away]. The [barbarian] situation has deteriorated to such an extent that a meeting like today's is called. After this [meeting], perhaps we will not even be able to see the princes!"

Prince Hui said: "The policy [of war and peace] should be confidential; why don't you prepare a memorial?"

I answered "yes" and left the room. As I looked at the imperial palace, sorrow rose from within and I wept in gushing tears.[83]

After this tempestuous grand meeting, Censor Yin complained to the throne that his voice was not heeded by the Manchu princes who kept matters entirely secret from him.[84] He wrote ruefully: "The various princes stood high above and would not listen [to voices] from below. Consequently your minister found no way of proffering his humble opinions." [85] However, Yin's reputation as a loyal official soared, a fact which did not seem to please the Manchu princes, and not long afterward Yin lost his position.[86] The defeat of the war advocates prepared the court to accept Kuei-liang's pleadings.

The above account may seem to lend credence to the common view that the Manchus, as an ethnic group, were more conciliatory than the Chinese. Actually such an impression is erroneous. The Manchus and Chinese were all anti-foreign, but the Manchu princes, being in closer contact with the emperor, enjoyed free access to the confidential reports from Kuei-liang, which gave them a clearer view of the gravity of the situation. Their intense concern for the safety of the dynasty compelled them to be more flexible in their response to the challenge of the time and more self-controlled in times of stress. On the other hand, most of the Chinese memorialists were censors and Hanlin scholars, men without the actual responsibility for formulating government policy and uninformed about the confidential reports on barbarian affairs. Their primary concern was not so much the safety of the dynasty as the preservation of the Chinese heritage and way of life. Their unrealistic, high-sounding pronouncements revealed their complete ignorance of the dangerous situation before them. For instance, even when Elgin was threatening to march on Peking, Censor Yin boldly asserted that fighting in Tientsin and Canton could exterminate the best barbarian troops and uproot their base. The dominant factor in determining individual reaction to the barbarian challenge, therefore, was not nationality, but knowledge of the impending danger. Kuei-liang, a Manchu, Hua-sha-na, a Mongol, and T'an T'ing-hsiang, a Chinese, all advocated peace because they realized the absolute futility of fighting. Prince Kung, a Manchu not in close touch with the emperor, and the censors and Hanlin scholars, mostly Chinese with no access to the confidential reports on barbarian affairs, all advocated war. There was no clear-cut line between the Manchus and the Chinese, as ethnic groups, in their response to the immediate barbarian challenge. Whoever was sent to the negotiation or was close enough to the throne to know what was actually going on advocated peace, and whoever did not face the barbarians or have access to confidential information advocated war.

The response of these men to the barbarian situation appeared spontaneous and lacking in centralized organization. Most of the memorials were sent in individually by the memorialists on their own initiative, except the joint one on June 23, quoted above. Even that joint memorial merely showed the sharing of similar views by the memorialists without indicating any organized efforts behind the move. No evidence has been found to suggest that Prince Kung, General Seng-ko-lin-ch'in, the censors and Hanlin academicians formed a party of war, while the two imperial negotiators, Kuei-liang and Hua-sha-na, and the three Manchu princes, Hui, I, Cheng, formed a party of peace. The common description of a "war party" and a "peace party" in Peking, so often seen in contemporary accounts, is too loose to be acceptable. "Party" implies an organized group, which did not exist. There were only war "advocates" and peace "advocates."

It has also been suggested that there existed in Peking a powerful "Council of Princes" (*Ch'ing-kuei hui-i*), which was influential in guiding the emperor on the course of war and peace. Some eighteen instances have been cited by a Japanese Sinologist to indicate that the Manchu princes, under the leadership of Prince Hui, had memorialized and received edicts conjointly during the period 1858–1861. This, he boldly asserts, proves the existence of the council.[87] A detailed and careful scrutiny, however, reveals that such was not quite the case. Of the eighteen instances cited, only four concerned the Tientsin negotiations in 1858: one pertinent to the appointment of the three Manchu princes as members of the Commission of Defense for the capital (*Hsün-fang ch'u*) in early June 1858; one relative to the June 23 grand conference; one relative to the punishment of Ch'i-ying; and one relative to the punishment of the officials who lost the Taku forts. This evidence is too sketchy and circumstantial to establish that they constituted a council. As confidential advisors to the emperor and members of the same Commission of Defense during the 1858 crisis, Princes Hui, I, and Cheng were doubtless a closely knit group in constant consultation with each other on matters of national defense and other important affairs relative to the imperial household, such as the trial of imperial clansman Ch'i-ying. While they memorialized jointly several times on the defense of the capital in 1858, they were rather quiet on foreign affairs. Sending memorials and receiving edicts jointly only suggests their close working relationship as an inner court circle without indicating any extra-official status. To refer to them as an advisory "council of princes" is to give them an added institutional status as members of a new government organ, which in fact did not exist. The notion of such a council is therefore misleading and must be discounted. It does seem, however, that the three Manchu princes rose to greater power in 1860, a fact to which many contemporary Chinese and Western records bore witness; for instance, H. B. Morse spoke of a "camerilla of three Imperial princes." [88] But to call them a council of princes is to stretch the imagination too far. There was no such council in 1860, much less in 1858.

The day after the grand conference, June 24, the court received an urgent request from Kuei-liang for instructions as to whether he should avert a break at the last minute by accepting the barbarian demands or resist to the end at the risk of an all-out war, in which case the Mongolian General Seng-ko-lin-ch'in had better come to Tientsin.[89] No direct reply came from the emperor, who merely restated that he had already saved the barbarian's face by allowing him to come to Peking once every three or five years on business visits, after the Russian fashion. "If the barbarian in question still insists on sending an envoy to the capital and building houses for permanent residence, you should tell him that this could never be done and that any unauthorized concession on your part will surely bring on severe imperial punishment and nullify completely all the previously granted articles. Further management [of the barbarians] will depend on the reply of the English and French barbarians. . . . You should confront them with forceful language and watch for their reaction. If they resort to force, we can only fight it out. But if they wish to keep the profits of the concessions already made by Kuei-liang and his colleague, which are indeed handsome, they will surely request mediation from the Russian and American barbarians. In that case we will act discreetly. The [situation] thus will not be entirely controlled by them and produce unending trouble." [90] Meanwhile, General Seng-ko-lin-ch'in and Viceroy T'an T'ing-hsiang were alerted to ready their troops and local militia for action.

In Tientsin, Lay and Wade continued to press Kuei-liang to sign the treaty, regarding which he had been stalling for over twenty days. Kuei-liang, literally an exhausted man now, informed the court that under the circumstances there was no alternative but to sign the treaty. Barbarian ships were in sight, and Lay permitted no further discussion. Nonetheless, he consoled the emperor: "At present the peace treaties with the two nations of England and France should not be taken as true certificates and real contracts, but a few pieces of paper by which the [enemy] warships could be made to withdraw temporarily from the harbor. In the future if the renouncement of the treaties and friendship is desired, your Highness needs only to charge your slaves with the crime of mismanagement; [the treaties] will immediately become waste paper." [91] To show that he had left no stone unturned, Kuei-liang further stated that he had applied for help from the Chinese scribes serving under the barbarians.[92]

On June 25, Kuei-liang begged Reed and Putiatin to intercede with Elgin on the resident minister issue which he said he could not grant except at the peril of his life.[93] On June 26, a warm but pleasant day, Putiatin asked Reed to join him in a formal protest to Elgin against the insistence on a resident minister, but Reed said later that while he was "very much inclined to such a step," it was "a very serious one, being in fact an appeal to the world against England." Reed asked for more time to think about it.[94] News of Ch'i-ying's death sentence arrived to lend weight to Kuei-liang's pleas. But Elgin refused to be moved. Frederick Bruce, Elgin's brother and secretary, accused Kuei-liang of temporization and bad faith, warning that if the treaty was not signed by that night, it would not be signed anywhere but in Peking. He denounced the court's opposition as an "utterly absurd and inadmissible" attitude of hostility toward England.[95]

Kuei-liang had no choice but to give in. He informed the court that the successive mismanagements of barbarian affairs in Canton, Shanghai and Taku had left him nothing to bargain with and that the barbarians had seen China's weakness. The views of the war ad-

vocates must be shunned, he stated, because fighting would only lead
to national destruction. He gave five compelling reasons why war
had to be avoided at all costs: (1) He himself had witnessed the
superior barbarian firearms and troop movements in Tientsin, and
was convinced of their ability to take Peking in case of war. (2) He
feared a domestic uprising in Tientsin and banditry around Peking.
(3) Depletion of the Chihli treasury, lack of munitions, and the flat
terrain in the Tientsin-Peking area made effective defense impossible. (4) The danger of the Taipings and the Nien rebels still
existed. (5) Peace with the barbarians would restore trade and enrich
the treasury to finance the internal campaigns. These considerations,
Kuei-liang stated, prompted him to accept the treaty as the only
alternative to an immediate barbarian onslaught. Fortunately, Elgin
was a man of some integrity, who had achieved the height of fame
and power in his own country and did not seek advancement through
foreign adventure. From his decision not to kill Yeh Ming-ch'en and
his promise to withdraw his troops and return Canton after the signing of the treaty, Kuei-liang surmised that Elgin's real intention in
insisting on the resident minister clause was not to make plots and
intrigues in the capital but to communicate with the court at a closer
distance so as to gain prestige among foreign nations.[96] The control
of these tens of barbarians was eased by the presence of their dependents, who could be looked upon as hostages. Their Chinese
employees and servants could also detect and report their movements. Moreover, Kuei-liang predicted that the barbarians might
even leave Peking on their own: "Barbarians dread most to spend
money. Let them pay their own expenses. Furthermore, they fear
wind and dust. With no advantages from residence [in Peking], they
inevitably will leave on their own. That is why I have granted the
issue of the residence in the capital at my discretion." [97]

The Treaty of Tientsin between China and Britain was signed
on that day, June 26, 1858, by Kuei-liang and Hua-sha-na for China
and Lord Elgin for Britain. The Chinese negotiators did not have
the previous consent of the court. When the report of the signing
reached the court on June 28, the emperor still ordered the negotiators to strive to add three articles to the treaty: (1) the English minister should make only occasional business visits to the
capital in the same way as the American minister, or wear Chinese
attire and accept Chinese ceremony if he was to stay in Peking; (2)

the opening of Chingkiang should be delayed until after the conclusion of the campaign against the Taipings along the Yangtze river; (3) Newchwang and Tengchow were to be opened only to foreign commercial ships, and not to battleships. This order reached Kuei-liang on June 29, three days after the signing of the treaty, and he could do nothing about it. On July 3, the emperor painfully approved the treaty.[98] The provisions concerning a resident minister in the British Treaty of Tientsin are as follows:

Article 2. For the better preservation of harmony in future, Her Majesty the Queen of Great Britain and His Majesty the Emperor of China mutually agree that, in accordance with the universal practice of great and friendly nations, Her Majesty the Queen may, if She see fit, appoint Ambassadors, Ministers, or other Diplomatic Agents to the Court of Pekin; and His Majesty the Emperor of China may, in like manner, if He see fit, appoint Ambassadors, Ministers, or other Diplomatic Agents to the Court of St. James.

Article 3. His Majesty the Emperor of China hereby agrees that the Ambassador, Minister, or other Diplomatic Agent, so appointed by Her Majesty the Queen of Great Britain, may reside, with his family and establishment, permanently at the capital, or may visit it occasionally, at the option of the British Government. He shall not be called upon to perform any ceremony derogatory to him as representing the Sovereign of an independent nation on a footing of equality with that of China. On the other hand, he shall use the same forms of ceremony and respect to His Majesty the Emperor as are employed by the Ambassadors, Ministers, or Diplomatic Agents of Her Majesty toward the Sovereigns of independent and equal European nations.

It is further agreed, that Her Majesty's Government may acquire at Pekin a site for building, or may hire houses for the accommodation of Her Majesty's Mission, and that the Chinese Government will assist it in so doing.

Her Majesty's Representative shall be at liberty to choose his own servants and attendants, who shall not be subjected to any kind of molestation whatever.

Any person guilty of disrespect or violence to Her Majesty's Representative, or to any member of his family or establishment, in deed or word, shall be severely punished.[99]

On the following day the Treaty of Tientsin with France was signed. Gros exchanged his signing pen for Kuei-liang's brush as a souvenir.[100] Like the American and Russian treaties, the French treaty did not contain a provision on permanent residence but only on occasional visits. Nevertheless, because of the most-favored-nation clause in their treaties, the French, Russians, and Americans all benefited by the British efforts.

The signing of these treaties was a milestone in Sino-Western relations. With an air of proud accomplishment Lord Elgin informed London that the concessions, though not extravagant in themselves, amounted to a revolution in the eyes of the Chinese, and that the resident minister clause was "pregnant with the most important consequences to China." [101] Although he now had the right to go to Peking to present the Queen's credentials, his political acumen told him to renounce it, feeling that such an act would be most distasteful to the Chinese emperor at that moment.[102] The British government approved of all his proceedings with great satisfaction, for he had indeed accomplished more than he was ordered to. The other foreign ministers were also happy about the newly won rights, though critical of Elgin's high-handed methods. Reed spoke of these new treaties as bringing "China into the great nations of the world," but expressed concern over the inevitable "perilous experiment" in the meeting of Christian and pagan civilizations, and wondering "whether the old system (in China) is to be totally demolished and then reconstructed, or whether it can be altered and renovated to adapt itself to new influences and institutions without undergoing the horrors of revolution." [103] The United States government approved Reed's work and stated that the treaty provisions were "as favorable to the United States as we had any just reason to expect." [104] The Chinese, of course, were bitter about this experience of *le pistolet sur la gorge.*

If Kuei-liang and Hua-sha-na signed the treaties with firm hands, they did it with wavering hearts. The gains and losses of the treaties would not be final before the exchange of ratifications a year later. Much could, and indeed would, happen during the interval. Lord Elgin took the precaution of suggesting an armed escort for the exchange of ratifications, and the Chinese sought hard for means to restore their losses. The highlight of the post-treaty period was the Shanghai Tariff Conference.

CHAPTER 4

The Shanghai Tariff Conference

Article 26 of the British Treaty of Tientsin required that a traiff conference be held in Shanghai. Kuei-liang, who in Tientsin had effected the withdrawal of the barbarians at a high price, counted on this occasion to win back some of the lost rights. On July 15, 1858, he and Hua-sha-na, together with the viceroy of Nanking, Ho Kuei-ch'ing, were appointed imperial commissioners to negotiate tariff regulations with Elgin in Shanghai. Two experienced Cantonese, Wu Ch'ung-yao, a leading hong merchant better known as Howqua, who held the brevet title of lieutenant governor, and P'an Shih-ch'eng, a salt comptroller, were sent to Shanghai to assist them.[1] Their appointment indicated the growing influence of commercial elements in Chinese foreign affairs. Kuei-liang and Hua-sha-na, however, did not proceed to Shanghai at once, but waited until August 27, 1858. What transpired during this interval of a month and a half?

a. The Secret Plan

The emperor's strong resentment against diplomatic residence was well known to all. He had accepted the Treaty of Tientsin only with the intention of breaking it at the first opportunity. A secret plan was proffered to him by someone who continues to remain unidentified, whereby he would offer to exempt the English barbarians from all customs duties in exchange for the abrogation of the treaty, or at least its four most obnoxious articles: the resident minister, inland trade, inland travel, and the indemnity.[2] The emperor embraced this plan with enthusiasm in the belief that it could solve the vexatious barbarian problem once and for all. Always regarding foreigners as mere profit-minded traders, he had no inkling of the political considerations behind Elgin's demand for diplomatic residence. He was convinced that the secret plan would bait the foreigners into renouncing the treaty.

The question of who originated this plan is of some interest. The emperor's unusual enthusiasm for it pointed to the possibility that he developed it himself. But Ho Kuei-ch'ing, the astute viceroy of Nanking and supposed executor of the plan, suspected it to have been masterminded by some venturesome foreign traders in Shanghai who, in the hope of profiting from tax-exemption, had sent traitorous Chinese "lobbyists" to Peking to plant the idea in high court circles. The basis of his reasoning was that foreigners in Shanghai knew all about this secret plan long before he did.[3]

Ho Kuei-ch'ing (1816–1862), the realistic and clairvoyant viceroy of Nanking since 1857, was well aware of the new forces at work in China. The strongest personality among the three commissioners, he was doubtless the moving spirit behind the diplomacy of the post-treaty period. Even before he learned of the secret plan, he had advised the government, in connection with the tariff conference, to deny coastwise trade to foreigners. They should be allowed to transport Chinese goods from *treaty* ports to *foreign* countries only, but not between the treaty ports themselves; this right should be reserved for Chinese traders.[4] The court, in its reply to this suggestion on September 12, first revealed the nascent secret plan: "All barbarian affairs should be managed according to the designated plan. Ho should not make arbitrary suggestions. If the plan meets local objections, he may consult with Kuei-liang and his colleague carefully about minor modifications. But the main body should not be changed."[5]

Undaunted by this rebuff, Ho Kuei-ch'ing sent another memorial advancing a new and somewhat unorthodox view that the essential aim of finance was to enrich people, and that the growing importance of Shanghai was a result of its income from foreign taxes and ship dues.[6] It was therefore necessary to keep trade profits for Chinese merchants. The court asked him to refrain from worries about losing profits from trade, which it said would not be entirely lost to the barbarians if the secret plan worked.[7] Two special emissaries, Mingshan, director of the Imperial Armory, and Tuan Ch'eng-shih, a second-class secretary of the Board of Punishments, were sent as couriers of the secret plan. They arrived at Changchow, where Ho was stationed, on September 20. Under Ho's influence, their preliminary report, which reached the court on September 29, already showed signs of doubt as to the workability of the secret plan:

If we can manage our affairs according to the original plan, it will certainly be best. But if minor modifications are necessary, we will make proper adjustment to suit the situation without daring to be overpunctilious. . . . With respect to the issue of total exemption from import duties, we dare not announce it too early, but propose to wait for the reaction of the barbarians after our explanation. Only then will we announce the imperial benevolence to win their gratitude. If we cancel only one or two important articles, *we may not even need to offer the total exemption of taxes.* Would it not be the safest device? [8]

The court, worried by this changed attitude, commented: "This way is not entirely safe. We must at once clearly announce the proposition of total tax exemption in order to make them realize China's generous treatment of them. Hereafter the barbarians will reap unending benefits; there will be no more reason for them to go to Tientsin for complaint. All the previously granted concessions should [naturally] be cancelled. Only this is the permanent solution. . . . Kuei-liang and his colleagues must manage [the affairs] properly according to the original plan. Ho Kuei-ch'ing has already been notified of the possibility of making minor changes if the plan interferes with local conditions. But the main substance should not be changed and must be carried out faithfully." [9]

Kuei-liang and Hua-sha-na, under Ho's influence, replied to the court that the secret plan would accord undue power and profit to foreigners and deprive the Chinese government of effective means of checking on them. Foreign dues, on the other hand, if collected, could be used to pay China's indemnity. The irate emperor scolded them: "When you left me, I ordered you to make a permanent solution [to the barbarian problem]. If you argue with them article by article, you practically give them a chance for unending bickering. The issue of indemnity is covered in the tax exemption plan. . . . You have made a bad start at the very outset! I am very much worried; I fear new troubles will arise before old ones die down. What will become of it? My only hope is that you, my ministers, will positively not deviate from the original plan and take an easy way out." [10] Kuei-liang and Hua-sha-na were admonished by the court not to overrate other people's opinions, which undoubtedly referred to Ho Kuei-ch'ing's.

Ho Kuei-ch'ing was now more determined than ever to shelve the secret plan. His close contact with Chinese merchants in Shanghai and his consultation with the wealthy Cantonese trader Howqua, who was now in his service, gave him an insight into the relations between the foreign traders and their diplomatic chiefs. He was far ahead of his contemporaries in expounding the idea that foreign traders and foreign chieftains were two distinctly different groups; tax exemption could win the gratitude only of the barbarian traders, but not necessarily of their chieftains, who would still demand the complete execution of the treaty. If Chinese traders were not to be exploited to exhaustion, he argued, the control of foreign dues must never be lost.[11] However, the court suspected Ho's motive in blocking the secret plan. It took his argument as an artful plea against the removal of his private source of income. The emperor chided him for selfish motives and told him once again that the secret plan must be carried out.[12]

Kuei-liang now tried to influence the emperor through his chief confidant and advisor, Prince Hui, who was his son-in-law. A letter about the unworkability of the secret plan was dispatched to the prince, who dutifully forwarded it to the throne. The emperor tartly reprimanded Kuei-liang for deviation before meeting with Elgin, and warned him of "severe punishment" if no permanent solution to the barbarian problem could be found. The Son of Heaven angrily reminded Kuei-liang that all the present troubles were due to his fatal concessions at Tientsin. The three commissioners were asked to reexamine the past edicts carefully and to stop thinking about shelving the secret plan.[13]

Hsüeh Huan, taotai of Shanghai and a close associate of Ho, reinforced Kuei-liang with a statement, born of long experience with foreigners in Shanghai, that tax exemption could not win Elgin's assent to abrogating the treaty. The emperor angrily asked: "Without meeting with the barbarians, how does he know they would not agree to it? Hsüeh Huan conducts himself truly like a traitor!"[14] Kuei-liang was admonished once again not to evade the difficult course lest heavy punishment be visited on him. The three commissioners explained to the court that their dissent from the secret plan was not motivated by obduracy or private considerations but by a stark awareness of its disastrous effects. It was illogical to levy tax on Chinese traders while exempting the foreigners. Moreover, the barbarians were not entirely profit-minded; the fact that they levied no tax in their colony [Hongkong?] showed that they were also prestige-conscious. It was not merely taxes that they wished to save, the commissioners said, but, more basically, the *established institution* of taxing foreign goods. The term "established institution," which the emperor so often used in rejecting foreign demands, was now used against him, and he was indeed hard put to find an answer. He could only respond with a laconic vermilion [imperial] remark: "*Chih-tao-liao*" [Noted].[15]

On October 27, 1858, a joint memorial came from the three imperial commissioners and the two special emissaries reaffirming their belief that the barbarians would most assuredly reject the secret plan and seize upon tax exemption as an extra imperial favor. Ten reasons were given for the impracticability of the secret plan: (1) The barbarians, who paid no tribute, must be required to pay taxes as an offering, the abolition of which would enhance their pride. (2) Tax payment compelled them to report their ships, commodities, sailors, etc., thus helping China to keep track of their activities. (3) Tax exemption would not benefit the barbarian chieftains but only their traders. (4) There was the danger that Chinese traders might join forces with foreigners to evade taxes. (5) Barbarians already settled in the interior would most certainly not move out even if they were given tax exemption. (6) Tax exemption would enrich and strengthen the barbarians by several million taels per year. (7) Faithful payment of dues tended to eliminate troubles at the outset. (8) Acceptance of the secret plan by the barbarians now would be no guarantee of their good behavior in the future. (9) Foreign dues could be used for China's indemnity. (10) The opium tax, not included in the exemption plan, would give the barbarians an excuse for complaint.[16]

While blocking the secret plan from all sides, the memorialists nevertheless reaffirmed their determination to retrieve some of the lost ground, such as the concession on diplomatic residence in Peking. The court was forced to reconcile itself to the failure of the secret plan.

b. *Kuei-liang Resumes Negotiations*

Having managed the court, Kuei-liang turned to negotiating with Elgin, who had just returned from a successful mission to Japan. Elgin was pleased by Kuei-liang's presence in Shanghai, which he took as a sign of the emperor's good faith in keeping the treaty obligations.[17] Kuei-liang, on his part, found the Shanghai atmosphere far more conducive to diplomatic activity: there was no Lay to raise his voice and no Bruce to threaten a march on Peking. He paid Elgin a courtesy call on October 16, which Elgin returned two days later.[18] The former enemies had become friends, and the polite preliminary exchanges augured satisfactory discussions.

On October 22, 1858, Kuei-liang reopened negotiations with Elgin by stating that the Treaty of Tientsin, exacted at gun point without the usual careful and fair-minded deliberations on both sides, contained some articles that were definitely injurious to China without being advantageous to England. The resident minister article, for example, contained a passage to the effect that the minister might reside permanently in the capital *or* visit it occasionally at the option of the British government. The word *or* indicated an ambiguity which Kuei-liang asserted should be rectified.[19] The old argument was repeated that the residence of foreign ministers in Peking was liable to stir up misgivings and trouble among the populace. On the other hand, if that article could be dispensed with, the emperor would appoint a high officer of the first rank to reside wherever else the British minister chose to stay, for the sole purpose of transacting business with him.[20]

Lord Elgin tactfully replied that since the treaty had been sent to the Queen for ratification, it was beyond his power to modify it. He reiterated that diplomatic accreditation, a common practice among Western nations, was not designed to hurt China but to avert future wars.[21] Lay was approached by Hsüeh Huan, the Shanghai taotai, to urge Elgin to comply with the only request of the emperor in order to avoid the stoppage of trade. Lay promised to speak to Elgin, but indicated that tax exemption could not replace the treaty.[22]

Kuei-liang now employed the new tactic of persuasion and praise. He wrote to Elgin on October 28: "The established reputation of your Excellency for justice and straightforwardness, for kind intentions and friendly feeling, makes us place the fullest confidence in your assurance that, when you exacted the condition referred to [i.e., resident minister], you were activated by no desire whatever to do injury to China. The permanent residence of foreign ministers at the capital would, notwithstanding, be an injury to China in more ways than we can find words to express. . . . It would entail, we fear, a loss of respect for the government in the eyes of her people; and that would indeed be no slight evil." [23]

Elgin was moved by the sincerity of this note, which he described as "very becoming in its tone." [24] The tragic fate of Ch'i-ying still lingered in his mind, and he could not but feel some concern for the future of Kuei-liang, whom he would be powerless to protect after he left China. He informed Malmesbury in London on November 5: "If, however, after having in terms so ample and language so respectful, acceded to my requirements, they are compelled to report to the Emperor that they have failed to obtain from me any consideration whatever for the representations urged by them on behalf of their sovereign, I fear that their degradation and punishment will be inevitable, and I need hardly say, that an occurrence of this nature would tend much to unsettle the Chinese mind, and to beget doubts as to the Emperor's intentions with respect to the new treaty." [25]

Lord Elgin was now inclined to accede to Kuei-liang's pleading for a variety of reasons. He knew that his exaction of the right to diplomatic residence *by force* was not authorized by his instructions. Although he had persuaded himself that the Canton affair had created a "state of war" which justified his exaction of this right by force, he nevertheless recognized that Baron Gros's description of the Canton affair as merely a local encounter was more apt.[26] There had been no declaration of war between Britain and China. Moreover, from exchanges with the Foreign Office, he gathered the impression that Lord Malmesbury, fearing that a resident minister might be "trapped" in Peking, was more inclined to establish the legation in Shanghai.[27] Elgin saw no point in waiving a right freely when the Chinese were willing to negotiate to pay.

Moreover, Elgin was anxious to inspect the new ports along the Yangtze that had been opened by the Treaty of Tientsin. Yet he lacked the legal right to make such a trip before the treaty ratifications were exchanged. Now was the best time to strike a bargain with Kuei-liang for the authorization of such a trip. The trip would have the added value of confirming to the public, Chinese and foreign alike, that the emperor had in principle conceded the opening of the river; it would thus induce the Chinese to take steps to effect the treaty.[28] Moreover, Elgin believed that such a trip would aid the imperial cause against the Taipings, since the "opening of the river ports is contingent on the suppression of the rebellion." [29]

Elgin was also aware of the extremely cold weather in Peking and the impossibility of sea communication during the winter. The presence of a minister in such miserable and isolated surroundings "would be to the mandarin mind less awe-inspiring than the knowledge of the fact that he had the power to take up his abode there whenever the conduct of the Chinese Government gave occasion for complaint." [30] In short, the threat of the exercise of this right could be equal to, if not more powerful than, its actual exercise. The fear of the growing Russian phantom in China also contributed to his more conciliatory attitude. [31] Above all, he realized that he had come to China to make a peace treaty. It was necessary to leave behind him a harmonious atmosphere conducive to the maintenance of that peace. [32]

Lord Elgin therefore replied to Kuei-liang gracefully that he would endeavor to "reconcile due consideration of the feelings of the Chinese Government with the satisfaction of the rights of his own," assuring Kuei-liang that he would "at once communicate" his views to London, and submit as his personal opinion now that "if Her Majesty's Ambassador be properly received at Pekin when the ratifications are exchanged next year, and full effect given in all other particulars to the Treaty negotiated at Tientsin, it would certainly be expedient that Her Majesty's Representative in China should be instructed to choose a place of residence elsewhere than at Pekin, and to make his visits to the capital either periodically, or only as frequently as the exigencies of the public service may require." [33]

Elgin made this concession in the face of strong opposition from nearly all the foreigners in China, and especially from Horatio Lay. [34] The Shanghai foreign body warned that the controversy over the right of entry into Canton ought to be a sufficient lesson to Elgin not to retreat now. [35] Alexander Michie commented: "In China a right conditionally waived is a right definitely abandoned." He charged that Elgin's action created the "necessity of making yet another war on China to recover what he was giving away." [36] But the Foreign Office approved of all his proceedings. [37] The American minister, who had not secured the right of diplomatic residence in his treaty, was "much gratified to find that after all, the English Plenipotentiary does not care to ask more than I obtained in terms of our Treaty." [38]

Kuei-liang was naturally pleased with this gentlemen's agreement, but the court was not satisfied with a partial success. The emperor sarcastically commented: "I sent Kuei-liang and his colleague to Shanghai and ordered Ho Kuei-ch'ing to join in the management, is it really for the sake of tariff? . . . Just consider this: In Tientsin Kuei-liang and his colleague made fatal concessions to the demands of the barbarians. According to their memorials, they originally planned to win back [the lost rights] later. If there is no recovery yet, they can not only not face me; can they face the nation? As a high provincial official, Ho Kuei-ch'ing was specially assigned to participate in this important matter; yet he stubbornly held to his own views without benefiting the nation in any way. Kuei-liang and his colleague followed him closely. In the depth of the night, they should search their hearts and be ashamed of themselves." [39]

On November 14, the emperor grudgingly and belatedly announced the demise of the secret plan. Approval was also given to Kuei-liang's suggestion to transfer the imperial commissioner in charge of barbarian affairs from Canton to Shanghai, there to take exclusive charge of barbarian affairs.[40] Kuei-liang had hoped that this transfer might obviate the need for the barbarians to go to Peking to exchange ratifications; he was even willing to wait in Shanghai himself to obligate the barbarian envoy to exchange ratifications on the spot.[41] The court warned that if the barbarians came north again with battleships, Kuei-liang was to be held responsible.[42] On January 24, 1859 Ho Kuei-ch'ing, viceroy of Nanking, was appointed concurrently "Imperial Commissioner in charge of the Affairs of the Various Nations." [43] To block the possibility of the barbarians sending one envoy after another to Peking on the pretext of business, the court asked Ho to inform them that Shanghai's proximity to Peking, as against Canton's great distance, should expedite the transaction of barbarian affairs and thus obviate their need to go to Peking.[44] The chief task of the new Shanghai commissioner, therefore, was to prevent the barbarians from going north.

c. *The New Imperial Commissioner in Shanghai*

The transfer of the imperial commissioner from Canton to Shanghai marked a step forward in the slow evolution of a modern Chinese foreign service. It was an intermediary between the Canton Viceroy System of the pre-Arrow War period and the formal establishment of the Tsungli Yamen in 1861. The idea of a Shanghai commissioner was not new, however. It was first suggested by Chin An-ch'ing, an expectant salt comptroller, on May 30, 1858, during the Tientsin negotiations. He advocated the appointment in Shanghai of a high-ranking agent, like the Canton Hoppo, to take charge of barbarian communications so as to remove their chief cause for complaint.[45] The court was not interested in the suggestion, but it was passed on to Kuei-liang in Tientsin for reference, and may well have been the seed of his later suggestion.

Ho Kuei-ch'ing, who did not relish this concurrent appointment, advised the court in great earnest that the new commissionership should be a full-time position to be filled by a high-ranking official from Peking. He argued that the viceroy of Nanking, who was regularly stationed in Nanking and now temporarily in Changchow because of the Taipings, was too far from Shanghai to keep in close touch with events there. Treaties, trade regulations, and local conditions, all complex and specialized matters well beyond the ordinary knowledge of viceroys and governors, required the mastery of a full-time appointee. Moreover, a trade commissioner should never be appointed on a permanent basis, as a viceroy was; like the foreign envoys, he should be limited to a specific term, so as to avoid either his attachment to foreigners, or slights by them through familiarity.[46]

Ho Kuei-ch'ing may well have been reluctant to accept the new commissionership because he feared involvement in foreign affairs. Few, if any, early barbarian managers fared well: Lin Tse-hsü was banished to Ili, Ch'i-shan's property was confiscated, Yeh Ming-ch'en was captured by the British, and Ch'i-ying was driven to suicide. But from the technical and administrative standpoint, Ho's suggestion of a full-time Shanghai commissioner appointed by Peking was a masterly stroke in modernizing the conduct of foreign affairs. The new appointee would still, if only barely so, be within the framework of the old system of managing the barbarians in a local port, but he would represent the policy of Peking rather than local interests. The Canton Viceroy System would thus come to an end, and the new situation, brought about by Kuei-liang's appearance in Shanghai as a Peking emissary in close working relationship with the local officials, would be regularized.[47] In this suggestion is seen

Ho Kuei-ch'ing's political genius, born of insight into the Peking mentality and the needs of the time.

This masterly idea, however, did not appeal to the emperor, who saw in the creation of a new Shanghai commissionership a mere act of transferring the seal of the barbarian manager from Canton to Shanghai.[48] Ho Kuei-ch'ing was informed by Peking that his not being in Shanghai need not disqualify him for the commissionership, since no viceroy or governor could receive foreigners in person on all occasions. He could delegate to his subordinates the power to receive them on less important occasions. Moreover, he should not accept indiscriminately all the barbarian communications, but only those not damaging to Chinese institutions and honor. The emperor refused to send any full-time appointee from Peking to fill the commissionership before the complete restoration of peace; instead he solicitously urged Ho Kuei-ch'ing to carry out his new duties for the benefit of the nation: "Your ability is quite equal to the task. I hope you will constantly bear in mind the importance of the overall situation . . . and strive to preserve our national honor, plan for the treasury, lay a foundation for the people's livelihood, and clean up official corruption and the greed of undesirable local gentry. I have great expectations of you." [49]

Lord Elgin, who had been notified by Kuei-liang on February 15, 1859 of Ho's appointment as Shanghai commissioner and the transfer of the seal from Viceroy Huang Tsung-han of Canton, greeted the move with delight and saw in it a restoration of liberal influence within the government, "indicative of a desire [of the Emperor] to maintain peaceful relations." [50] On the transfer of the seal from Huang Tsung-han, whose removal Elgin had long urged in the belief that he was the evil instigator of troubles in Canton, Elgin now wrote to Kuei-liang: "It is gratifying to the Undersigned to learn that His Majesty the Emperor has seen fit to sanction a measure so long since proposed by the Undersigned as the surest measure of preventing further recourse to hostilities in Kwantung." [51]

Elgin, however, was concerned over a statement in Kuei-liang's communication to the effect that the appointment of Ho and the transfer of the seal would make "Shanghai the point at which *all* business relating to foreign trade will henceforth be transacted." [52] Suspicious of Chinese duplicity and mindful of the forthcoming arrival of his brother, Bruce, as minister plenipotentiary to exchange the ratifications, Elgin found it necessary to restate his position on the resident minister issue:

Her Majesty has been pleased to direct that if her Representative be properly received at Pekin, when the ratifications are exchanged, and full effect given in all other particulars to the Treaty of Tientsin, he shall be authorized to choose a place of residence elsewhere than at the capital, and to make his visits there either periodically or as frequently as the exigencies of the public service may require. It must, however, be distinctly understood that Her Majesty's right to direct her Minister to reside permanently at Pekin, as provided by the Treaty of Tientsin, remains inviolable; and that this right will not fail to be insisted on, should the conduct of His Imperial Majesty's servants at the ports, or in the interior, be such as to render its exercise, in the opinion of Her Majesty's Government, essential to the continuance of peace between England and China.[53]

In closing his farewell message to Kuei-liang, Elgin offered a piece of advice on the nature of international relations: "Between equal nations there is no plan for management — as man is to man, so is nation to nation. There is peace so long as each respects the rights of the other." [54]

Baron Gros also served notice that the place for foreign transactions, whether Shanghai or elsewhere, was a matter to be decided not by China but by Britain and France.[55] Kuei-liang commented: "This is a particularly unwarranted assumption of self-importance." [56]

The Shanghai negotiations having been concluded, Lord Elgin returned to England on May 19, 1859. His China mission placed him in the national limelight. He had become a popular hero and was rewarded with the position of postmaster general. He later defeated Disraeli for the rectorship of Glasgow University.[57]

The Shanghai Tariff Conference virtually returned the resident minister issue to where it had been before the Tientsin negotiations. There would be no diplomatic residence in Peking, although the treaty provisions were not formally canceled. What were the larger factors prompting Elgin to retreat from the exercise of a right which he had so forcibly exacted a few months before? And what was the secret of Kuei-liang's diplomacy?

CHAPTER 5

Personality and Diplomacy: A Study in Leadership

Inasmuch as policies are made and executed by men, the study of personalities is a useful pursuit in diplomatic history. This is particularly true in the case of Lord Elgin, who was given complete control over his mission several thousand miles from home. It was he who decided to go beyond his instructions during the Tientsin negotiations to insist upon the right of diplomatic residence in the Chinese capital; it was he also who decided, during the Shanghai Tariff negotiations, to waive the exercise of this right, in all but theory. Such actions certainly appear strange even in the light of the immediate circumstantial motivations. A more complete and satisfactory explanation is impossible without reference to the larger forces operating on Elgin's mind, and these forces include his personality, his attitude toward the mission, his relations with his subordinates, his views of the Old China Hands, and his relationship with the Allied representatives.

Lord Elgin was a lonely man, torn between a number of contradictions. He was divided between a sincere desire to be just to China and an obligation to fulfill the objectives of his mission, between his aristocratic contempt for his overseas countrymen and his sympathy for the mellow civilization of defenseless China. He was also torn between his desire for a quick settlement and his admiral's slow cooperation, between his dislike of petty consuls on the spot and his dependence upon their service, and between his inclination to independent action and the necessity for cooperation with the Allies, who criticized his method but shared the fruits of his labor. Resting on the solitary pedestal of supreme leadership, he allowed himself no friends and took no one into his confidence except Bruce, his brother, and Oliphant, his private secretary. Wade and Lay were merely useful local personalities.

To begin with, Elgin had no sympathy with the origin of his mission. He frankly admitted that "nothing could be more contemptible than the origin of our existing quarrel [i.e., the *Arrow* incident]."[1] He was chosen as the expeditionary leader by the government in deference to the powerful minority wing of British political circles, which was in favor of a more moderate settlement with China. The scathing and disparaging criticisms directed against Consul Harry Parkes in Parliament reinforced his natural aristocratic distaste for local men, whom he described as "very bloody" and dominated by the immediate facts before their eyes.[2] His personal sympathies were, strangely, with the Chinese, whom he found "peaceful, industrious and often pathetically friendly even to his military mission."[3] His visit to the treaty ports gave him a firsthand view of the deep wrongs being visited upon the helpless Chinese by his countrymen. "I thought bitterly of those who, for the most selfish objects, are trampling under foot this ancient civilization," he wrote, "certainly I have seen more to disgust me with my fellow-countrymen than I saw during the whole course of my previous life."[4] His distrust of local British officers was evinced by his refusal to take along with him in his northern campaign Harry Parkes, the British consul in Canton, who he thought was "violent and domineering," the "very incarnation of the man on the spot."[5] He was very much afraid that the Old China Hands would abuse the fruits of his success. Diplomatic representation, however, was the one right that they could not abuse;[6] on the contrary, he believed that a good minister could restrain the ever-demanding traders and the fire-eating consuls. This was an important factor in his thinking when he insisted on diplomatic residence in Peking.

Parkes and the British community, in return, had no kind words for Elgin. Parkes chafed at Elgin's unnecessary hauteur and considered him supercilious and essentially weak, lacking in the qualities of a great man.[7] The Shanghai British community, through an editorial in the *North China Herald*, satirized him: "We admire his wit . . . but of China in general, and of the past and present state of affairs between the English and the Chinese, he exhibits a deficiency of information, which is greatly to be wondered at, and much to be deplored."[8]

At a party given in Elgin's honor, the representatives of many British firms — Jardine, Matheson and Co., Dent and Beale, Moncrieff Grove, Gibb and Livingston, for example — expressed a hope that "the result of Your Excellency's exertions, we trust, may be more fully to develop the vast resources of China, and to extend among the people the elevating influences of a higher civilization." [9] Elgin blandly reminded them that the Chinese civilization was not one of "barbarism" but an ancient one which, although in many respects "effete and imperfect," was not "without claims on our sympathy and respect." [10] His farewell message to the British community in China once again called their attention to the importance of making good use of the newly-won rights: "Neither our own conscience nor the judgment of mankind will acquit us if, when we are asked to what use we have turned our opportunities, we can only say that we have filled our pockets from among the ruins which we have found or made." [11]

Elgin's lack of sympathy with his mission, coupled with his repugnance at wresting concessions from the defenseless Chinese, whom he pitied, for the benefits of the British traders, whom he despised, created in him a yearning to leave China at the earliest moment. While in Canton he wrote to his wife: "If I can only conclude a treaty at Shanghai, and hasten home afterwards!" [12] The refusal of Yü-ch'ien to deal with him in Shanghai shattered his hope, and he had to go north. Speedy completion of the northern expedition required naval cooperation, and this brought him into conflict with his naval aide, Admiral Michael Seymour, whom he accused of not giving him the necessary whole-hearted support. There was no denying that Seymour spent more than two months transferring his ships from the South to North China, and this Elgin could not tolerate. Without Seymour's knowledge, he repeatedly complained to Clarendon and Malmesbury, on April 23, April 29, and May 9, 1858, of the lack of assistance from Seymour, who regarded his request as supererogatory. Elgin commented, "It is indispensable that those who control the material force of Great Britain in this quarter should lend to those who direct its diplomacy a vigorous and intelligent support." [13] Sharp words were exchanged between him and the admiral. When Elgin demanded naval escort on his trip to Tientsin on May 15, 1858, Seymour declined on the ground that he would not "expose the persons of the Ambassadors" [i.e. Elgin and Gros] to dangers while the Chinese still held the Taku Forts. Elgin lost no time to inform London of Seymour's failure to send up gunboats "at the time originally agreed on between us," and insisted that this unforgivable act of omission had deprived him of a golden opportunity for action.[14] The Admiralty in London called Seymour to account. Seymour defended himself on the military grounds that the conditions under which Elgin wanted to act were unfavorable for naval operations, and that if anything happened, it was he, rather than Elgin, who would have been answerable to the Admiralty and the country. He expressed surprise that Her Majesty's noble diplomatic agent should speak ill of the naval agent behind his back.[15] His explanation was found satisfactory, and Sir John Pakington, First Lord of the Admiralty, resolved the case in Seymour's favor.[16] The Admiralty's full approbation of Seymour's course of action was announced, perhaps for the sake of revenge, without first informing Elgin, who, feeling slighted, responded sarcastically: "It does seem to me to be a most unusual proceeding when differences have occurred between two persons in any position of life, that a verdict should be given in favor of one of the parties without the other being informed either of the result which has been arrived at or of the grounds upon which it is based." [17]

Disharmony was not limited to Elgin's relations with his naval aide; it extended to his relations with the Allied and netural representatives as well. Although his mission was supposed to be a joint undertaking with Baron Gros, Elgin was reluctant to let the French in on what he thought was basically a British quarrel with the Chinese. He never failed to impress upon his Allied colleagues his indisputable position of leadership in this Chinese embroilment, intimating all along that, whatever his methods, the fruits of his labor would be claimed by them all, whether they agreed with him or not. His revised instructions were said to have been kept secret from the French, and his decisions to resort to fighting and to seize Chusan and the Yangtze ports were made without consultation with the French.[18] The British were irritated by the French cannoneers' demand for a proper place in the attack on the city of Canton in December 1857, and by the antics of a French marine who hoisted the French flag on the Canton city wall before the British soldiers had a chance to hoist theirs.[19] Such experiences, reinforced by Gros's different stand on the full powers and resident minister issues, strained Anglo-French relations. The coldness in the Anglo-French entente can best be seen in the fact that Baron Gros was not informed of all the provisions of the British Treaty of Tientsin.[20] The *North China Herald* represented the British stand well when it editorialized that it was humiliating for Britain to depend upon France for political results.[21]

The long-standing Anglo-Russian antagonism predisposed Elgin to strong feelings against Putiatin, whose presence in China as a "mediator" was enough cause for suspicion. Elgin never discussed any policy of common interest with the Russian diplomat, in the belief, as expressed by the *North China Herald*, that Russian "policy was doubtless to exclude other nations from Peking and to prevent any port being opened in the North." [22]

Elgin's attitude toward Reed was one of haughty indifference. He would not come off his high stool to discuss matters with his American "cousin"; even those captured Chinese documents on the management of the American barbarians in Canton were kept secret from Reed during the Tientsin negotiations. Their belated disclosure on October 21, 1858 — some three months after the treaty was signed — aroused no small resentment in the American diplomat, who, very visibly enraged, informed his Secretary of State: "Perhaps no stronger illustration could be given of the awkward and partial cooperation and semi-confidence of last summer than that such papers should have been in the hands of the allies, and yet not have been communicated to me." [23] Reed felt, and rightly so, that Elgin had done him a great injustice in withholding such vital information to which he, more than anyone else, was entitled.

Reed's confidential reports to Washington frequently contained such expressions as "His Lordship's tone is not agreeable to me" and "nothing of an official character passed between the English and French plenipotentiaries and myself, and little in the way of conversation on public affairs." [24] He surmised that the seed of Elgin's attitude was the irritation created by his country's failure to embroil the United States in its China adventure.[25] His criticism of Elgin on the full powers issue and his separate interview with T'an T'ing-hsiang further deepened their estrangement. Reed's intercession on China's behalf against Lay's overbearing conduct drew a curt reply from Elgin that America surely wanted to share the fruit of Lay's work. Neither Elgin nor Reed made a secret of the discord between them, and Reed described it by observing: "The negotiations here have been as distinct from each other . . . as if their representatives had been separated by a wide distance." [26]

Isolated from his Allied colleagues, embittered by his encounter with his naval aide, distrustful of the local petty officers, contemptuous of the British traders, ashamed of the origin of his mission and yet obliged to fulfill the orders of the Queen, Lord Elgin was full of inner conflicts and antagonisms. Without the benefits of mutual consultation and collective thinking he worked out the solution to the China riddle himself: a British resident minister in Peking to help the Chinese regulate foreign communities and to restrain the petty consuls in the ports. Perhaps, psychologically, his browbeating of the Chinese into conceding the right of resident minister was an escape from his fretful relations with his aide and Allied colleagues. It is even possible that unconsciously he felt such a resident minister would eliminate the need to send any more extraordinary missions whose leaders, like himself, might not be in sympathy with their missions' objectives. He knew full well that diplomatic residence was extorted from the Chinese through fear,[27] yet he truly believed he was "China's friend in all this." [28] Reed shrewdly remarked that Elgin was a man who had "an irksome task in protecting the Chinese against themselves, and maintaining his own opinions against the impatience of military men, and amidst the cavils and criticism of the querulous merchants around him." [29] On the other hand, if he were truly the friend and protector of the Chinese, he certainly could not push them so hard as to endanger the safety of their dynasty. This element was possibly uppermost in his mind when he made the Shanghai concession with Kuei-liang.

Elgin's position may be summed up in the witty words of Reed: "In fact he was not unlike the Scottish post-boy in the Antiquary, a whip in his hand and a tear in his eye, and he could hardly conceal his repugnance at what he had to do." [30]

Elgin's Chinese counterpart, Kuei-liang, was as flexible and mellow as Elgin was stiff and fretful. The role into which the aged Manchu negotiator was cast called for the combined qualities of a skillful diplomat, a clairvoyant statesman, and a sly political maneuverer. He had to placate the "unreasonable" enemy, to manage the stubborn court, and to overcome a recalcitrant officialdom. He saw realistically that under the threat of a barbarian advance and naval bombardment, the exposed position of Tientsin left him little room for diplomacy. The locale and atmosphere of the negotiations had to be changed if better results were to be expected. The first essential, therefore, was to rid Tientsin harbor of enemy ships and to avert an Allied march on Peking. To this end he knew, if the court and the censors did not, that he had to pay the high price of diplomatic residence in the capital. Yet a day of delay in paying this price was a day gained for General Seng-ko-lin-ch'in to strengthen the defenses of Peking. With no knowledge of modern diplomacy and with no effective military support, the old Manchu, by sheer native intelligence and personal charm, managed to stall the signing of the treaty for nearly a month, in spite of Lay's browbeating and Bruce's coercion. And in the changed atmosphere of Shanghai three months later, he succeeded in freezing the exercise of this coveted right by the British.

Kuei-liang's chief asset was his flexibility. To the barbarians he magnified the fiery opposition of the emperor to diplomatic residence and the tragic fate that awaited him, as it had Ch'i-ying, if he gave in on that point. To the court he minimized the dangers of foreign residence in Peking and maximized the striking power of the enemy. He not only urged the emperor unremittingly to approve his concessions so as to avert the immediate danger, but he exercised pressure on the court through the reports of Prince Seng-ko-lin-ch'in, the commanding general, to whom he never failed to furnish information on the gravity of the situation in Tientsin. He also kept up correspondence with his two powerful sons-in-law in the capital, the venerable Prince Hui, who was the leading prince of the blood and confidential advisor to the emperor, and Prince Kung, the then anti-foreign younger brother of the emperor.[31] Because of these connections and manipulations, Kuei-liang knew that he was not entirely alone in steering a dangerous course between Scylla and Charybdis. If anything should happen, he would not be so helpless as Ch'i-ying. Perhaps because of this realization, he dared to give Lay the June 11th note and sign the Treaty of Tientsin with Elgin without the previous assent of the court, which was secured later.

A treaty in Kuei-liang's eyes was but a means to an end, never an end in itself. He used it to accomplish a specific purpose in the light of a specific condition, and when that purpose had been achieved or that condition had changed, he saw no point in honoring the treaty any more. This Machiavellian approach to international agreements was doubtless unethical, but to him good faith to the barbarians could be superseded by loyalty to the emperor and considerations of dynastic security. Confucian ethics applied only to the Chinese themselves; it was not "wrong" to rule the unassimilated barbarians with misrule.

Yet in his dealings with Elgin, Kuei-liang proved to be a diplomat *par excellence*. Never sycophantic, as Ch'i-ying was, he did not ingratiate himself with the enemy, but combined sincerity with a dignified deportment. Lord Elgin always treated him with honor, and in none of his elegant dispatches to London did he ever speak ill of Kuei-liang. If the arts of diplomacy involve the creation of a harmonious atmosphere for the transaction of business, and the convincing of the opponent of one's sincere inclinations, Kuei-liang undoubtedly had mastered these. When speaking to his enemy, he continuously uttered the pleasant word "yes, yes" until his secretary intervened, whereupon he stiffened his stand a little,[32] implying that he himself was anxious to reach a settlement, but that the presence of someone else made it difficult. When Ch'i-ying was found unacceptable to Lord Elgin, Kuei-liang petitioned his recall, and when Ch'i-ying was thrown into prison, Kuei-liang did not defend him. He also permitted a wealthy Chinese merchant in Tientsin, Chang Chin-wen, to become for all practical purposes, a quartermaster for the invading armies. He did this with the dual purpose of winning the good will of the foreigners and saving the local populace from foreign disturbance.[33] These facts could not fail to impress Elgin with his cooperativeness. By these tactics he made himself *persona grata* to Elgin, and in the end he was able, by a mixture of praise and appeal to Elgin's sense of mercy, to win back virtually the right of diplomatic residence during the Shanghai Tariff Conference.

Kuei-liang was a superb diplomat and a deft manipulator. He was able, without imperial sanction, to make the institution-shaking concession on diplomatic residence in the capital without being decapitated by the emperor. He was also able to make Elgin renounce this coveted right in Shanghai in all but theory, without employing a soldier or firing a bullet, and without Elgin's feeling a breach of faith on the part of the old Manchu. It is entirely possible that if the court had accepted with grace his Shanghai agreement with Elgin and treated Bruce with due courtesy in Peking when the ratifications were exchanged, there would have been no diplomatic residence in the capital and foreigners would have been kept in Shanghai, which, though not so ideal as Canton from the court's standpoint, would nevertheless have been preferable to Tientsin or Peking. But such was not the course of history. The court was not satisfied with Kuei-liang's accomplishments in Shanghai, and was determined to block Bruce's northern trip, in defense of the Chinese *t'i-chih*.

CHAPTER 6

The Resident Minister Issue after Taku

Although Kuei-liang scored an impressive victory on the resident minister issue in Shanghai, he did not succeed in modifying the other three "obnoxious" items — inland trade, interior travel, and the indemnity. Mindful of the impending arrival of Bruce and the emperor's warning that if the barbarians came north with warships again he would be held responsible, the old Manchu once again busied himself concocting plans to block Bruce's journey to Peking. However, he was well aware of the strong English determination to exchange the ratifications nowhere but in Peking. On the one hand he took pains to explain to the court that this occasion was different from either permanent residence in the capital or occasional visits; on the other, he suggested that the emperor ratify the treaty and send it to Shanghai in advance, so that he might attempt to oblige Bruce to exchange the ratifications there. If this worked, Bruce's future visits to the capital could also be blocked by the Shanghai commissioner.[1] The emperor rejected the suggestion, refusing to ratify the treaty before the definite settlement of the four items, and emphasizing that if the barbarian envoy must proceed to Peking, he was to come with a small retinue of less than ten men. They must be unarmed, they must not sit in the sedan chairs or tarry long in Peking, and they must leave the capital as soon as the ratifications had been exchanged. Kuei-liang was also told that the barbarian envoy must not be permitted to establish his future residence anywhere in the capital province of Chihli. Meanwhile the emperor transferred troops from Manchuria to Tientsin and alerted General Seng-ko-lin-ch'in against any crisis.[2]

Kuei-liang reassured the court of his readiness to fight any barbarian attempt to settle in Chihli, and his determination to reopen the four invidious issues with Bruce in Shanghai. He intimated that the barbarians might pick Nanking or Hangkow as a place to reside.[3] Meanwhile, ten barbarian ships and two thousand troops were reported as preparing to escort Bruce on his northward trip.[4]

Frederick Bruce, who had been sent home as courier for the queen's ratification of the Treaty of Tientsin, was appointed British Envoy Extraordinary and Minister Plenipotentiary to China on March 1, 1859. He was instructed to resist "firmly but temperately" any Chinese attempts to dissuade him from going to Peking to exchange the ratifications. Although his future official residence would be in Shanghai, he was to inform the Chinese that "Her Majesty's Government do not renounce the right of permanent residence, and, on the contrary, will instantly exercise it, if at any time difficulties are thrown in the way of communications between Her Majesty's Minister and the Central Government at Pekin, or any disposition shown to evade or defeat the objects of the Treaty." Should the Chinese object to his not having the rank of ambassador, the instructions continued, new credentials would be sent to him at once, in which case permanent residence in Peking must be established. He should be treated better than any of the envoys from the tributary states, and not worse than any other envoy of the Christian powers. He was also to inform the Chinese that if he was well received this time his future visits to the capital would be rare, more in the nature of presenting compliments than of transacting business.[5]

On his arrival in China, Bruce announced to Kuei-liang on May 16 his intention of making the trip to Peking.[6] Kuei-liang replied on May 28 that owing to the excessive heat and the long distance by land from Shanghai to Tientsin, he could not possibly catch up with Bruce, who travelled by ship. Bruce, refusing to delay his northern trip, reaffirmed his position and expressed regret that his mission was not met at the outset with "a cordial and frank invitation to the capital, but with delays and hesitations, ill-calculated to cement a good understanding." [7] He was determined "to establish, on a proper footing, once for all, our [the British] diplomatic relations with the Court of Pekin" and to show the Chinese that his visit was "a matter of right, not of favor." [8]

On June 18, 1859, the court learned from Kuei-liang that Bruce refused to receive him in Shanghai and was gathering a large number of ships and soldiers for the northward journey. Preparing for the worst, the court ordered the preparation of three large houses of seventy or eighty rooms for the envoys of the three maritime nations, after the fashion of the tributary practice.[9]

Bruce proceeded north and reached the mouth of the Peiho on June 18–20. The story of his repulse at Taku is too well known to need retelling here. Suffice it to say that he refused to take the Chinese-assigned route, approaching Peking via Pei-t'ang, north of Taku, for fear of being put in circumstances that would be unfavorable to his dignity in the capital. He chose, rather, to ignore the Chinese warning and force his way through their blockade. Thereupon the Chinese in the forts opened their unusually deadly fire, killing and wounding some 434 British soldiers, sinking four British ships, and badly damaging two more. The French losses were also heavy. It was at this moment that Commodore Tatnall of the neutral United States went to their aid in the belief that "blood is thicker than water." [10] The Chinese lost thirty-two men in the encounter.

a. The British Response

In England the news of the Taku repulse brought forth heated criticisms of Bruce. Lord Malmesbury, who drew up Bruce's instructions, thought Bruce "exhibited too much precipitancy." [11] Sir George Lewis criticized his rashness and implied that he was not acting according to international law.[12] Elgin defended his brother by arguing that Bruce had no choice but to act swiftly because the deadline for the exchange of ratifications was fast approaching.[13] Lord Russell, Foreign Secretary, while openly declaring that Bruce "acted exactly according to his instructions," [14] secretly criticized him for imprudence and overreadiness to use arms. In a secret memorandum of September 22, 1859, Russell conceded that the Treaty of Tientsin did not specify the route to be taken for the exchange of the ratifications, and according to common international practice, the inland waterways of a nation were usually not open to foreign warships in time of peace. "If we can import into the treaty or attach to its execution what it does not itself contain, do we not have to allow the Chinese to do the same? . . . [It is] doubtful whether [under] the law of nations, however understood or applied, we could be justified in treating the absolute refusal of a particular route [presuming that fact to be established, which it is not] as an absolute refusal of access to the capital and consequently a breach of engagement." [15]

Since Russell had declared that Bruce had faithfully followed his instructions, which unfortunately had not anticipated the events in China, it was hard for him to decide what attitude to take toward Bruce. On September 26, 1859 he informed Bruce that Her Majesty's Government "deeply regrets the loss of life" but did not diminish its confidence in him.[16] On November 10, 1859, after long delay, Russell finally came to the decision that Bruce deserved a mild reprimand: "Although the denial of a passage to the capital by the usual and most convenient route would have been evidence of an unfriendly disposition, yet it was a matter upon which you might have remonstrated and negotiated, without having recourse to force to clear the passage." [17] Bruce acknowledged his mistake, admitting that the old treaty did not give him the right to go to Peking, and that the new treaty, under which he would have the right, was not yet operative.[18] The cabinet disowned Bruce's act, yet it did not censure or recall him.[19]

Sidney Herbert, Minister of War, speaking in the House of Commons in defense of Bruce, stated that it was always easy to be wise after the event, and that if Admiral Hope had succeeded in silencing the Chinese fire, nothing derogatory would have been said about Bruce's bad judgment.[20] Lord Clarendon voiced his views in a similar vein: "If Bruce and the Admiral had succeeded, people would have said they had done the right thing in the right way, but having failed and John Bull as usual wanting a victim, they are generally blamed and there certainly are one or two pegs on which criticism may be hung." [21]

While London was critical of Bruce's rash action, it also decided that the Chinese must be punished for their "outrageous" attack. On October 29, 1859, Lord Russell informed Bruce that the personal understanding between Lord Elgin and Kuei-liang in Shanghai had come to an end, and that permanent diplomatic residence in Peking must be insisted upon, although personal interviews with the emperor need not be compelled.[22]

The Taku repulse put the issue of diplomatic residence in an entirely new light. Members of Parliament began to doubt the wisdom of having exacted this right in the first place. The halo that surrounded Lord Elgin after his return to England quickly disappeared amidst a barrage of criticism, charging him with showing "undue harshness to the Chinese, and with having pressed demands upon them, which some of the representatives of other nations did not venture to put forward." [23] Baillie Cochrane, Speaker of the House of Commons, attacked Elgin in the Commons on February 13, 1860, for reserving to himself the power of wresting the right of diplomatic residence in Peking, which had unfortunately sowed the seed of Bruce's defeat.[24] Sidney Herbert conceded, "It is possible that there is no necessity that there should be a minister resident at Pekin." [25] John Bright, a member of Parliament, pointed out Elgin's "grave error" in insisting on an English minister in Peking, where he would be least comfortable and least wanted. "That clause was inserted in the treaty, I believe, with the special object of humiliating the Chinese, and to give a proof of the absolute supremacy and triumph which the arms of England had obtained over the feeble government of China." [26] The Earl of Ellenborough also stated that he could never "comprehend why so much importance has by some persons been always attached to the presence of a British Minister at Pekin." [27]

Elgin lost no time in defending himself: "My accuser(s) might have been reminded that I did not go to China without instructions; that it was not altogether a matter of choice to me whether I should make this or that demand upon the Chinese Government." [28] Then, apparently, he recalled that the resident minister clause was exacted by force at his discretion in excess of the authority granted by his instructions. He quickly made a clever turn:

> I do not mean to rest the justification of my demand for a resident Minister in Pekin upon the fact that such was my instruction. I am ready to justify that demand upon its merits; for I am confident that if we intend to maintain permanent pacific relations with some 400,000,000 of the human race, scattered over a country some 1,500 miles long by as many broad; if we intend that our merchants shall conduct their trade and commerce with that vast population in peace, in some shape or other, under some modification or another, we must establish direct diplomatic relations with the Imperial Government of Pekin.[29]

Because such a resident minister could force the Chinese to conduct foreign affairs responsibly and could also restrain the foreign consuls from using force, Elgin asserted that diplomatic representation in Peking was "the greatest kindness that you can possibly confer upon the Chinese Emperor." [30]

Viscount Palmerston rose to defend Elgin by stating that England was asking no more than the Chinese emperor had already granted to Russia, who, though she had fewer subjects in China than England, "had for some time a diplomatic agent resident in Pekin." [31] To have neither a resident minister in Peking nor the right to visit there was "to be placed in a position of inferiority in regard to the Chinese Government." [32]

T. Baring, a member of Parliament, attacked Palmerston's stand: "The noble Lord said . . . Russia has a minister in Pekin, therefore we must have a minister at Pekin too. Now I do not want a Minister at Pekin unless it will benefit British interests although Russia may have a Minister there. . . . We do not want diplomacy, but trade, in China, and we want protection in those places where trade is carried on. This is not to be gained by forcing the entrance of the Peiho or establishing a Minister at Pekin." [33]

In view of the heated debate, Lord Russell, Foreign Secretary, felt impelled to clarify the government's stand on the resident minister issue:

> Our business in China is commerce. A Minister residing there would not have the same duties to perform as a Minister residing at any European Court. His chief business would be to treat of matters of commerce, to protect his own countrymen residing in the country, and to obtain reparation for them if any of them chanced to sustain injury; and it is a serious question to consider whether this could best be done by a Minister residing at Pekin, or at one of the outports, and going to Pekin occasionally. These are matters which require grave consideration.[34]

On March 16, 1860, he finally took a decisive stand that the purpose of trade as well as the security of the persons and property of British subjects in China could best be served, not by occasional visits to Peking as provided for in the American treaty, but by free access to the highest Chinese authorities. Therefore, "the condition which Lord Elgin inserted in the Treaty is essential and ought to be insisted on." [35]

However, the government felt that Bruce, whom the Chinese had successfully repelled, was not the best man to carry out its policy. On February 13, 1860, Lord Russell told the House of Commons that he was thinking of sending another emissary, with more authority than Bruce, to settle the difference with the Chinese emperor.[36] This proposal later materialized as Lord Elgin's second China mission.

Baillie Cochrane attacked the government's policy as a vain "gratification of the national pride." He argued that the demand was made "not because it was a wise or prudent one, but simply as a punishment to them [the Chinese] for their misconduct." He moved on July 13, 1860, that Lord Elgin be instructed not to insist on the resident minister issue.[37] Lord Russell reminded him that Parliament had no right to instruct the servants of the crown directly, and that he, Cochrane, could petition the crown to achieve his object. Moreover, the Russians had already sent a resident minister to Peking who had been accepted by the Chinese without causing the downfall of the Chinese empire and the degradation of the emperor. The presence of the Russian envoy should deprive the Chinese of any excuse to refuse a British envoy, whose presence in Peking was "a condition which had been agreed to by the Emperor himself." [38] Cochrane's motion for dismissing the article on diplomatic residence was negated in the Commons.

b. *Elgin's Second Mission*

Bruce was informed by Lord Russell on February 7, 1860 of Lord Elgin's reassignment to China "to renew peace and avoid effusion of blood," with the explanation that this decision stemmed not from a diminished confidence in Bruce, but from the fact that Elgin was the original negotiator with the Chinese.[39] For the "outrageous" Taku attack, Bruce was ordered to deliver an ultimatum to the Chinese on March 8, 1860, demanding: (1) ample and satisfactory apology, (2) the exchange of the ratifications in Peking by way of Taku and Tientsin, and (3) an indemnity of four million taels.[40]

Emperor Hsien-feng, with renewed confidence after the Taku victory, dismissed the ultimatum with a laugh. China was not in the wrong, why should she apologize and pay an indemnity? Moreover, the new state of affairs had nullified the need for diplomatic residence in Peking or anywhere else. Confidently he told Ho Kuei-ch'ing, viceroy of Nanking and Shanghai commissioner in charge of barbarian affairs: "Although this communication of the nation in question reveals no intention of begging for peace, we can well imagine their inner weakness [camouflaged] under a strong appearance. The whole issue now hinges on your proper management and guidance as occasions present themselves. Only so will you not betray my trust." [41]

Bruce was notified by the Chinese that there would be no apology, no indemnity, and no entry to Peking via Taku and Tientsin. He could come north with a small retinue, unescorted by ships, and wait for the exchange of ratifications at Pei-t'ang.[42] This, of course, was unacceptable, and Bruce awaited the arrival of Elgin to take action.

Lord Elgin received his instructions on April 17, 1860, from Lord Russell, who, in view of the unforeseen events that confronted Bruce, politely described the instructions as "suggestions rather than directions." Elgin was authorized to act as he saw fit, and while stressing the necessity of his going to Peking and being received there with honor, Lord Russell cautioned him to refrain from shaking the foundations of the ruling dynasty. "Her Majesty would see with great concern such a state of things." Elgin was to make three major demands: an apology, an indemnity, and the ratification of the Treaty of Tientsin.[43]

Elgin undertook his second mission in a subdued mood. He was quite aware that his departure from England meant the sacrifice "of a seat in Her Majesty's Council." Moreover, a mission to rectify errors, for which he was partly responsible, offered neither the glamor nor the excitement of the first mission. He accepted the appointment reluctantly and only after the government reassured him that his mission did not reflect diminished confidence in his brother, but was an acknowledgement of his own special qualities: his acquaintance with English sentiments and the Chinese situation, his conciliatory attitude, and the fact that he was the original signer of the Treaty of Tientsin.[44] His spirit was further dampened by a shipwreck, in which his credentials and decorations were all lost. Rescue operations recovered only a few cases of champagne, which offered some minor consolation; he had to send for new credentials.[45]

The French government concerted action with the British by again sending Baron Gros. The British expedition consisted of 11,000 men under General Sir Hope Grant, Elgin's brother-in-law, and the French expedition of some 6,700 men under General de Montaubon.[46] Actually Britain and France were not on good terms in Europe. Their relations had been strained by the French annexation of Savoy in 1860, and there was a general English fear that the French ally in China might become an enemy at any time.[47]

Peking, confident after Taku, was certain that the barbarians would not dare to start a war again. However, Ho Kuei-ch'ing, the

Shanghai commissioner, realized the futility of empty confidence. He urged the court not only to appease the barbarians in order to avoid a national disaster, but to seek their cooperation in suppressing the Taipings. The emperor was irritated by this undignified suggestion and removed him from the Shanghai commissionership, which was given to Hsüeh Huan.[48] On July 27, 1860, the court received a detailed report on barbarian affairs from Hsüeh, interpreting the Taku fighting as having been ordered not by the British and French governments but by Bruce and Bourboulon themselves. To rectify the wrong, Hsüeh said, Elgin and Gros had been sent again to China to negotiate a peace, but Bruce, out of personal pettiness and a desire to hide his mistakes, was attempting to block a meeting between the Chinese and Elgin.[49] The emperor ordered Hsüeh to leave the door open for Elgin so as not to fall into Bruce's trap.[50] Appreciatively the vermilion remark read: "Hsüeh Huan's investigation and interpretation of foreign affairs this time truly contains many points. Since the two nations of England and France have changed their envoys . . . it can generally be surmised that they do not intend to fight." [51] The court was convinced that Elgin came to seek peace.

Determined to settle the matter with Peking once and for all, Elgin and Gros on their arrival in China ignored the Shanghai commissioner altogether and proceeded north in July 1860, planning to occupy Tientsin before negotiations. The history of the subsequent military operations is beyond the scope of this study. Only a glimpse of the major diplomatic events is presented here to preserve the chronological order.

The Allies attacked Pei-t'ang and the Peiho in August, thus threatening Peking directly. Kuei-liang was again rushed to Tientsin to negotiate, and Heng-fu, viceroy of Chihli, was twice ordered by the court to invite Elgin to Peking with a small retinue.[52] Elgin refused to accept the invitations, for fear of repeating the fate of John E. Ward, the American minister, who had gone to Peking on Chinese invitation but, in Elgin's view, had not been honorably received.[53]

Elgin insisted that the ratifications must be exchanged in Peking in the company of four or five hundred soldiers. To guard against Chinese duplicity, he demanded that the roads leading to Peking and the housing conditions in the Chinese capital be subject to inspection by a group of Englishmen under Harry Parkes, the thirty-two-year-old British consul in Canton, whom he had recently called into his service.[54] Kuei-liang had no alternative but to accept the demands, and to avoid misunderstanding and accident in Parkes' trip, he assigned two mandarins as the Englishman's escorts: Heng-ch'i, the former Hoppo in Canton and now director of the Imperial Armory and assistant negotiator, and Ch'ung-hou, the Ch'ang-lu salt comptroller.[55]

The court, while conceding that a small number of foreign personnel might be tolerated in Peking if the article on the permanent residence of foreign diplomats could not be canceled, was adamant on the point of Parkes' inspection trip. It instructed Kuei-liang that no such trip could be allowed since it was not the Chinese practice to let foreigners select their own lodgings. Fearful that Parkes would not leave once he came, the court considered his trip no different from Elgin's forcible entry into Peking under armed escort for the exchange of the ratifications.[56] Strict orders were given to Kuei-liang and Heng-fu prohibiting the assignment of the two escorts to Harry Parkes. The emperor was exasperated by Kuei-liang's concessions; he angrily remarked: "The great minister in question must have gone blind in both eyes!" [57] He ordered General Seng-ko-lin-ch'in to intercept Parkes, should he come, and send him back to Kuei-liang in Tientsin.[58]

In Tientsin, Kuei-liang diligently applied himself to dissuading Parkes from making the trip, but to no avail. Parkes ignored the pleadings and was determined to go ahead on his own.[59] At this point, Elgin suddenly considered Kuei-liang's powers insufficient as a negotiator and broke off the negotiations in Tientsin on September 7, 1860. He decided to advance his army northward and negotiate a convention with a new full-powered Chinese commissioner in Tungchow, whence he intended to go to Peking to present the queen's letter to the Chinese emperor in person.[60] To prepare the reception of his embassy in Tungchow, he dispatched Harry Parkes there ahead of the army.[61] Meanwhile, the Chinese court had relieved Kuei-liang of his assignment and appointed Prince I, Tsai-yüan, as the new imperial commissioner on September 10.

Parkes arrived in Tungchow on September 14 and was received by Prince I despite a court order that the exalted prince should not receive the barbarian in person but should assign an assistant to see him with a view to sending him back or detaining him in Tungchow.[62] The court apparently was still under the impression that Parkes had come to inspect the roads and houses in Peking, not knowing that a new situation had arisen after the breakdown of the negotiations in Tientsin and the subsequent renewal of military activities by Elgin. Parks's mission now was not to inspect the houses in the Chinese capital but to prepare Elgin's reception in Tungchow. An unfortunate incident was to arise from this misunderstanding.

During the September 17 meeting between Parkes and Prince I, great opposition was offered by the Manchu prince to Elgin's personal presentation of the queen's letter to the emperor. "I tried to avoid the question . . . ." Parkes wrote, "I distinctly declined further discussion on the ground that I was not authorized to speak on the subject." [63] Prince I replied: "You can settle the point at once yourself; but you will not do this." [64] A Chinese record described the meeting in a most interesting way. Parkes, it said, was disgusted by the protracted debate on this point. Appearing to be exhausted from the meeting, he told Heng-ch'i, the assistant negotiator: "I am tired. Get me a sleeping couch at once." Heng-ch'i had no alternative but to set up a couch, on which Parkes threw himself, turning a deaf ear to the Chinese pleadings. [65] The insult and the embarrassment can be imagined.

The following morning news arrived that the Tientsin prefect, Shih Tsan-ch'ing, had been kidnapped by the British soldiers. Thinking that the peace talks had completely broken down and probably with a view to revenge, Prince I notified General Seng-ko-lin-ch'in that Parkes was to be arrested. [66] The general, who was still under the old court order to detain or block Parkes from his inspection trip, easily accomplished this objective. [67] The court was now determined to fight for its survival. An order was given on September 18, 1860, to the effect that anyone who killed a black barbarian [Indian?] soldier would be rewarded with 50 taels, a white barbarian soldier, 100 taels, a barbarian general, 500 taels, and anyone who burned and destroyed a barbarian ship would receive 5000 taels. [68]

The arrest of Parkes spelled an end to the negotiations and Elgin advanced his army to the vicinity of Peking. The emperor fled to Jehol in panic and blamed himself for having believed Hsüeh Huan's misinformation that Elgin had come to seek peace. [69] Prince Kung, his younger brother, was ordered to stay in Peking as the new imperial commissioner to sign a treaty with Elgin.

At this critical moment General Nikolai Ignatiev, the Russian ambassador, walked into the political limelight as friend of both China and the Allies. He had originally come to China in the summer of 1859 as chief of a Russian military mission, which owed its existence to a suggestion by Admiral Putiatin after the Treaty of Tientsin that Russia seize the leadership in Eastern affairs through military aid to China. Grand Duke Constantin Nicholaivich heartily agreed with him and picked the shrewd General Ignatiev, once an aide-de-camp to the Tsar, to perform this difficult and delicate assignment (*trudnoe i shekotlivoe delo*).[70] However, because of China's disinclination to accept the proffered Russian aid, Ignatiev was given the title of ambassador on May 7, 1859.[71]

Muraviev had advised his government to surround Ignatiev with a number of military officers to impress the Chinese.[72] Ignatiev came with five officers — experts in infantry, military engineering, mounted artillery, gunnery, and topography, respectively — and a fund of 500,000 rubles.[73] He was instructed to settle the Sino-Russian border problems and to play the role of "mediator" between the Chinese and the Allies. Because all the Russian treaties with China were signed with the existing Manchu government, he was asked to see to it that the Allied military activities did not become a threat to the existence of the dynasty.[74] But if the Manchu government should collapse, he must keep Manchuria, Mongolia and Kashgar for Russia.[75]

Ignatiev negotiated with Su-shun, president of the Li-fan-yüan, from July to September 1859, and from December 1859 to April 1860, about border affairs, but without success.[76] Yet he was prevented by his instructions from applying force to China or from joining the Anglo-French allies. His diplomatic talents were held in abeyance until the Allies had reached the Peking area, when he suddenly appeared as the man of the hour. He befriended General Hope Grant, the British commander, to whom he offered a detailed map of Peking, showing the northern gate of the Chinese capital as the weakest spot. Grant considered him "a straightforward gentleman" and remarked that the map was of "great value." [77] On the other hand, Ignatiev informed Prince Kung of his willingness to mediate and to rid Peking of the Allies.[78] The court authorized Prince Kung to accept Russian mediation.[79]

Determined to read the Chinese a lecture first, so as to vent his wrath against the dilatory tactics of Su-shun, Ignatiev announced to Prince Kung's emissary that because of the Chinese stupidity in not accepting him earlier, the best time for a bargain with the Allies had passed. Condemning the Chinese for the arrest of Parkes and the mistreatment of the prisoners of war, he said Russia would not hesitate to join the civilized nations of the world in taking punitive action in order to uphold the dignity of international law. However, he would exert his influence to save the capital from Allied destruction on the following conditions:

1. That Prince Kung should send me immediately a written request for the mediation so that I can enter into official relations with him.
2. That the Chinese government, during the negotiations with the Europeans, should consult with me about everything in advance without hiding anything from me.
3. That the Chinese government should satisfy all the demands presented by me during the first time of my stay in Peking: a) to approve and fulfill the Treaty of Aigun; b) to agree to settle an eastern border line along the Ussuri River to the limits of Korea, and in the north, along the line of the permanent Chinese picket; and c) to allow the establishment of Russian consulates in Kashgar, Urga, and Tsitsikhar." [80]

Prince Kung, though a tyro in international diplomacy, was aware of the Russian designs. Yet in his fear of goading Ignatiev into the Allied camp and his desire to effect an early withdrawal of the Allied troops in Peking he was forced to accept Ignatiev's demands. [81]

It was said that when Lord Elgin occupied Peking and found that the emperor had fled, he was exasperated and intent upon overthrowing the Manchu dynasty in favor of a Chinese one. The idea was abandoned only after strong opposition from General Ignatiev and Baron Gros. [82] Instead, the Summer Palace was burned, to vent his wrath.

On October 24, 1860 Elgin dictated the peace terms to Prince Kung and the Convention of Peking was signed, establishing once and for all the principle of diplomatic residence in the Chinese capital. Ignatiev was anxious to get rid of the Allies so as to be left alone to deal with the Chinese. [83] As the "never-failing counsellor" to General Grant, he warned that Peking was unsafe in the winter because the Peiho would soon freeze. [84] General Grant then clamored for an early departure and set November 8 as the deadline. [85] Spreading the word that he would soon leave Peking for the winter, Ignatiev urged

Elgin to spend the winter in Tientsin rather than in Peking.[86] On November 7, Baron Gros also asked Elgin to pull out of the capital to permit the return of the emperor, who might otherwise establish himself in the interior. Gros suggested setting up the legations temporarily in Tientsin and proceeding to Peking after the return of the emperor, in which case, "il les *recevra* au lieu de les *subir*, et cela ne vaudrait-il pas mieux pour lui comme pour nous?"[87] Elgin accepted the advice and instructed Bruce to take up his abode in Tientsin until the next spring. A student interpreter, Thomas Adkin, was left in Peking to prepare the legation house.[88]

The departure of the Allies gave Ignatiev a free hand to exact a high price from the Chinese for his services. He succeeded, within a few days of the Allies' departure, in signing the supplementary Treaty of Peking on November 14, 1860, which cost China 400,000 square miles of territory.[89] His mission accomplished to his great honor, Ignatiev proudly told the Tsar that the task of a diplomat should never be merely to transfer documents like a machine, which any secretary could do, but to exert an influence equivalent to fifty thousand soldiers.[90]

After all the troubles over the resident minister issue had been smoothed out, the British government unexpectedly showed a disinclination to exercise such a right. On December 23, 1860, Lord Russell informed Elgin that in view of the mistreatment of the prisoners of war and the arrest of Parkes, he doubted "whether any European is safe whose liberty and life are dependent on the mercy of the Chinese."[91] He would rather see Bruce established in some easily accessible place like Shanghai or Tientsin than in Peking, which was "liable to outrage or insult, only to be avenged by a fresh war, or to be submitted to in a spirit of humiliation."[92] On January 9, 1861, Lord Russell, in congratulating Elgin on the success of his mission, praised his accomplishments in securing the indemnity, the additional ports, and the new position of Hongkong as "solid and real advantage"; but he failed to mention in any particular manner the resident minister issue.[93] This is further proof that London did not consider diplomatic representation in Peking a *sine qua non*.

c. *The Legations and the Tsungli Yamen*

When the Allies occupied Peking, Lord Elgin turned the official residence of Prince I, who had ordered Parkes's arrest, into his temporary headquarters, and Baron Gros took the Hsien-liang Monastery.[94] After the Convention of Peking, Elgin formally proposed that the residence of Prince I be rented to the British as the future legation quarters, at 1500 taels per annum.[95] Prince Kung politely replied that because the princely residence was bestowed by the emperor, it could not be rented out on a monetary basis.[96] The house of the Duke of Liang was instead assigned to the British at 1000 taels per annum, with the first two years' rent earmarked for renovating the place.[97]

Permission was also granted to the Russians to build new legation quarters on the open ground adjoining the Northern Quarter of their religious mission.[98] The buildings of the Russian religious mission were formerly the Southern Hostel of the Hui-t'ung-kuan of the Ming dynasty, which, being government property, were rent free.[99]

The French request for a legation quarter was made a little later because of Gros's early departure from Peking. On December 20 Baron de Meritens informed Prince Kung that he wanted to rent the *Ching-ch'ung fu*, in lieu of the original request for the residence of the Prince of Su, at a rent of 1000 taels per annum until France built her own legation quarters in the western garden of the *fu*.[100] The French legation site, not as large and dignified as the British, was more attractive and had a beautiful garden.[101]

The American legation was not set up until two years later, because of Minister Ward's retirement from China to join the American Confederacy late in 1860.[102]

The personnel of the various legations came to Peking the following spring. M. Bourboulon of France, after sending his first secretary, Count Kleczkowski, to the capital on February 5, 1861 to make a final check of the legation quarters, arrived himself on March 25, and was received by Prince Kung three days later.[103] Bruce arrived on March 26 in the company of Colonel Neale, and was received by the Prince on April 3.[104] The Russian minister, Colonel Balluzeck, who had served in the famous siege of Sebastopol and had been Ignatiev's military attaché the year before, arrived on July 8, 1861.[105] The American minister, Anson Burlingame, arrived in China in October 1861 and went to Peking the next summer, living at first in the French legation, as his own residence was not yet ready.[106]

The establishment of these legations and the arrival of the foreign diplomats necessitated a reexamination of the Chinese institutions of foreign intercourse. The upshot was the establishment of the Tsungli Yamen, commonly known as the Foreign Office, to centralize the management of foreign affairs.[107] Yet living with these barbarian chieftains was unpleasant enough. The deep-seated desire to *éloigner* the barbarians continued to exert its influence, and the ingenious Prince Kung, though devoid of military power or a legal basis for ridding the capital of the foreigners, dreamed up a new device by which he hoped to make the foreigners leave Peking on their own initiative. He suggested installing a new trade commissioner in Tientsin to draw away business from Peking, so that the foreigners in the capital might become sufficiently bored by the emptiness of their lives there to think of leaving. "If Tientsin can manage properly," he memorialized, "then, even though the barbarian chieftains live in the capital, they must be depressed with having nothing to do and finally think of returning home. Hence the Tientsin commissionership is most important." [108] The court approved this clever device; furthermore, it appointed another commissioner in Shanghai in charge of the southern ports. Orders were given to the provincial authorities to treat foreign cases themselves, and not to refer them incessantly to the Tsungli Yamen, so as to minimize the occasions for foreign visits to Peking.[109]

Later, when a strong man like Li Hung-chang was installed as Superintendent of Trade for the Northern Ports in Tientsin, he practically superseded the Tsungli Yamen as China's foreign representative. The endless cross-reference of cases between the Yamen and the venerable port commissioner so annoyed the foreigners that they were prone to deride the low administrative and organizational abilities of the Chinese, little realizing the secret motives behind such maneuverings.

Prince Kung's ingenuity, however, did not escape the watchful and perceptive eyes of Horatio Lay in England. He told Lord Russell in 1864 that the Chinese intention in creating the port commissioners was "to prepare the way for evading the treatment of foreign questions at Pekin." [110] He accused the Tsungli Yamen of constantly referring matters to the commissioners to wear out the patience of foreign ministers — "in the hope of convincing them that there was no real advantage in living at Pekin after all, and inducing them to abandon Pekin and take up their residence at one of the ports." [111] To remedy the situation, he suggested that Britain demand an end to this practice as the price for continuing to aid China against the

Taipings.[112] For some reason, the suggestion was not acted upon.

From the standpoint of sheer logic, the establishment of the Tsungli Yamen in Peking countered the original secret purposes of the ports commissioners. The very existence of a Foreign Office attracted foreign diplomats to Peking. They did not dream of returning home as the Prince had expected; in fact, they began to enjoy the social life among high court officials like the Prince himself and the affable Wen-hsiang, senior minister of the Yamen. They even developed a psychology of not wanting to deal with local Chinese officials. As a result, the port commissioners did not achieve the desired result of drawing the foreigners away from the capital, neither did the foreign ministers in Peking lead a life of boredom. Prince Kung's original purposes were partially defeated from the very beginning because they were illogical.

The establishment of the Tsungli Yamen pointed up a phenomenon which no keen student of history can afford to ignore: the impact of foreign affairs on native institutions. Foreigners in the pre-Opium War period were quarantined in Canton and were "managed" by the Hoppo through the local hong merchants. With the opening of the five ports after the Treaty of Nanking in 1842, Peking felt the need to appoint the viceroy of Canton concurrently imperial commissioner in charge of foreign affairs in the five ports. This Canton viceroy system persisted during the inter-war period, but after the Treaty of Tientsin in 1858 the imperial commissionership was transferred to Shanghai. With the establishment of foreign legations in Peking in 1861 came the creation of a centralized foreign office, the Tsungli Yamen. The traditional Chinese institutions of foreign intercourse were shattered by the advancing West, which moved step by step from Canton to Shanghai to Peking. In collaboration, the Russian land power thrust downward from the north, meeting the maritime nations in Peking, like a pair of pincers pointing at the heart of the Sick Man of the East.[113] Indeed, China was inextricably drawn into the world stream.

Peace had returned, but the emperor did not return with it. Ashamed of his flight and fearful of the foreigners' new coercion after his return to Peking, he stayed in Tartary and soon passed away. A chapter of history thus came to an end.

CHAPTER 7

The Ideological Issue:
Diplomatic Representation vs. T'i-chih

The forcible imposition of foreign legations on China raises the inevitable question of whether a state, under the law of nations, has the right to compel another state into diplomatic intercourse. Students of international law and diplomacy for the most part agree that no state is bound to receive permanent envoys from other states.[1] However, R. R. Foulke, a writer on jurisprudence, while condemning compulsory diplomatic relations as "a plain act of aggression," concedes that the phrase "right of legation" in the final analysis signifies the "power of legation." When a state has developed its resources and power to a certain extent, it is bound to expand its influence and contact with other states. The necessities of commerce, civilization, and self-interest compel states into relationships with one another.[2] The question of compulsory diplomatic representation is therefore one of national power as well as one of legality. On the one hand it portrays an inevitable and even progressive trend in international living, and on the other it points up the ugly phenomenon of imperialism.

The "unequal" Treaties of Tientsin and Peking left an indelible mark of injustice on the Chinese mind. Nationalist writers for decades angrily denounced the Western record in China as nothing but imperialism and exploitation at the expense of the poor Chinese, but they generally refrained from attacking the British for imposing diplomatic relations on China. Rather, they assailed the stupidity and blindness of the corrupt Manchu rulers in resisting this innocuous issue while readily giving away such important sovereign rights as extraterritoriality, tariff autonomy, and the most-favored-nation treatment. Communist writers today, however, not only attack the British imposition of diplomatic residence as a naked act of imperialism, but go farther still to assail the Manchu ruling class for accepting this arrangement. Fan Wen-lan, a leading Communist historian, denounces the Treaty of Tientsin as a "sell-out of the Chinese people by the Manchu overlords." [3] Hu Sheng, a propagandist writer, portrays the acceptance of foreign envoys in Peking as an act of Manchu surrender to the imperialist world order and of affording imperialist nations a commanding position in China. "Foreign envoys who forced their way into the (Chinese) capital were not to be ordinary diplomatic representatives, but masters of China. The reason that foreign ministers insisted on the right to apply their own ceremony in the audience with the Chinese emperor was to consolidate their position in Peking." [4]

The propriety of these views is a moot point, but the fact remains that Elgin's action was imperialistic by any standard; it left behind bitter memories which have lasted even until today. When the price for resident ministers was so high, one wonders whether the gain was worth the effort. Judging by the nature of the modern world, it appears that no nation could live long in isolation, but had sooner or later to come into relationship with others. Compulsory diplomatic intercourse forced the pace of progress in international living and impeded the growth of harmonious relationships among states. It could not be justified by the principle of sovereignty, upon which the modern community of nations is founded. Thus, while diplomatic representation was an accepted practice in international law, compulsory diplomatic representation was not sanctioned by it.

Probably because of this, the London government was not too anxious to force a resident minister on China. Lord Elgin, although led by his China experiences to believe it the sovereign cure for all the troubles in China, was nevertheless conscious of its precipitant and illegal nature. Hence he was willing to tone it down in Shanghai. However, such Britons on the local scene as Lay and Parkes and other Old China Hands, who had no idea or intention of applying international law or justice to China, were intent upon humiliating the Chinese emperor by demanding exactly what he feared most: residence in the capital. Three levels of attitude toward the resident minister issue could therefore be observed on the British side: London was not too anxious about it; Elgin was willing to hold this right in abeyance; while the Old China Hands pressed for its immediate realization. Distance from the China scene and position in the British official hierarchy seemed to constitute the two overriding factors in determining attitudes.

If compulsory diplomatic representation ran counter to the principle of sovereignty in international law, it contradicted even more drastically the political and social systems of Imperial China. The expression "incompatibility with the *t'i-chih*" inevitably appeared in all Chinese rejections of foreign demands. What did it mean? Literally, *t'i* means "base," "essence," "form," or "prestige," and *chih* "institution," "system," or "polity." The combination *t'i-chih*, in a narrow sense, meant "basic institution," with the implication that its maintenance was a matter of prestige and face. The larger meaning of this term, however, went far beyond the above description to include virtually the Chinese way of life and the proper manner of doing things from the Chinese standpoint. It was in essence the Chinese counterpart of the English unwritten constitution: both being the sum total of all tangible and intangible traditions, beliefs, codes, statutes, governmental systems, and religious observances. To demand of the Chinese a change in their *t'i-chih* would be tantamount to demanding of the English a change in their common law or Magna Carta. The Western practice of exchanging resident ministers was alien to the Chinese mind and totally incompatible with the Chinese institutions of foreign intercourse as recorded in the Collected Statutes of the Great Ch'ing Empire (*Ta-Ch'ing hui-tien*). It was impossible to accede to this foreign demand without amending the *Ta-Ch'ing hui-tien*, and any such amendment would be an acknowledgement of the impropriety of the Chinese system that had proved adequate for the past two thousand years.

The underlying spirit of *t'i-chih* was the concept of *li*, or propriety, which, together with *jen*, or benevolence, formed the two basic tenets of Confucianism. *Li* in a narrow sense meant ritual ceremonies, or court formalities; in a broader sense, the whole corpus of governmental laws, regulations, social institutions, and proper human relationships.[5] The aim of *li* was to achieve social stability, and the means to such an end was to make a distinction between men. Everyone had an assigned station in this society, including the barbarians, and the highest was that of the emperor, to whom everyone must bow. To demand equality and to refuse to *kowtow* to him was a worse crime than *lèse majesté*. *Li* was the deepest bond between the mem-

bers of the Confucian patriarchal society, and the censors were entrusted with its guardianship.

The international relations of the Far East were regulated by
a product of *li*, the tributary system. No foreign resident ministers
were ever received in the Chinese capital, and no Chinese resident
ministers were ever sent abroad.[6] To demand a resident minister at
the capital was to disrupt the tributary system externally and to
preempt the concept of *li* internally, thereby shaking the very foundations of Chinese society. The question involved was not ritual formality, as it might appear on the surface, but the basic fabric of
Chinese society and government. Therefore, the demand had to be
resisted to the bitter end.

Filial piety was another cause for the strong imperial resistance
to diplomatic representation. The emperor was head of the state, but
not head of the imperial family. He could say: *"L'état, c'est moi;"*
but not: *"La famille, c'est moi."* This was especially true during the
Ch'ing dynasty, when imperial "family laws" reigned supreme. The
emperor, although above state laws, was under ancestral instructions.
Filial piety demanded that he preserve the institutions set up by his
forefathers, and that he place his duty to the family above all else.
Since childhood he had been taught to "revere Heaven and emulate
ancestors" (*ching-t'ien fa-tsu*). Ancestral admonitions, edicts, de-
crees and practices were presented to him as sacred and inviolable,
as the constitution was in a Western state. Constantly he was reminded that the dynasty was the property of the founding fathers
and that the chief function of later emperors was to preserve the
dynasty for their ancestors. The founding fathers of a dynasty far
exceeded their offspring in greatness and foresight; for later emperors
to try to change ancestral practices was to invite confusion, disorder,
chaos, and even extinction of the dynasty. Thus, the basic principle
of ancestral laws must be kept by later emperors at all times; only
minor adjustment could be allowed after careful consideration.[7]
Shackled by this kind of imperial familial system, only the extremely
strong-willed emperors dared to challenge the established practices:
K'ang-hsi introduced Europeans into the Chinese bureaucracy, and
Yung-cheng allowed the establishment of a Russian religious mission
with a language school in Peking. Lesser emperors dared not deviate
but strove to preserve the established order; Hsien-feng belonged to
this category, and the hand of the past lay heavily on him. The

double demands of *li* and filial piety left him no alternative but to resist the foreign demand of diplomatic residence in Peking. *T'i-chih* was a two-edged sword; it served strong emperors and enslaved weak ones.

It is indeed unfortunate that in her hours of great need China had no great emperors like K'ang-hsi or Ch'ien-lung. Yet a mediocre emperor might still have been rescued from the tragedy of history had there existed a galaxy of able and perceptive advisors like the Meiji statesmen in Japan. Unhappily such was not the case with the Ch'ing empire during the Hsien-feng period. The Grand Council, which usually assisted the emperor in deciding national policies, had declined greatly in power during the latter part of Hsien-feng's reign. The emperor took personal direction of the vexatious, pressing barbarian affairs and was virtually his own foreign minister.[8] Selections and dismissals of imperial commissioners as negotiators with the barbarians were made by himself. He gave them instructions during the negotiations and read their memorials in detail with marginal or interlinear comments; occasionally he even wrote edicts himself with the vermilion pen. The proud dualistic approach to the barbarian problem was formulated by the emperor, who also took the initiative in calling the June 23 grand conference to mollify the belligerent feelings of the advocates of war. It was he also who sponsored the secret plan.

Emperor Hsien-feng's personal direction of foreign affairs could not but prove a disaster for China. His refusal of Lord Elgin's initial request for negotiations in Shanghai was a grave tactical error. It not only deprived China of a golden chance to keep the scene of negotiations, and hence barbarian pressure, far from Peking, but in fact precipitated Elgin's northern thrust. It goaded him into the demand for direct contact with the court as a punitive measure to offset the slight he had received. If the Ch'ing court had accepted his proposal, he would probably have been pleased by the Chinese cooperative response and in all likelihood would have been less belligerent and insistent upon a resident minister in the Chinese capital. Moreover, without the experience of storming the Taku Forts and occupying Tientsin with only limited forces, Elgin could not so easily have discovered China's weakness. Peking, on its part, would also have enjoyed a much stronger bargaining position when it was not under the direct threat of the enemy. Thus, hindsight reveals that insofar as China was concerned, Shanghai was by far preferable to Tientsin as a site for negotiations. Kuei-liang realized this, as he repeatedly complained to the court that the successive mismanagement of barbarian affairs in Canton and Shanghai had left him no basis for bargaining with Elgin in Tientsin. Ho Kuei-ch'ing also discovered this tactical error when he expressed regret to the court over his failure to persuade Huang Tsung-han, viceroy of Canton who succeeded Viceroy Yeh, to open negotiations with Elgin in Shanghai.[9] Later, when reflecting on the course of Chinese foreign affairs in 1867, Prince Kung, head of the Tsungli Yamen, remarked: "We should never [repeat] the old mistake of passing the responsibility from Canton to Shanghai and from Shanghai to Tientsin. When trouble began, people watched from the side and congratulated themselves that they were luckily not involved." [10] For this tactical error China paid dearly.

This tactical error was followed by the even greater strategic mistake of having no definite overall policy toward the barbarians. The emperor's vacillation between the course of war and peace was, in the opinion of both Marxist and non-Marxist writers, the basic weakness of Chinese diplomacy.[11] His inability to take a definite stand had a demoralizing effect on the nation, and while he talked in stern tones his secret hope was to make peace through appeasement. It was not until the very last moment, when Elgin was marching on Peking in 1860, that he determined to give up this wavering attitude in favor of fighting. All during the negotiations of 1858–1860 he took no definite position as to whether he would fight the barbarians to the end or accept their peace terms, but he repeatedly warned Kuei-liang of severe punishment if he failed in the management. No comprehensive, definite instructions were ever given to Kuei-liang as a guide in his negotiations; there was only piecemeal approval or disapproval of his intercession for the barbarians at each point in the negotiations. Edicts to Kuei-liang abounded in such expressions as "watch for his [Elgin's] reaction and then quickly memorialize me for instructions." [12] The imperial commissioner was consequently in an impossible position. Not infrequently, before Kuei-liang had received the anticipated instructions from the emperor, a new situation had come into existence, in which he could only put off the barbarians with vague promises while waiting for new instructions. These, when they arrived, might order him to reverse completely his stand of the previous day and the barbarians would then accuse him of bad faith. He had either to think up new excuses to muddle along, or accept the barbarian demand in order to prevent the breakdown of the negotiations, and then confront the emperor with a *fait accompli* so as to force him to approve it.

It has been suggested that the emperor's vacillation stemmed from the indecision of Su-shun, president of the Li-fan-yüan and a powerful personality whom the emperor had taken into his confidence.[13] Although usually assertive and articulate in his views, Su-shun was divided on the barbarian problem, caught as he was between the opposite views of his two most trusted friends and advisors: the one, Censor Yin Keng-yün, who strongly urged war to resist foreign residence in Peking, and the other, Kuo Sung-t'ao, later first minister to England, who advocated peace.[14] The emperor, used to having Su-shun's advice, suffered from the lack of it during this period, and was therefore hampered in making up his mind. No doubt he was also a victim of China's traditional attitude toward the barbarians.

Historically, China never had a positive long-term policy toward the barbarians, except the vague principle of playing them off against one another known as *i-i chih-i*. She dreamed of getting nothing from them but peaceful coexistence. As a result she developed toward them only a negative attitude of watchfulness and *ad hoc* "management" when troubles arose. This traditional attitude was sufficient to cope with her border tribes but proved inadequate for the well organized new nation-states of the West. The emperor in particular and the Chinese in general suffered from this tradition.

In the larger context of social and cultural backgrounds, Sinic ethnocentrism accounted for the general xenophobia so clearly exhibited by the censors and Hanlin scholars, who formed the most articulate sector of Chinese society. While all nations exhibit pride in their culture and a certain degree of ethnocentrism, the Chinese version went far beyond a mere state of mind or sense of pride. It became, in fact, an established philosophy toward foreign countries. It has been asserted by an able modern historian that since the Southern Sung (1127–1280 A.D.) Chinese xenophobia has been intensified and transformed by Neo-Confucian philosophers into a national policy of self-defense. The realization of China's inability to cope with constant foreign incursions prompted them to develop a defensive dogma, which asserted that "national security could only be found in isolation, and stipulated (that) whoever wished to enter into relations with China must do so as China's vassal, acknowledging the supremacy of the Chinese emperor and obeying his commands, thus ruling out all possibility of international intercourse on terms of equality." [15]

Although Ch'ing intellectual trends on the whole rejected metaphysical Neo-Confucianism,[16] this defensive dogma remained embedded deep in the minds of the literati. In fact, anti-foreignism was sensitized by the alien rule of the Manchus. The Chinese became more appreciative of their culture and traditions, and the extensive research on ancient classical texts (*k'ao-cheng hsüeh*) reflected their ardent interest in their cultural past. They were ever ready to defend their way of life against foreign infiltration. The Manchu overlords won Chinese cooperation by identifying the dynastic interest with the Confucian order. But Western nations made no such commitment. Their demands for diplomatic residence and inland trade exceeded the bounds of propriety, challenged the established order, and threatened the basic Three Bonds and Five Relationships of the Confucian society. It was only natural that the censors and Hanlin scholars, whose duty it was to safeguard social order and the principle of *li*, should react violently against foreign contravention of the Chinese way of life and time-tested institutions. Here we discern the delicate difference between Chinese and Manchu motives in resisting the foreign challenge; the Chinese literati were basically against foreign pollution of their culture in order to preserve the old way of life; the Manchu officials were against the foreign threat to the dynasty in order to preserve their political interest. But this does not mean that the Chinese did not care at all for the dynasty or that the Manchus did not care for the Chinese way of life. The Chinese scholar-official class, inextricably intertwined with the government bureaucracy, did have a vital interest in the continuance of the Manchu dynasty. It would be hard to believe that men like T'an T'ing-hsiang and Ho Kuei-ch'ing, both viceroys, did not have a vested interest in the existing political order. Among the Chinese themselves, those who were in the government were probably more identified with the dynastic interest than the literati who were not in the government. The Manchu overlords, on the other hand, having committed themselves to the Confucian order, also wanted to maintain the Chinese culture which, though alien to them, was infinitely preferable to Western ways. Yet these considerations were far less *basic* than culturalism for the Chinese and dynastic interest for the Manchus. However, when threatened by the more fundamental problem of immediate extinction, the Manchus and the Chinese, regardless of the differences in their ethnic backgrounds, alike gave in to foreign pressure. As we have seen, Kuei-liang, a Manchu, Hua-sha-na, a Mongol, and T'an T'ing-hsiang and Ho Kuei-ch'ing, both Chinese, all advocated peace in order to avert a barbarian march on Peking.

While the alien rule served as a stimulus to Chinese ethnocentrism, it was also a constant reminder to the Manchu rulers of their insecure position. The maintenance of dignity before the Chinese subjects was essential to effective control of their teeming millions; any concession to foreign demands under the threat of force was a blatant admission of weakness. It lowered the Chinese esteem for the Manchu ruling class and exposed its inability to defend the established order. This was tantamount to an invitation to Chinese rebellion, which certainly could not be allowed to happen. At a time when Tseng Kuo-fan and Chinese scholars rallied under the slogan of preserving the traditional order to save the almost-lost imperialist cause from the Taipings, what alternative did the Manchu rulers have but to do their part in upholding the old order? They had to reject foreign demands on the grounds of "incompatibility with the established institutions."

Moreover, domestic disorder was believed to be directly or indirectly related to external trouble. The Manchus, having entered China themselves when the Ming was troubled by internal disorder, were well aware of the lurking dangers from the Taipings within and the barbarians without. Only by reasserting the Confucian moral order could they renew their spiritual strength, and this order could not coexist with the foreign demands for residence in Peking, which must therefore be resisted to the bitter end. On the other hand, commercial interests and trade profits were trivial matters of far less importance than the basic problems of ceremony and dignity, and could therefore be sacrificed more easily under the euphemistic pretext of "benevolence toward men from afar." Hence the secret plan of 1858.

Thus a multitude of factors — institutions, filial piety, imperial familial law, Neo-Confucian ethnocentrism, Chinese culturalism, and the alien Manchu rule — were operating on the Chinese scene during the 1858–1860 negotiations. Only by taking them into account can one understand why Peking resisted so stubbornly what seemed to be a most innocuous issue, diplomatic representation.[17]

The establishment of foreign legations in Peking signified the victory of the expanding Western family of nations in the East. China was brought half-way into this family. Her complete entrance into it was achieved after she developed a due regard for international law as the basis of state relationships and established her legations in foreign nations in the 1870's.

PART II

THE INTRODUCTION OF INTERNATIONAL LAW 1862-1874

The Translation of International Law into Chinese

Modern Chinese have often deplored China's ignorance of international law in her early days of negotiation with the West. Writers have been prone to condemn the decadent Manchu government for signing away lightly what should not have been signed away and keeping stubbornly what should not have been kept.[1] The easy concessions on such vital issues as tariff autonomy, extraterritoriality, and the most-favored-nation treatment in the Treaty of Nanking in 1842, and the mulish resistance to such common practices as diplomatic representation and audience in Peking during the negotiations of the Treaty of Tientsin in 1858 are frequently quoted as proof of the Manchu ineptness. These writers have also accused the West of having exploited China's ignorance. The Chinese feeling that they had been tricked by the West was evident as early as 1873 in a letter from Li Hung-chang, the great viceroy of Chihli, to the Tsungli Yamen: "China and Japan first entered into treaty relations with the West in a most reluctant way, and being unfamiliar with European customs and habits they often got cheated. After the ratifications were exchanged, nothing could be done about them. Every time I see the haughty pretensions of foreign consuls, my heart really cannot bear it."[2] Hsüeh Fu-ch'eng, Li's subordinate and later minister to England and France, also observed in 1880 that China's unawareness of international law victimized her "in such a way as is not known within the realm of international law of this globe."[3] Similar writings of more recent date could be quoted *in extenso*. All seem to imply that China's miseries could have been avoided by a knowledge of international law.[4] Undoubtedly such a knowledge would have considerably mitigated China's diplomatic blunders. The interesting point is, why, after the introduction of international law into China, did she still fail to use it as an instrument to assert her sovereignty and recover her lost rights?

Though a product of the Western European Christian states, international law was conceived, by such early jurists as Grotius, as applicable to all mankind. Its extension into the Chinese empire, which contains one-fifth of humanity, was therefore a highly important event in the annals of the expansion of the West into the non-Western world, and also from the standpoint of intercultural exchange.

In view of the rather common assumption that China's acceptance of the treaty system after 1860 meant her automatic adoption of international law because treaties form a part of international law, the first necessity is to examine the specific nature of China's treaties with the West. Important multilateral treaties, such as the Treaty of Paris of 1856, which declared the principle of blockade and the abolition of privateering, may properly be considered part of general international law. Bilateral treaties, unless later acceded to by many other states, are usually not considered part of general law, since they only bind the contracting parties. Treaties between China and foreign powers were almost all bilateral, containing only a few principles of international law, such as the exchange of envoys, full powers, credentials, exchange of ratifications, and freedom of religious belief. The great bulk of general international law remained untouched.

Moreover, these treaties, known in China as "unequal treaties," imposed on her such obligations as tariff restrictions, consular jurisdiction, and the most-favored-nation treatment, which normally do not exist among sovereign states under international law. They limited rather than asserted China's sovereignty as a state, and as such they ran counter to the basic spirit of international law, partaking of the nature of exceptions to, rather than parts of, the general law. Commenting on the relation between treaties and general international law, J. L. Brierly of Oxford says: "The ordinary treaty by which two or more states enter into engagements with one another for some special object can very rarely be used even as evidence to establish the existence of a rule of general law; it is more probable that the very reason of the treaty was to create an obligation which would not have existed by the general law, or to exclude an existing rule which would otherwise have been applied. Still less can such treaties be regarded as actually creating new law." [5] Thus, China's acceptance of the treaty system must be regarded as her adoption not of international law, but only of some of its principles that happened to be embodied in her several treaties. The major corpus of the general law remained unknown to her.

a. *Lin Tse-hsü's Attempt to Translate Vattel*

International law was formally introduced into China by the American missionary W. A. P. Martin in 1864, but the need for it was realized long before Martin undertook his monumental task. As early as 1839, during his opium-suppression campaign in Canton, Imperial Commissioner Lin Tse-hsü had applied to the American medical missionary Dr. Peter Parker (1804–1888) for a translation of three paragraphs of Vattel's *Le droit des gens*. Parker interestingly recorded this event in his *Tenth Report of the Ophthalmic Hospital*, Canton, 1839:

> Case No. 6565. Hernia. Lin Tsihseu, the imperial commissioner. . . . His first applications, during the month of July, were not for medical relief, but for translation of some quotations from Vattel's *Law of Nations*, with which he had been furnished: these were sent through the senior hong-merchant; they related to war, and its accompanying hostile measures, as blockades, embargoes, etc.; they were written out with a Chinese pencil.[6]

Parker's translation appears in *chüan* 83 of Wei Yüan's celebrated *Hai-kuo t'u-chih* (An illustrated gazetteer of maritime countries), edition of 1852, with Vattel's name transliterated as Hua-ta-erh, and the book title rendered as *Ko-kuo lü-li* (Laws and regulations of all nations). The translation was not literal but paraphrastic, and the translator's comments were in a labored and unliterary style, which is a travesty of Vattel's perspicuity. For instance, Vattel says:

> Every state has, consequently, a right to prohibit the entrance of foreign merchandises, and the nations that are affected by such prohibitions have no right to complain of it, as if they had been refused an office of humanity. Their complaints would be ridiculous, since they would only be caused by a want of that gain, refused by a nation that would not suffer it to be made at its own expense.[7]

Parker's rendition of the above lucid paragraph, when "re-translated" literally into English, appears as follows:

> It is known that all nations have prohibitory laws on foreign merchandises which foreign nations should not complain against and violate; nor

should they seek pretexts to evade them on ground of human feelings. If they do complain, they are motivated by nothing but profit. A nation certainly cannot let others make profit at the expense of her prohibitory laws. Let it be understood, when a nation establishes a prohibition, it has a purpose! [8]

The last sentence, which does not appear in the original Vattel, is apparently a comment by Parker himself. The rendition of the above paragraph, though not literal, is the best of the three paragraphs he attempted. The other two deal with the right of a state to confiscate smuggled goods and contraband and to wage war; [9] the last paragraph on war is almost unintelligible. On Parker's performance, a modern Chinese political scientist has remarked: "The rendering is thus a mockery of Vattel's precision and clearness, and a few notes added to make it more intelligible only serve to increase the confusion. One is forced to conclude that Parker did the work by himself, without seeking counsel from any Chinese." [10]

Apparently Commissioner Lin had some difficulty in understanding Parker's translation, or it may have been for the purpose of double-checking that he had a Chinese interpreter, Yüan Teh-hui, translate the same passages over again. An additional paragraph was translated by Yüan concerning the need to appeal to foreign rulers for the redress of wrongs done by foreigners before a local official took punitive action himself. Yüan's translation also appears in the *Hai-kuo t'u-chih*, placed immediately after Parker's section. Yüan had studied Latin at the Roman Catholic School in Penang and had been a student at the Anglo-Chinese College in Malacca. One of his classmates at the college was William C. Hunter (1812–1891) who later became a very rich trader, and through Hunter's good offices and the arrangements of the influential Chinese trader, Howqua, Yüan secured an appointment as interpreter in the Court of Colonial Affairs [*Li-fan-yüan*] in Peking. In 1838 he was sent to Canton to buy foreign books. While there he was temporarily placed on Commissioner Lin's staff, and one may suppose that "it was he who, in view of the impending trouble with the British, first called Lin's attention to the authoritative work of Vattel." [11]

Yüan's translation is somewhat smoother than Parker's, though it is still not very literal or very polished. The one additional paragraph attempted by him was of some importance in view of later events, and that translation reads: "In a conflict with foreigners, it is necessary first to bring the matter to the foreign ruler or high officials of the opposite side. Only when they refuse to take notice of it may one turn to his own ruler to request protection." [12]

The translations by Parker and Yüan undoubtedly had a decisive influence on Lin, as he later followed exactly the course of action discussed in them. He proclaimed opium a contraband in 1839 and demanded its destruction; he wrote to Queen Victoria requesting her to order the stoppage of opium traffic.[13] When these measures failed to bring the desired results, he resorted to force, fully confident of both the moral and legal correctness of his action, even in the context of Western international law. One may say that the initial effect of international law in China was a strengthening of Lin's determination to take a firm stand against the English.

With the removal of Lin from his post in 1840 and the cessation of hostilities in 1842, interest in international law subsided. It was not until twenty years later that W. A. P. Martin rekindled it.

b. *Martin's Translation of Wheaton*

In the general atmosphere of Sino-Western cooperation after the Convention of Peking in 1860, the Chinese became aware that some knowledge of Western law was necessary in dealing with the West. Prince Kung, chief of the newly founded Tsungli Yamen, commonly known as the Foreign Office but in fact a subcommittee of the Grand Council, reported to the court in August 1864:

The spoken and written language of China is earnestly studied by foreigners without exception, and the craftiest of them even immerse themselves wholeheartedly in exploring Chinese books. Very often they have argued with quotations from Chinese institutional and legal codes to embarrass us. When we want to defeat their statements with [citations of] their practices and precedents, we suffer from not knowing the foreign languages in which all foreign codes and regulations are written. The students at the T'ung-wen kuan still need time to master the [foreign tongues]. Nevertheless, your ministers, exploiting the occasions when the various nations were at odds with each other, have made inquiries and investigations. We learn that there is such a book as the *Laws and Regulations of All Nations*, but if we bluntly ask for it and request them [foreigners] to translate it, we fear they may hold it as a secret and not reveal it.[14]

On the other hand, foreigners were also conscious of the Chinese need for international law. Having witnessed numerous Chinese blunders in diplomatic transactions, W. A. P. Martin, an Indiana-born missionary in China who served as interpreter to Minister William B. Reed in 1858, was in sympathy with the Chinese need for a translation of a work on international law.[15] Before Martin had a chance to do such a translation, Robert Hart, chief assistant to Horatio N. Lay, inspector-general of the Chinese Customs, succeeded in translating for the Tsungli Yamen twenty-four sections on the rights of legations from Henry Wheaton's *Elements of International Law*,[16] with the express intention of persuading the Chinese to send diplomatic representatives abroad. When Martin began his translation in 1862, he was encouraged by Hart, now inspector-general of the Chinese Customs.[17]

Born April 10, 1827 in Livonia, Indiana, Martin was the eighth of the Rev. W. W. Martin's ten children. After graduating from the University of Indiana and the Theological Seminary in New Albany, Indiana, which later moved to Chicago as the new McCormick Seminary, he went to Ningpo, China, in 1850 as a missionary. After many years' service there, he earned a trip home on furlough, and when he returned to China in 1862 his mind was set upon opening a mission in Peking.[18] However, the sudden death of Dr. Culbertson, supervisor of the mission press in Shanghai, detained him in that great metropolis, and while there he employed his time in translating parts of Wheaton's *Elements*, a choice advised by John E. Ward, United States Minister to China during the turbulent years 1859–1860, who considered Wheaton's book more up to date than many other great European works.[19]

In introducing international law to China, Martin was acting on the conviction that he was giving the best fruit of Christian civilization to the Chinese, and that through this work the Chinese government might be brought closer to Christianity. He wrote of it, to his friend Walter Lowrie on October 1, 1863, as "a work which might bring this atheistic government to the recognition of God and His Eternal Justice; and perhaps impart to them something of the Spirit of Christianity."[20] He insisted that his undertaking was "not unsuitable for a missionary who feels in duty bound to seek the welfare of the country he has chosen for the seat of his labors."[21] On the selection of Wheaton, he said: "For the choice of my author I offer no apology. My mind at first inclined to Vattel; but on reflection, it appeared to me, that the work of that excellent and lucid writer might as a practical guide be somewhat out of date; and that to introduce it to the Chinese would not be unlike teaching them the Ptolemaic system of the heavens. Mr. Wheaton's book, besides the advantage of bringing the science down to a very recent day, is generally recognized as a full and impartial digest, and as such has found its way into all the Cabinets of Europe." [22] With the further knowledge that Wheaton was a requirement in the training of interpreters in the West and almost a "must" for many European and American diplomats, he determined to benefit the Chinese with this accepted work. [23]

Wheaton's *Elements of International Law*, the first work of its kind in English, was published in 1836 and received with high favor in the West. A copy was sent by the Department of State to the American commissioner in China in 1855, but it never arrived. Not wishing to be deprived of the benefit of such a useful aid, William B. Reed, the American minister, purchased another copy in 1857 at official expense. [24] The popularity of Wheaton may well be imagined.

Martin secured the aid of some Chinese scholars in his translation. [25] He labored with the intention of showing the Chinese the Western principles by which international relations were governed; he expected no patronage from the Chinese government at all. But luck was with him. In the summer of 1863, while the Chinese were having difficulties with the French, Wen-hsiang, a leading minister of the Tsungli Yamen, asked the American Minister Anson Burlingame to recommend an authoritative work on international law that was recognized by Western nations. Burlingame suggested Wheaton and promised to have some portions of it translated. He wrote to Consul George Seward in Shanghai about it, and happily was informed that Martin was coincidentally doing the work. He gave Martin what encouragement he could, and Martin came north in June 1863. [26] Ch'ung-hou, minister-superintendent of trade for the Three Northern Ports, upon seeing Martin's manuscript, was impressed by "its adaptation to the wants of China in her new relations," and promised to write to Wen-hsiang about it. [27]

Burlingame succeeded — rather against the Chinese custom — in arranging for Martin an interview with four ministers of the Tsungli

Yamen on September 11, 1863.[28] When presented with the manuscript in four tomes, Wen-hsiang asked: "Does it contain the 'twenty-four sections'? This will be our guide when we send envoys to foreign countries." [29] By "twenty-four sections" he meant, of course, Hart's translation. In the course of conversation, Martin assured them that "this book would be appropriate reading for all countries having treaty relations with others. In case of dispute, it also can be used for reference and citation. But because its [the translation's] text and meaning do not flow very smoothly and satisfactorily, he requested our [Chinese] corrections and revision with a view to publication." [30]

Prince Kung had already heard about the manuscript from Burlingame and was secretly anxious to read it. Upon perusal he found it useful but hard to comprehend; he reported to the throne: "Examining this book, I found it generally deals with alliances, laws of war, and other things. Particularly it has laws on the outbreak of war and the check and balance between states. Its words and sentences are confused and disorderly; we cannot clearly understand it unless it is explained in person. We may just as well take advantage of this offer and comply with his [Martin's] request." [31] Four secretaries of the Yamen were assigned by the prince to edit the text, one of whom was a Hanlin scholar.[32] Half a year's collective effort polished the manuscript into good literary form, and at the instance of Robert Hart the prince appropriated five hundred taels for publication. Three hundred copies were distributed to the provinces for the use of local officials.[33]

As patron of this whole project, Burlingame expressed great gratification at the Chinese enthusiasm and reported to the State Department: "I responded, thanking them for what they had done, commending the book as the repository of the rules which govern nations in their intercourse with each other, and stated that although its prescripts had not the force of statute law, or the obligations of treaties, still a thorough examination of the book could not fail to be of vital importance to them. The work was printed according to promise, and published by being sent in large numbers to their officials on the coast and in the interior of the Empire." [34] Martin dedicated the work to Burlingame. To celebrate its completion, a picture was taken of the prince and his suite, with Tung Hsün, chairman of the Board of War and a minister of the Yamen, holding a copy of Martin's translation in his hand.[35]

c. *A Textual Criticism of Martin's Translation*

Martin's background as a close associate of the Natural Law School of international law was clearly reflected in his translation, which is more strongly tinged with Natural Law than the original Wheaton, also a product of that school.[36] Although the accuracy of Martin's translation leaves much to be desired, he is still to be commended for a splendid performance, if one takes into account the unusual difficulties confronting a pioneer intercultural disseminator. Judging by present standards, however, his work cannot strictly be considered a translation, but rather a paraphrastic interpretation of Wheaton. Conscious of this, Martin himself explained in the English Preface: "The translation here offered to the public is not properly an abridgment, though I have thought it fit to omit certain prolix discussions, such as that relating to the immunity of the dwelling occupied by Mr. Wheaton when Minister at the court of Prussia; and also sundry unimportant details such as the particular stipulations regarding the navigation of the Rhine, the St. Lawrence, and the Mississippi. In some cases, I have condensed a little to avoid unnecessary minuteness, and in others, I have amplified somewhat, with a view to perspicuity." [37]

The edited text of the translation is in good, semi-classical style, which posed no problem for the Chinese literati, but when it was introduced into Japan in 1865 the Japanese were confronted not only with many strange new concepts but with a difficult text as well. "International law" was rendered by Martin as *Wan-kuo kung-fa*, or Public Law of All Nations, because "it is commonly used in various nations and is not a monopoly of any single state. Moreover, it is like the laws and regulations of the various states, hence it is also called *Wan-kuo lü-li*" [38] (*lü-li* means laws and regulations).

At the beginning of the translation was a two-page essay, describing the various nations of the world, followed by two simple maps of the Eastern and Western hemispheres, which do not appear in the original Wheaton.[39] Martin's renditions of terms, though imprecise, were understandable, but most of them are now out of date. "International law," rendered as *Wan-kuo kung-fa*, is now translated *Kuo-chi-fa*, a term coined by Dr. Mitsukuri Rinsho of Japan in 1873.[40] "Principle," rendered as *li-i*, is now *yüan-li*; "neutrality," as *chü-wai*, is now *chung-li*. Other discrepancies are shown in the following list:

English terms	Martin's renditions		Present translations	
Natural law	Hsing-fa	性法	Tzu-jan-fa	自然
Self-preservation	Tzu-hu	自護	Tzu-pao	自保
High seas	Ta-hai	大海	Kung-hai	公海
Equality	P'ing-hsing	平行	P'ing-teng	平等
Mediation	Chung-pao	中保	T'iao-chieh	調解
Treaty of Peace	Ho-yüeh chang-ch'eng		Ho-yüeh	和約
	和約章程			

At times Martin's renditions were so free as to be explanations rather than translations; for instance, "Congress of Verona" was rendered as "Four countries controlling Spain." But some of his translations were quite good; for instance, *chu-ch'üan* for sovereignty is still in use today.

Martin's free translation of long sentences may be seen in a comparison of an excerpt from his work with the original passage from Wheaton. The subject under discussion is the lack of universality of international law; Wheaton, after quoting the views of Grotius, Bynkershoek, Leibnitz, and Montesquieu, says:

> There is then, according to these writers, no universal law of nations such as Cicero describes in his treatise *De Republica*, binding upon the whole human race — which all mankind in all ages and countries, ancient and modern, savage and civilized, Christian and Pagan, have recognized in theory or in practice, have professed to obey, or have in fact obeyed.

Martin's rendition of this paragraph, when literally re-translated into English, appears as follows:

> Judging from them there is no universally practiced law as is said in *Te-li* [De Republica], for there has never been a case that is accepted by all nations at all times, barbarian or civilized, within or without the Church.[42]

Such free translation ran through the book, but fortunately the general meaning of the original was not lost. Nishi Amane of Japan aptly commented on Martin's work in a critical but restrained tone: "Translating is such a difficult task that even if no serious errors are involved, one cannot help feeling that there are differences in the shades of meaning, and in the expressiveness of the text."[43] How

:ver, Martin was unafraid of critics, announcing that the difficulties
ie encountered could only be appreciated by those who were "best
icquainted with Chinese." "Their criticisms on my performance will
)e listened to with deference, when they shall have executed an
:qually arduous task with as few imperfections." [44]

CHAPTER 9

Success and Failure: China's Limited Application of International Law

While gratified at the offer and services of Martin and Burlingame, the mandarins were uncertain of the real intentions of these foreigners and of the usefulness of the book. They feared that this product of seeming goodwill might be a trap, and suspected it "as the Trojans did the gifts of the Greeks." [1] Their deep-rooted suspicions of the West made it hard for them to believe that foreigners would benefit China without profit to themselves. Full acceptance of the work was contingent on its merits.

a. *Reactions to Martin's Translation*

When Burlingame brought Martin to the Yamen with the unfinished manuscript in 1863 and stated that all nations would profit from reading it, the mandarins were instantly on their guard. "Your ministers," Prince Kung wrote in reporting the occasion to the throne, "[in an attempt] to forestall their demand that we act according to the said book, told them at once that China had her own institutions and systems, and did not feel free to consult foreign books. Martin, however, pointed out that although the Collected Statutes of the Great Ch'ing Empire [*Ta-Ch'ing lü-li*] had been translated by foreign countries, China never forced them to act by it. How is it possible [that foreign nations] will force China, in turn, to act by a foreign book? He appealed in this way repeatedly. Your ministers suppose his intentions are, first, to boast that foreign countries have laws also, and second, the said scholar wants to follow men of the past like Matteo Ricci to make a name in China." [2]

While the manuscript was being edited in the Yamen in 1864, a diplomatic incident arose which afforded the mandarins an opportunity to test its usefulness. It was a time when Prussia and Denmark were at war in Europe. When the new Prussian minister to China, von

Rehfues, arrived in China in a man-of-war in the spring of that year, he found three Danish merchant ships off Taku. He at once seized them as war prizes. The Tsungli Yamen protested against the extension of European quarrels to China, as it feared that China's indifference would invite foreign nations to claim that area of water as high sea, which, according to Western law, belongs to no country.[3] "Foreign countries have the view," Prince Kung explained to the court, "that oceans and seas over 10 *li* [one marine league] from the coast, where it is beyond the reach of guns and cannon, are common area of all countries. [The ships of] any country may come and go or stay in that area at will." [4] Therefore he must protest to the Prussian minister in order to establish China's jurisdiction in that area and to forestall possible foreign claims.

The Prussian minister argued that the place of seizure was far enough from the coast to be allowed by the European law of war in time of hostilities.[5] Prince Kung insisted that the place was not high sea but China's "inner ocean," meaning territorial waters. "Inner ocean" is an indigenous Chinese term for the ocean area on the coast, equivalent to the Western "maritime territory." Martin translated the latter term as "ocean area within the jurisdiction of a nation," which is not so concise as "inner ocean." [6] Although Prince Kung was applying international law for the first time, he did not openly declare it. His covert use of the principle of maritime territory was supported by an even more effective weapon, namely, the treaty between China and Prussia. He told von Rehfues: "The various [inner] oceans under China's jurisdiction have, as a rule, been specifically stipulated in all her peace treaties with the foreign nations, and in the peace treaty with your nation, there is such a term as 'Chinese ocean.' You know this more clearly than any other country and how can you say it is beyond your comprehension? As to the European law of war, China cannot be obliged to know all." [7] Prince Kung reinforced his written protest with a refusal to receive the new Prussian minister, condemning him for the unbecoming way in which he was beginning his ministerial duties.[8] Von Rehfues saw the seriousness of the situation and released the three Danish ships, with a compensation of $1,500.[9]

Martin was naturally overwhelmed by the result of this application of his translation, and he lost no time in informing his friend Walter Lowrie on July 19, 1864: "By citing a passage from it [Wheaton], the Chinese lately compelled a Prussian man-of-war to relinquish three Danish vessels captured on the coast." [10]

By the combined use of the principle of maritime territory, a treaty, and the refusal to recognize Von Rehfues' ministerial status, Prince Kung scored a diplomatic victory for China. The usefulness of Wheaton having now been established, the Yamen decided to request imperial sanction for its publication. Prince Kung memorialized: "Your ministers find that although the said book on foreign laws and regulations is not basically in complete agreement with the Chinese systems, it nevertheless contains sporadic useful points. For instance, in connection with Prussia's detention of the Danish ships in Tientsin harbor this year, your ministers covertly used statements from that law book in arguing with him [Von Rehfues]. Thereby, the Prussian minister acknowledged his mistake and bowed his head without further contention. This seems to be proof [of its usefulness]." [11] The imperial sanction was duly granted, and the manuscript was printed and distributed.

When the revised translation was being printed, Martin asked the Tsungli Yamen to favor him with a foreword containing the names of the four editors. Prince Kung interpreted his intentions as a desire to win honors in China and to attach himself to the illustrious civilization of the Celestial Empire. The writing of the foreword was entrusted to Tung Hsün, a minister of the Yamen noted for his literary accomplishment, and the names of the four editors were mentioned in it.[12] Prince Kung's failure to write himself was possibly due to his apprehension over possible attacks from the ultra-conservatives and his reluctance to associate himself with foreigners on familiar terms. Whatever disappointment Martin may have felt must have been somewhat offset by a second long foreword from Chang Ssu-kuei, a foreign affairs expert and later associate envoy to Japan.

Tung Hsün's foreword was succinct and noncommittal. "Nowadays," he wrote, "there are many nations outside China. If there is no law to regulate them, how are nations possible? This is why Missionary Martin has translated the *Laws and Regulations of All Nations*. Martin can speak Chinese, yet he presented the book for improvement. I ordered Ch'en Ch'in of Li-ch'eng, Li Ch'ang-hua of Chengchow, Fang Chün-shih of Ting-yüan, and Mao Hung-t'u of Ta-chu to edit it and then return it to him. I know of Martin's interest in ancient history and he is a well-informed scholar." [13]

Chang's foreword was several times longer, discussing at some length the general situations of the West. After paying tribute to the power and prosperity of England and France, he praised Russia's Westernization as an admirable way to self-strengthening and eulogized Washington for his selfless devotion in leading the American people to independence without creating a personal dynasty. Modern Europe was compared to China of the pre-Ch'in period: Russia was likened to Ch'in, England and France to Ch'u and Chin, the United States to Ch'i, Austria and Prussia to Lu and Wei, and Turkey and Italy to Sung and Cheng. Then, in a masterly turn, he suddenly changed the tone to expound the magnanimity and liberality of China: "Now the American Missionary Martin has translated this book, hoping that we may stoop to understand its practices and condescend to follow its propositions. We of China see things with uniform benevolence; his sayings will perforce be studied . . . . All who come from distant lands will not fail to be awed by our prestige and embrace our virtue. But this book can serve as a useful aid to China in planning border defence." [14]

These two forewords revealed an improvement in the Chinese view of the West. Both openly recognized the existence of strong and independent nations beyond China, which amounted to a revolutionary departure from the conventional Chinese claim to universal supremacy. The high tone and overbearing expressions in the latter part of Chang's foreword were probably face-saving devices to offset the luster of Western prowess by emphasizing China's liberality. It was also a good way to avoid attack from the conservatives. Curiously enough, there was no overt and concerted opposition to the introduction of this foreign knowledge, due probably to the general belief that to know one's enemy was the first step toward winning the battle. Only once was there an indirect sign of criticism. In a secret memorial of 1867 Prince Shun criticized Tung Hsün for "ingratiating himself with the barbarians by writing a foreword and publishing a book for them." [15] On the whole, the court and the conservatives could not help being pleased by the palatable words of Prince Kung's masterly memorial, drawn up along the favorite line of playing off the barbarians against one another: "In this book there are quite a few methods of controlling and bridling the consuls, which may be useful [to us]." [16]

Martin appears to have been carried away by his initial success;

he heartily lauded the Chinese for their ability to digest new concepts and ideas unknown to them in the past two thousand years.[17]
He remarked optimistically in his English preface to the translation:
"To its [international law's] fundamental principle, the Chinese mind
is prepared to yield a *ready* assent. In their state ritual as well as their
canonical books, they acknowledge a supreme arbiter of human
destiny, to whom kings and princes are responsible for their exercise of delegated power; and in theory, no people are more ready to
admit that His law is inscribed on the human heart. The relations of
nations, considered as moral persons, and their reciprocal obligations as deduced from this maxim, they are *thoroughly able to comprehend*." [18] In an expansive mood, he even wrote: "I am not sure it
[his translation] will not stand second in influence to the translation
of the Bible!" [19]

Martin's material reward for his work was gradual and lasting.
When he presented the finished manuscript to Prince Kung, he said
jokingly: "You will, of course, give me a decoration for it. I take no
other pay," [20] little realizing that this work contributed to his very
successful later career. He was made president and professor of international law at the T'ung-wen kuan, 1868–1894, first chancellor of
the Imperial University in Peking, 1898–1900, and the recipient of
many other high honors.

Quick to claim credit for his role in the work of translation, Burlingame lost no time in telling Secretary Seward that it was he who
succeeded "in getting the Chinese Government to adopt and publish
'Wheaton's International Law.'" [21] He sent to the Department of
State what he called the first copy of the translation, and another as
a personal gift to the Secretary, who gratefully acknowledged it and
remarked that "the learning and zeal of the Chinese Government in
connection with this matter cannot be too highly commended." [22]
S. W. Williams, chargé d'affaires at the American Embassy, expressed
concern over the book's effect on extraterritoriality: "An authentic
study of this work by the officials in both China and Japan will probably lead them to endeavor to apply its usages and principles to their
intercourse with foreign countries. This will gradually lead them to
see how greatly the principle of extraterritoriality contained in their
treaties with those countries modifies the usages in force between the
Western and Christian powers." [23] Then he went on to express a
wish: "How desirable it is that the latter [Western powers] should

aim rather to elevate these eastern peoples to their own level than to urge this principle of extraterritoriality to the subversion of the native." [24]

Secretary Seward replied to Williams that he regarded the Chinese enthusiasm as "proof of the advance in China of the sentiments of Western civilization." [25] In a dispatch dated December 15, 1865, he instructed Burlingame to invite China to send a diplomatic representative to Washington: "As the empire may now be disposed to respect the obligations of public law, it strikes us that the Emperor's government would be consulting their own interest, and would also be reciprocating that which, to a degree, at least, is a courtesy on our part, by having a diplomatic agent here, whose province it would be to see that our obligations toward China, under the treaties and law of nations, are fulfilled, and who might report to his government that and other interesting topics." [26] Such a Chinese envoy would be able to look after the Chinese subjects in California to the mutual advantage of America and China. Seward went so far as to offer an American warship to carry the first Chinese diplomat to the United States.[27]

Nothing came of this friendly gesture. The Chinese were reluctant to take such a revolutionary step so soon, in defiance of the old established institutions of foreign intercourse. Their stand was probably strengthened by their reading of Martin's translation, which offered such comforting passages as the following: "If a nation is unwilling to send envoys abroad, other nations cannot force it. But according to general practices, one would say that non-exchange of envoys tends to give an appearance of unfriendliness. Nevertheless, exchange of envoys is a matter of comity; there should definitely be no compulsion. Whether or not it should be done depends on the nature of friendship and the urgency of business." [28]

Frederick Bruce, British minister in Peking, lent his encouragement to Martin from first to last, remarking that "the work would do good by showing the Chinese that the nations of the West have principles by which they are guided, and that force is not their only law." [29] The Russian minister, Colonel Balluzeck, told Burlingame in 1863 that his government wished to see China move into closer ties with the family of nations and become subject to the obligations of international law. Thus, Martin was encouraged to write in his preface: "The Three Great Powers [Britain, France, Russia], hitherto

the dread of China, have laid aside, if they ever entertained it, the
petty ambition of seeking their own aggrandizement at the expense
of this empire; while they unite in the nobler enterprise of endeavor
ing to confer a boon on mankind by elevating and blessing the oldes
and most popular member of the family of nations." [30]

On the other hand, hostile responses were not lacking. M. Klecs
kowsky, chargé d'affaires at the French legation, as reported by Mar
tin, angrily asked Burlingame: "Who is this man who is going to
give the Chinese an insight into our European international law?
Kill him — choke him off; he will make us endless trouble." [31] The un
official foreign community responded to Martin's work with mixed
feelings. As the self-appointed vanguard and promoters of Western
civilization in the East, they assumed a patronizing attitude; but a:
the beneficiaries of the unequal treaties, they entertained misgiv
ings lest the Chinese use Western methods to repulse the West. A
Shanghai view was well reflected in an editorial in the *North China
Herald*: "Whether we are supplying weapons which may at some
future period be directed against ourselves, or which will only be
turned to the acquisition of new conquests, cannot at present be de
cided. To stem the stream while it is still near its source, and guide
it into proper channels should now be our aim." [32]

b. *The Failure to Make Positive Use of International Law*

In addition to Wheaton's *International Law*, Martin also trans
lated several other works in the same field, with the assistance of hi
students at the T'ung-wen kuan. In collaboration with Wang Feng
tsao and others, he translated Theodore D. Woolsey's *Introduction
to the Study of International Law* under the title *Kung-fa pien-la*
in 1877, and the Institut de Droit International's *Le manuel des loi
de la guerre* in 1881. Under Martin's guidance, Lien-fang and Ch'ing
ch'ang of the T'ung-wen kuan translated George Friedrich de Mar
tens' *Guide Diplomatique* under the title *Hsing-yao chih-chang i*
1877, and Johann Kaspar Bluntschli's *Das moderne Völkerrech*
(from a French version) under the title *Kung-fa chien-chang* in 1879

These translations should have given the Chinese a fair knowl
edge of international law, which could have led to a movement fo
the abolition of unequal treaties. But it did not, why? The explana
tions may be sought in China's attitude toward her lost rights, he

attitude toward the treaties, and her overall foreign policy during the latter half of the nineteenth century.

Because of their peculiar history, culture, and institutions, the Chinese of the mid-nineteenth century did not seem to consider tariff restriction, consular jurisdiction, and the most-favored-nation treatment to be serious infringements on national rights. On the other hand, they considered such ceremonial matters as diplomatic accreditation and audience without the *kowtow* grave humiliations.

The idea of sovereignty and territorial jurisdiction did not exist in traditional China. Law, as in the Ottoman empire or medieval Europe, was considered personal rather than territorial.[33] While the government of China recognized the status of foreigners in Chinese society, it usually exempted them from its law. This was done not with any sense of loss of dignity or power, but in the condescending belief that the less civilized aliens could not understand the highly complex Chinese rule and must therefore be given a chance to learn the civilized way of life through gradual observation and slow assimilation. Needless to say, it was also an expedient device by which the Chinese officials could avoid the troublesome task of governing men of different tongues and modes of life. The laws of the T'ang dynasty allowed foreign chieftains in China to adjudicate cases where only their tribesmen were involved, while keeping the power of adjudication for the Chinese officials where Chinese were involved as a party to the dispute. This may be said to be the beginning of extraterritoriality in China. The Sung dynasty followed the T'ang practice; the Arab traders in Ch'üan-chou [Zayton] were allowed autonomy in their own quarters. Although the Ming dynasty in principle governed the foreigners with Chinese law, the tradition of non-interference in foreign lives was so strong that the Ming law may be said to have been honored more in the breach than in the observance. The same is true of the Ch'ing period, which witnessed the outright granting of extraterritoriality to the Russians in the Treaty of Kiakhta in 1727: Article 10 stipulated that China would send Russian culprits to Russian authorities for punishment.[34] So strong were these precedents that when the maritime nations demanded extraterritoriality during the negotiations of the Treaty of Nanking and the subsequent treaties, the Manchu negotiators readily assented to it. Viewed in this historical context, extraterritoriality was to the Manchu of the mid-nineteenth century but a new variation of an old practice toward the aliens and was not an infringement of dynastic dignity or national sovereignty, as it became to the modern Chinese.

The idea of protective tariff was also absent in traditional China. The Manchu negotiators did not think of a fixed tariff rate as detrimental to Chinese rights but as a convenient and expedient device.[35] The official tariff of Imperial China had always been moderate, although the irregular fees were high. In the Sung period customs duties at Ningpo and Canton averaged six to ten per cent *ad valorem*, and in the K'ang-hsi period (1662–1722) of the Ch'ing dynasty import duties averaged only four per cent, while export duties averaged sixteen per cent.[36] The new rates after the Opium War were about five per cent *ad valorem*, in principle, but this agreement was not formally set down in the tariff regulations of 1843.[37] In actual practice the rates were fixed on the basis of the old imperial tariff of regular duties, exclusive of local charges and irregular fees. The new rates, while hurting the private coffers of the local customs officers, actually worked in favor of the imperial treasury. For instance, the new rate for tea, 2.5 taels per picul, was 25 per cent higher than the old rate of combined imperial and local charges.[38]

The most-favored-nation treatment was accepted by the Chinese in part as an expedient measure and in part as an expression of the emperor's traditional equal benevolence toward all men from afar, regardless of culture and nationality. When the United States and France asked for the same privileges that the British had obtained in the Treaty of Nanking in 1842, I-li-pu, the Manchu negotiator, asked the court at Peking to comply with their request, on the grounds that their physical similarities to the British made it extremely difficult for the Chinese to differentiate them from one another, and that a refusal would drive them to seek British permission to trade under the British flag. In that case they would be grateful to the British rather than to the Chinese, who would also lose a means of detecting their movements. Granting them equal rights with the British, on the other hand, would win their gratitude and lead them to cut into the British trade profit, to no disadvantage to China; it made no difference whether the China trade, which had a limit, was totally monopolized by the British or shared by them all. Since the English did not object to the extension of the rights to other countries, I-li-pu saw no reason for the court to refuse the American and French requests.[39]

Thus, within the historical context, these concessions were made as temporary and expedient variations of old established practices without any sense of serious loss of Chinese national rights. Of course, nobody in Ch'ing officialdom was anxious to make these concessions to the barbarians, but the sense of bereavement was not as acute as it would have been with modern Chinese. Without the conception of sovereignty, the Ch'ing officials seemed to consider their concessions not so much serious reductions of their national powers as expressions of China's liberality toward the aliens. Their attitude reflected the traditional impractical views on trade and unwillingness to quibble about profits. But they did resent foreign exaction of these rights at gunpoint, for it hurt the Chinese pride. The tone of the numerous documents on barbarian affairs gives the impression that the mandarins did not regret the loss of these rights as much as they regretted the way in which they were lost. Hence, their desire for revenge was far stronger than their will to recover the lost rights.

Years later, when the evils of these concessions became all too obvious, the mandarins still took no measures to rescind them; they merely tried to improve the conditions within the framework of the treaties. The Alcock Convention of 1869, the first "equal" treaty that China had negotiated with a Western maritime nation, can best illustrate this attitude. The occasion was the official revision of the 1858 Treaty of Tientsin, but no attempts were made by the mandarins to remove extraterritoriality, the most-favored-nation treatment, and the tariff restrictions. Rutherford Alcock, British minister, considered it "a matter of congratulations" that the Chinese did not "insist upon" the abolition of consular jurisdiction, which was known to be their "cardinal" desire.[40] The most-favored-nation principle was only conditionally limited by Article 1 of the Convention, which stipulated that British subjects henceforth, in order to enjoy the rights granted by the Chinese to other nations, must also accept the conditions under which such grants were made. The tariff restrictions were slightly relaxed to allow China to increase the export duty on silk and the import duty on opium (Articles 12, 13).[41] Although these were handsome accomplishments of Chinese diplomacy, they were only minor improvements within the vast network of foreign shackles. No attempts were made to remove the shackles themselves. Even in the seventies and eighties, when China's knowledge of the West was far improved, there were still no concrete plans to abrogate the unequal treaties, as there were in Japan. The mandarins merely urged the use of international law to restrain the "wild" foreign consuls, but they never strove to deprive the consuls of the basic *raison d'être* of their "wildness," namely, the right to control their own citizens. The mandarins complained about the low assessment of the five-per-cent *ad valorem* import duties, but when Marquis Tseng Chi-tse in 1889 suggested tariff revision in concert with Japan, the Tsungli Yamen did not accept it for fear of trouble.[42] Why did the Chinese government not press for the abrogation of the treaties when it had become fully aware of the evils of these concessions? The answer lay in its attitude toward the treaties and in its general foreign policy.

To the Chinese of the mid-nineteenth century the Treaty of Nanking, which contained these concessions, was known as the *Wan-nien ho-yüeh*, or Peace Treaty of Ten Thousand Years, which was supposedly unalterable and forever valid. The treaty was a means to bridle the foreigners tactfully (*chi-mi*); it was the price for peace. As anti-foreign a monarch as the Hsien-feng emperor did not take the rash step of abrogating the treaty unilaterally; he merely encouraged blocking its fulfillment through the obstructionist tactics of the Canton viceroy, Yeh Ming-ch'en, and the Canton populace. The Tsungli Yamen wrote in 1867, "once an item enters into a treaty, every word of it becomes ironclad." [43] Even such a well-informed man as Li Hung-chang believed that once the treaty ratifications were exchanged nothing more could be done about it. In fact, the Chinese came to view treaties as a necessary evil that must be endured in order to keep the barbarians within bounds, because treaties, though costly to China, set the maximum limits beyond which the foreigners could not legally go.[44] Prince Kung, after dealing with Lord Elgin and Baron Gros in Peking in 1860, reported to the court that the barbarians were not totally devoid of reason and understanding; if China kept the peace treaty faithfully, they would do the same and peace would be insured. Feng Kuei-fen, in his famous *Protests from the Chiao-pin Studio*, emphasized the importance of getting along with the enemy: "Now that a peace has been negotiated, we had better keep it unswervingly and treat them [barbarians] with candor and utmost sincerity, without entertaining the least idea of suspicion and distrust." [45] Any attempt to recover China's lost rights would necessarily entail a treaty revision which the government was afraid would upset the peace and open to the foreigners new opportunities to make demands. The safest policy was to keep the status quo and, with a knowledge of international law, to forestall trouble by avoiding diplomatic blunders and not goading foreigners into quarrels and thus into making new demands.

The mandarins' fear of new foreign demands was so great that they did not even consider turning to their advantage the official occasions for treaty revision. The Old China Hands' constant clamor for more concessions had created a tense psychological atmosphere that put the mandarins on the defensive. They were terrified by such fire-eating pro-consuls as Harry Parkes, and so busy ferreting out the foreigners' next moves in order to devise means of blocking them, that they hardly had the time or the will to demand restitution of lost rights. Treaty revision was a one-way affair to the officials of the T'ung-chih period: it was an occasion for the foreigners to make new demands, but not for the Chinese to reduce the foreigners' rights. All China could do was to bargain with the foreigners about the new concessions. For instance, in preparation for treaty revision in 1868, the Tsungli Yamen stated in a memorial of June 16, 1867 that foreigners not only would not assent to the modification of any existing treaty provisions, but would even attempt to add something not already included in the treaties." [46] The Yamen solicited advice from viceroys and governors on such issues as audience without the *kowtow*, Chinese diplomatic representatives abroad, telegraphic lines, and mines, but it did not ask for advice on the recovery of the lost rights; nor did any of the officials consulted volunteer any advice. Burlingame was sent abroad by China to dissuade foreign governments from forcing the pace of progress in China, but he was never instructed to negotiate with them about the recovery of the lost rights. It never occurred to the mandarins that the treaty revision could be maneuvered in China's favor also, and it was not until about 1880, when China had already established legations abroad and learned more about the West, that men like Marquis Tseng Chi-tse, under the tutelage of such foreign advisors as Halliday Macartney and James D. Campbell, gradually realized that treaty revision could be a two-way affair: China could notify foreigners of her intention to terminate a certain treaty one year before its expiration, just as foreign nations could propose to make a new treaty. Tseng remarked in his *Diary*, which was forwarded to the Tsungli Yamen, that trade regulations, as opposed to ceded territory, could be adjusted periodically to the mutual advantage of all parties, and old injurious provisions could be revoked upon expiration of the treaty.[47]

Historically, the Chinese had always felt that external troubles were a manifestation of internal weakness. If China was strong, barbarian problems would be solved before they arose. Self-strengthening was therefore a more important and basic solution to the barbarian problem than piecemeal abolition of unpleasant treaty provisions. Moreover, at a time when foreign assistance and cooperation were needed for self-strengthening and the suppression of domestic rebellions, a movement to cut foreigners' rights would be impolitic. Under the system known as the Chinese-Manchu-Western synarchy during the T'ung-chih period, the development of a nationalistic movement for treaty revision seemed hardly possible.[48]

Thus, the Manchu foreign policy of the T'ung-chih period was observance of treaties and avoidance of *faux pas*. This approach did produce good results but it was fundamentally *defensive* in nature and lacked the positive and dynamic spirit required in any nationalistic movement toward the abolition of the unequal treaties. There was in China a conspicuous absence of any such attempt to develop into a modern state as existed in Japan. There was only a strong and deep, if subdued, vindictive desire to avenge the burning of the Summer Palace and the hurried flight of the Emporor Hsien-feng to Jehol in 1860. One day, the mandarins rationalized, the self-strengthening movement would enable China to efface these dynastic humiliations and drive away the foreign devils, but until that day the treaties must be endured as facts of life.

Viewed from a larger perspective, the Ch'ing dynasty, by and large, seems to have spent much of its lifespan and arrived at what the Chinese call "the pre-ordained finale." The problem was one of survival, not of improvement of its lot. This was particularly true after the British failure to ratify the Alcock Convention of 1869. There grew a general feeling that piecemeal improvement of China's position was futile, and a wave of inertia set in after 1870. There was no desire to assert China's rights as a sovereign state; there was only a pious hope that she might be left alone to work out her salvation in her own way. International law, which recognized national sovereignty as well as the sanctity of treaties, alone was not enough to offset the onerous weight of China's history, institutions, and inveterate habits of thought. Without the dynamic motivating power of nationalism, international law was merely a diplomatic reference book with which the Ch'ing officials might restrain "wild" foreign consuls and avoid diplomatic mistakes. Japan, in contrast, had the force of nationalism, which turned her knowledge of international law to active use, resulting in a successful revision of the treaties, although the road was by no means an easy one.

While knowledge of international law did not give birth to a movement for treaty revision, it did restrain China from many diplomatic *faux pas*. The conduct of Chinese foreign affairs was on the whole much improved during the T'ung-chih period. Benjamin P. Avery, the United States minister in Peking, aptly attributed the general improvement in Sino-Western relations to "a better understanding by the foreign office here [Peking] of international law and comity as slowly acquired through intercourse and discussion with foreign representatives." [49]

PART III

THE ESTABLISHMENT OF PERMANENT CHINESE LEGATIONS ABROAD

CHAPTER 10

Early Approaches to the Problem

Diplomacy was an honorable and popular profession in ancient China. The *Chou-kuan* (Officials of Chou) describes the director-ships of State Ceremonies and of Emissary Affairs (*Ta-hsing-jen, Hsiao-hsing-jen*) as important positions filled by men of unusual knowledge and ability.[1] Training in the art of "diplomacy" was part of the regular curriculum for students during the Spring and Autumn and the Warring States periods, and the ability to fulfill foreign mis-sions for one's prince was considered by Confucius a higher quality than filial piety to parents, fraternity with countrymen, or sincerity in speech.[2] A disciple as able as Tzu-kung was commended by the Master as fit to be an envoy; the high regard for the diplomatic pro-fession may thus be imagined. The ancient emphasis on eloquence of speech and respect for diplomacy is further seen in two sayings of Confucius:

> Though a man may be able to recite the three hundred odes, yet if . . . when sent to any quarter on a mission, he cannot give his replies unassisted, notwithstanding the extent of his learning, of what practical use is it? [3]
> He who in his conduct of himself maintains a sense of shame, and when sent to any quarter will not disgrace his prince's commission, de-serves to be called a scholar-official.[4]

However, the Ch'in unification of China in the third century B.C. dealt a mortal blow to diplomacy. The disappearance of the con-tending states destroyed the *raison d'être* of the diplomatic profes-sion, which plunged into an eclipse from which it did not recover for two millennia. Although the Han dynasty sought extraordinary men to be emissaries to foreign lands — Chang Ch'ien to the West-ern Region [Sinkiang] and Su Wu to the Huns — the old glamor of diplomacy was not revived. Foreign assignments to uncivilized, nomadic peoples offered little attraction to men of ability and ambition, who looked upon them as a modified form of banishment. In contrast, the flourishing Chinese civilization and its pervasive influence on the neighboring states lent credence to the belief that China ruled supreme in the whole known world, and that the Chinese emperor was the universal overlord. There was nothing that did not belong to him, hence under the heaven of this universal state nothing could strictly be called "foreign" or "diplomatic."

Diplomacy degenerated from a regular function of state to an *ad hoc* device required periodically by immediate exigencies. It came to be identified with the investiture of tributary kings when China was strong, and with supplication for peace from the marauding barbarians when she was weak. Supervision of investiture, no great honor in itself, involved a long trip and a hard life, and supplication for peace from the barbarians was humiliating and disgraceful. Neither type of appointment offered any glamor or romance, and ambitious men managed to keep aloof from them as a political liability. The following episode illustrates the Chinese attitude toward foreign missions.

a. *China's Traditional View of Foreign Missions*

In 1406 Chang Hung, a Hanlin compiler in the Ming court, was sent on a good-will mission to the tributary state of Burma with an entourage of seventy men. His *Shih Mien lu* (Mission to Burma) records that the Chinese generally regarded Burma as an uninhabitable land of miasma, from which few civilized visitors ever returned. The mission left China to the cries and wails of its members' dependents, who acted as if their dear ones were heading toward the grave. Upon arrival in Burma, the mission was informed that most Chinese who had come there had died within three days and that not one out of ten could expect to survive the air. Taking precautions, Chang Hung ordered a thorough cleaning of the camps to "disinfect" the air, and forbade soldiers to fraternize with Burmese women, who were called "human miasma." Special attention was devoted to sanitation and the food offered by the Burmese government was declined for fear of poison. The members of the mission lived in constant fear of death, and it was not until three days had passed with no deaths that they began to have some peace of mind. The end of the mission brought joy to all, each member congratulating the

other for not having been the one unfortunate member who suc-
cumbed.[5]

This account, reprinted in 1833, epitomizes the Chinese idea of
the dangers and hardships of foreign missions. It is small wonder
that the Chinese government and officials felt that foreign missions
were to be sent only under the direst necessity. Throughout the first
two hundred years of the Ch'ing dynasty, only two missions were
dispatched to the "West": both to Russia in 1729 and 1731, sent by
the Emperor Yung-cheng in search of a counterpoise to the "perni-
cious intrigues of the Jesuits" in China and Russian aid, or promise of
neutrality, in the Manchu campaigns against the Jungars.[6] Apart
from these two instances, there was no indication of Chinese willingness to conduct international relations by diplomacy. The general
feeling was: since China had nothing to ask from the foreigners, why
should she send missions abroad? This being the attitude toward
temporary missions, the issue of permanent legations took on added
difficulty because of the lack of precedent.

Unlike the industrial nations of the West, the agricultural Confucian state of China, self-sufficient and nonexpansive, saw little need
to sell products to, or seek raw material from, foreign lands. Confucianism, lacking the aggressive dynamism of Western religions, never
urged people to go abroad as missionaries to convert others; it rested
content with the notion that those who wanted civilization should
come to China to be assimilated. Without Chinese traders and missionaries in the Western world, the Ch'ing court saw little reason
for China to send envoys abroad. Neither was it concerned with the
protection of overseas subjects, who had gone astray from the fatherland in pursuit of gain, with no respect for their ancestral tombs at
home and no regard for the government's prohibitory laws. Besides,
many of them had anti-Manchu leanings. Men of such dangerous
background, low motive, and poor quality naturally did not deserve
the attention of the Son of Heaven. When William B. Reed, American minister to China in 1858, suggested to T'an T'ing-hsiang, viceroy
of Chihli, that China send ambassadors abroad to protect her overseas subjects, he received a summary reply that bountiful China had
nothing to ask from her emigrants and cared not about their welfare.[7]

As a result, although the Convention of Peking in 1860 had
crushed the walls of the Chinese Jericho, only foreigners took advantage of it. Into the once mysterious Middle Kingdom poured foreign

diplomats, traders, missionaries, tourists, adventurers and exploiters, but the Chinese themselves were slow to emerge from behind the broken walls. The government still regarded foreign missions in the traditional light of tribute and homage, and the literati still looked with disdain and horror upon foreign assignments, for which no respectable men would volunteer.

Because of the fundamentally different concepts of the role of diplomacy — the Chinese regarded it as an act of submission and the Westerners regarded it as a normal function of state — the article on the exchange of envoys in the 1858 British Treaty of Tientsin was as galling an obligation to the Chinese as it was a valuable right to the West. This right was exercised by Western nations almost immediately after the cessation of war in late 1860, with foreign legations established in Peking in 1861. But China was slow to reciprocate. Nevertheless, the need for diplomatic representation abroad was increasingly felt as a result of a series of events, such as the persuasion and urgings of Robert Hart, inspector-general of the Chinese Maritime Customs, and Sir Thomas Wode, Counsellor of the British legation, the discussion of treaty revision in 1867, the Formosa incident of 1874, and the Margary affair of 1875. No attempts, however, are made in the following pages to examine all aspects of these events but only those which bear on the envoy issue. It is important to note that in the discussion of these issues the court repeatedly deferred to the opinions of provincial authorities. These local officials had acquired great power since the suppression of the Taipings, and no important national issues could be decided without their participation. The power of the empire now lay in their hands and the central government was powerless to decide policy alone. It had almost become a rule for Peking to refer important issues to the provinces under the euphemistic pretext of "getting the benefits of collective thinking." As we will see in the following pages, the voices of Viceroys Li Hung-chang, Tseng Kuo-fan, and Tso Tsung-t'ang were particularly weighty.

b. *Early British Proposals, 1858–1866*

During the negotiations of the Treaty of Tientsin in June 1858, the British, while persisting in the demand for a resident minister in Peking, had also expressed a wish that China would send an ambassador to England. Kuei-liang and Hua-sha-na informed Lord Elgin on June 11, 1858, that after the peace settlement "His Majesty the Emperor will select an officer to proceed as Imperial Commissioner to England with the compliments of His Majesty, in token of the friendly relations existing between our two governments."[8] This statement looks like the polite expression of persons vanquished in war and anxious to create a harmonious atmosphere in which to conduct difficult negotiations, rather than a policy statement, but it was nonetheless the first indication of the possibility of a Chinese mission to the West. Elgin apparently took it seriously and, on leaving Tientsin after signing the treaty, asked Hua-sha-na if he would be China's first ambassador to England. The sedate Mongol replied that he would not volunteer but would go on the emperor's order.[9]

The ink on the British Convention of Peking had hardly dried in 1860 when Westerners began to urge China to send diplomatic missions abroad. In the general concern to learn about the West, Prince Kung listened with close attention to the suggestion of Frederick Bruce, the British minister, that China send an embassy to England as a pledge of her intention to conduct foreign affairs in a new spirit.[10] It was in an effort to acquaint the Chinese with the details of diplomatic missions that Robert Hart of the Chinese Maritime Customs translated in 1862 twenty-four essays on the rights and duties of legation from Wheaton's *Elements of International Law.*

Becoming appreciative of the usefulness of international law and the modern functions of diplomacy, and receptive to the persuasions of foreigners in Peking, Prince Kung often inquired of them as to the details of sending embassies abroad.[11] But momentum was slow to gather in the tradition-bound society of China; time was needed to overcome the mental opposition and the general inertia of Confucian officialdom before any radical departure from the established institutions could be attempted. Wheaton's exposition of the exchange of envoys as an act of etiquette rather than a requirement, and the successful Chinese delay in granting an audience to foreign ministers during Emperor T'ung-chih's minority, did not help to promote an early decision on the dispatch of diplomatic missions.[12]

The mandarins' chief concern at this point was not China's international position in the community of nations, but the discovery of a way by which they could effectively check the headstrong, arrogant and ever-demanding foreign diplomats in China without sending Chinese envoys abroad. Anson Burlingame offered some solid advice to Tung Hsün, a minister of the Tsungli Yamen, on March 6, 1865. One good method, Burlingame stated, was to send copies of correspondence on the issue at stake to all foreign representatives not involved in it, with a request that they make public its contents in their countries. "The fear of public opinion would prove a wholesome safeguard against violent or unjustifiable proceedings" on the part of the haughty foreign ministers in Peking. But the most effective way was to go over the heads of foreign diplomats in China altogether by accrediting Chinese envoys directly to their governments. Burlingame hoped that Tung Hsün could be China's first ambassador.[13]

Robert Hart was untiring in his efforts to draw China out of her shell. Ever since he had gone to Peking in 1861, he had urged Prince Kung to move in the direction of progress as understood in the West, and to establish Chinese legations abroad as a means to free China from the maneuvers of foreign diplomats in Peking. "I regard representation abroad as of paramount importance," Hart wrote, "and as, in itself, progress, for, while I thought that I saw in it one of China's least objectionable ways of preserving freedom and independence, I also supposed it would constitute a tie which should bind her to the West so firmly and commit her to a career of improvement so certainly as to make retrogression impossible."[14] To the Tsungli Yamen he explained that foreign diplomats would have their own way as long as China was not in direct communication with their governments. The best way to check them was to enter into direct communication with foreign governments, whose views could be learned through China's own representatives rather than through the foreign diplomats in China.[15] Hart's pleading was convincing and persuasive, yet the mandarins were slow to act on it. In then occurred to him that a formal disquisition on the importance of Westernizing China and diplomatic representation would be more potent than oral advice.

On November 6, 1865 Hart presented to the Tsungli Yamen an essay entitled "Observations by an outsider" (*Chü-wai p'ang-kuan lun*) which, in sincere but pointed language, expounded the interlocking nature of China's domestic and foreign affairs. Just as China's past internal policy was responsible for the present state of her foreign relations, so would her future internal conditions be determined by her present foreign policies.[16] Former mistreatment of foreigners as barbarians, and resistance to the establishment of foreign legations in Peking were "all attributable to [China's] lacking wisdom yet desiring to slight others, and being weak in power yet wishing to subdue others." [17] For her own good China had better accept the new situation with grace and adopt such Western practices as building railways, steamships, telegraphic lines, and sending diplomatic representation abroad, all of which were indispensable to a strong state. His old argument was reiterated: "The accrediting of high officials to foreign nations will do China much good. If the [foreign] ministers in the capital make some reasonable requests, China should naturally comply with them; but if some unreasonable requests were made, China, having no high officials stationed in foreign countries, would have difficulty in not complying with them." [18] He tactfully warned that acceptance of his advice could turn China into a leading nation in the future, whereas nonacceptance might result in international servitude. Disclaiming any discourteous intention in presenting this straightforward and unpalatable essay, he explained that "the view of an outside observer is neither unconsidered nor coercive. What the foreign nations will demand in the future does not aim at hurting China; they merely hope that peace and friendship with her may be maintained." [19]

The Tsungli Yamen did not inform the throne of Hart's essay until half a year later, when Thomas Wade of the British legation presented a similar but more pointed disquisition. Prince Kung then felt called upon to present both memoranda to the throne with the following explanation of the delay: "On November 6th last year [1865], Hart, inspector-general of the Customs, presented an essay entitled 'Observations by an outsider.' Your ministers carefully studied his arguments and found him quite capable of making vigilant examination of Chinese and foreign situations, but it is, after all, an outsider's view and, what's more, cannot be put into practice at once. Therefore we dared not trouble your Imperial Highness with it." [20]

Although his exposition had been sidetracked, Hart was not discouraged. On his trip home in 1866 he offered to take a few Chinese to Europe with him as a first step toward sending official missions. Alive to the possibility of learning more about the West, the Yamen agreed. Prince Kung explained to the court that a mission of petty officials and students, in sharp contrast to a regular embassy, would not raise the touchy problem of *t'i-chih*, national polity, and it could still bring back information about the West. Furthermore, the display and high cost of an embassy could be dispensed with.[21] The court gave its approval and the result was the first investigatory mission under a sixty-three-year-old Manchu, Pin-ch'un. It was not an official diplomatic mission, and its leader was only an ex-prefect presently in Hart's employment as a secretary for Chinese correspondence. Nevertheless, he was given the temporary third civil rank to impress foreigners. The mission was accompanied by E. C. Bowra and E. de Champs of the customs service and a few T'ung-wen kuan students, one of whom, Te-ming, later became Chinese minister in London under the name Chang Te-yi. This investigatory mission visited London, Copenhagen, Stockholm, St. Petersburg, Berlin, Brussels, and Paris, but it did not go to Washington. It created quite a sensation in Europe and the stately, polite Pin-ch'un left behind him a very favorable impression. The members came back with three diaries describing the customs and machines of Europe but with little information on Western political systems.[22] These were read and quickly forgotten, and the mission seems to have had little impact on the Chinese mind.

Thomas Wade's note, entitled "A brief exposition of new ideas" (*Hsin-i lüeh-lun*), was described by himself as a memorandum prepared originally for Sir Rutherford Alcock, the British minister who succeeded Frederick Bruce in 1866. Impressed with its usefulness, Alcock prepared a translation for Prince Kung as a reference.[23] Wade added a preface to the Chinese translation, explaining that honest advice might not be pleasant to the ears and that the different expressions in English and Chinese might even make for unpalatable reading. "If a man manages his affairs improperly," he wrote, "he may not be able to help feeling displeased in his heart by the remonstrance of his friends even though it is made with good intention. Yet an observer cannot discharge his duties of friendship unless he frankly and directly points out the dangers as he sees them." [24] After this introduction came a lengthy exposition of the need for the railway, telegraph, mining, schooling, and army training in the Western ways. He then proceeded to a discussion of diplomatic missions abroad:

What was the intention of foreign nations in accrediting high officials to the capital of China? England and other countries alike fear that disputes may arise abroad which cannot be settled, and would thus be liable to lead to a resort to arms. In the past five years, disagreeable deeds have admittedly often been committed, which would have been likely to brew trouble under the old system, when there were no high officials representing their sovereigns in the capital. Luckily this has been avoided through the medium of [such representatives]. Its effects on friendship and the general situation were beneficial to both sides alike. But should a foreign minister make a decision at variance with the Chinese standpoint, China, having no high official stationed in his country, could only let the very foreign minister in question represent [her views] to his own government. Who else in his country could argue for China? [25]

The fact that such a suggestion for checking foreign maneuvers in Peking came from no other person than the British minister himself was proof enough of British friendship, Wade said, as it was also a good answer to the usual Chinese charge that no foreign suggestion was made without some ulterior, malicious motive. "If China is still unwilling to realize it [the value of sending an embassy]," he added pointedly, "then the only conclusion foreign countries can come to is that the residence of foreign ministers in the [Chinese] capital is unpalatable, and was accepted only as a temporary arrangement to keep things straight for the time being so that plans might be worked out to oust them eventually. I am not sure that such is not her intention!" [26] He pleaded with the Chinese to see for themselves the benefits of diplomatic representation:

The Western nations traditionally regard the exchange of high officials as a comity of intercourse. Those within the same comity are joined into a circle, and those not within the comity are regarded as outside of it. Should China consent to exchange [envoys] as other nations do, the advantages would be twofold: at the present China stands alone, and does not communicate with neighboring states; every nation cannot but have some cool feelings [about her]. If there were communication, then warm feeling would replace the cold regard, and the various nations would have a concern for her. Then it would be easier to prevent or block any aggressive designs at the outset. Even when [China] was embroiled in a quarrel with a certain country, if she was in the right, other nations would of course come forward to assist her with good offices, if not with armed assistance.[27]

The basic trouble with China, as Wade diagnosed it, was her predisposition to look to the past for guidance rather than to the future for inspiration. Exactly because of this attitude, no period in Chinese history could surpass its predecessor. In glaring contrast, the West made progress by leaps and bounds, and it had now reached a point far beyond China's grasp. The foreigners of today were surely not the Huns of the past. Unless she sought progress and caught up with the West, China could only seal her fate.[28] However, if diplomatic representation abroad was too novel an undertaking for the moment, Wade concluded, China should at least explain to the foreigners the reasons for her delay so as to allay their suspicion.[29]

c. *The Court's Response*

Wade's memorandum created a stir in the Chinese court. While acknowledging some truth in Wade's essay, Prince Kung felt that his real motive was to pave the way for future demands.[30] In his memorial to the throne, the prince emphasized the importance of self-strengthening to counter foreign designs: "Your ministers think that without a doubt China needs self-strengthening. We generally scorn others' methods as unusable, while we do not anxiously seek good methods to put into immediate practice. . . . Although the various points raised by the envoy in question contain much that is presumptuous, objectionable, and hard to put into practice, they nevertheless touch upon matters that the various nations have long planned with deep intentions and that they will eventually strive for with all their might. It is to be feared that in the future, acting on the pretext of protecting foreign trade, they will start [trouble] from the treaty ports." [31] And in such a case, the Yamen would be too far away to control the situation. Prince Kung therefore asked the court to alert local authorities against possible trouble.

An edict was hastily issued on April 5, 1866 by the frightened court: "Having read [the foreign memoranda], can we not devise precautionary measures in advance? The military campaigns [against the Nien and Moslem rebels] in China have not yet been concluded, and the national treasury is still not opulent. Foreigners are already taking advantage of this situation and becoming covetous!" [32] The views of the Tsungli Yamen were quoted at length and the local governors were instructed to improve their efficiency so as to forestall trouble. "Only thus can we avoid foreign slights, eliminate troubles before they brew, and block their designs before they start;" the edict went on to say, "as to the various points on foreign affairs, such as the sending of Chinese envoys to the respective nations, we ought to do something about them too." [33] Copies of the memoranda by Hart and Wade were sent to the provincial authorities, whose comments were urgently solicited.

Ch'ung-hou, minister-superintendent of trade for the Three Northern Ports, answered the call first. More cosmopolitan and better informed than most of his contemporaries, he astutely declared that the foreigners were of such a stubborn nature that the more China resisted the more they would insist. An effective way to deal with them was to devise long-range policies covertly so as not to arouse their suspicion. On the envoy issue he stated: "It is a subject that deserves top priority. It is a means to cultivate friendship with, and transmit [Chinese] ideas and views to Western nations having treaty relations [with China]. China has never had such a practice, and they [the Western nations] look upon this with suspicion." [34] Thus, the first essential for the Chinese government should be to disperse their suspicions by sending embassies abroad.

Li Hung-chang, acting viceroy of Nanking and soon to be transferred as viceroy of Hu-kuang, also took a liberal view of Wade's note: "Surely, the purpose of the said chieftain in making these repeated requests is to impress upon China that sending envoys is a sign of true intention of friendship and peace, and to demonstrate to us the wealth and power (of Western nations). He wants to let us know the benefits of their railways and telegraphs so that we may copy and adopt them without further obstruction. Actually, from our standpoint this is not without advantages too." [35]

An interesting contrast to these liberal views were those of Liu K'un-i, governor of Kiangsi, and Ma Hsin-i, governor of Chekiang. Liu opposed diplomatic representation on the reasoning that it would send useful men to useless places, where they would serve only as hostages of the Western barbarians.[36] Ma based his opposition on the mistaken idea that Western practices permitted foreign diplomats to exercise great power in the governments to which they were accredited. If the barbarians were to give the Chinese envoys the titular status of "power-wielder" (*ping-cheng*) at their courts and demand of the Chinese government the same status for their envoys, what disorder they would create! [37] He condemned Westernization as a diabolic barbarian scheme to sow dissension among the Chinese and to plant agents in China's self-strengthening enterprises.

Most of the other memorials dealt with the problems of Westernization rather than the envoy issue. According to Kuan-wen, viceroy of Hu-Kuang, the fact that the English suggestions were not made in 1860, when China was at their mercy, but now when the Taipings had been defeated indicated their dual motive: (1) they feared that China might soon turn her guns against them, and (2) they felt insecure about their employment in the Chinese service. To hide their inner fear, they exposed China's weakness; and to insure their continued employment, they exaggerated the importance of Westernized enterprises.[38] A third motive was added by Tso Tsung-t'ang, viceroy of Min-Che, who stated that Hart and Wade, both being British, apparently wanted to seize a position of leadership for their country in widening the Chinese market for foreign goods, thereby winning gratitude from other trading countries.[39]

Private individuals, as well as the official circles of China, were also stirred by Wade's essay. A certain Chiang Tun-fu drafted an answer to Wade accusing him of being a wolf in sheep's clothing whose intention was to dupe the Chinese. He wrote of Wade's memorandum: "In name it looks like an impartial exposition; in reality it is the display of a man's wit, bluffing and threatening us all the way through. Ah! This is much too much." [40] Communist writers today assert that foreign diplomats strove for Chinese diplomatic missions abroad out of a desire to "infiltrate their influence into the Manchu ruling groups through all possible channels," and that Hart's memorandum was but a textbook of instructions for the Manchus, prepared on behalf of foreign legations with a view to subjecting China to foreign domination.[41]

While the court remained inert after reading the memorials from the provincial authorities, the Tsungli Yamen became increasingly aware of the need for a diplomatic mission abroad. Hart reported that after his return from England in 1867, every time he went to the Yamen he was asked detailed questions about sending missions to the West.[42] To pave the way for such an eventuality, the Yamen in 1867 submitted a secret memorial expounding its ideas on the subject. It may be recalled that the Yamen's earlier memorial on the memoranda from Hart and Wade urged vigilance against trouble in the treaty ports and the need for self-strengthening, but it did not specify the methods of self-strengthening or touch on the envoy issue in any particular manner. Now this long secret state paper stressed three concrete subjects as being of the highest importance and urgency: (1) envoys to the West, (2) proficiency in foreign languages, and (3) the manufacture of Western guns. It recognized the need for change to meet the challenge of the time even at the risk of contravening traditions and established institutions, and the famous saying from the *Book of Changes*, "When a series of changes has run all its course, another change ensues," [43] was quoted to support the advocacy of new undertakings. The foreign ministers in China were crafty and demanding, said the Yamen, and China had no way of knowing whether they were truly representing the attitudes and policies of their governments; nor could she be sure of their honest representation of China's position to their governments. The only way to free China from their maneuvers in the impending treaty revision in 1868 was to bypass them by sending a Chinese mission to foreign countries directly, to explain China's position and discuss with them the various difficult problems. Such a step could serve as a warning to the foreign diplomats against misrepresentation of China's stand, and it could also enable China to learn of the relative strengths and weaknesses of Western states. China had better exercise the right of legation, as stipulated in the British and French Treaties of Tientsin, for her own good.

However, many difficulties must be expected in such a venture. The expenses of an embassy would be high; salaries, traveling expenses, rents, stationery and other daily expenditures must all be taken into account. Suitable men for a mission were also hard to find. An unsuitable man would invite slights from the foreigners and, living alone in a strange land, would be liable to fall easy prey to Western duplicity, not to mention the possibility of his being held as a hostage. Nevertheless, these difficulties could be offset by the many advantages that would come with a mission. First, it could learn about Western policies toward China firsthand and spread Chinese civilization to win foreign admiration, to the end that Sino-Western relations might be improved. Secondly, skillful and ingenious technicians could accompany the mission to learn of Western technology and the manufacture of guns, so as to destroy the Western monopoly of power. Thirdly, the mission could use this opportunity to investigate the possibility of recruiting overseas Chinese, who had mastered foreign techniques, into Chinese government service. Lastly, it could even enlist foreign support in case of dispute between China and another nation. The long memorial closed with an urgent plea that the matter of a foreign mission should not be further delayed, and the court was requested to instruct high officials both in and out of the capital to recommend suitable men.[44]

The Yamen was thus prepared to take the bold step of sending a temporary, explanatory mission to the West, as suggested in Wade's note, to dissuade the various powers from being too demanding in the forthcoming treaty revision. In addition, the Yamen turned to important provincial authorities, who had acquired great power since the suppression of the Taipings, for advice on the various issues that were likely to come up in the treaty revision. It is to this domestic discussion that our attention is now directed.

CHAPTER 11

The Envoy Question as a National Issue, 1867–1876

a. The Treaty Revision, 1867–1868

Article 27 of the Treaty of Tientsin with Britain, which was signed in 1858, stipulated that a treaty revision might be made at the end of the tenth year, that is, 1868. As the time for treaty revision approached, the atmosphere in Chinese officialdom became increasingly tense. A sense of national crisis was apparent in Peking high circles, and preparations were made to weather the storm. The Tsungli Yamen, in anticipation of strong foreign demands as implied in the Hart and Wade memoranda, took measures to gather the best minds in the nation to meet this ominous challenge. A secret circular was prepared by the Yamen containing its views on such issues as the audience, the sending of diplomatic missions, telegraphs, railways, inland navigation, mining, and missionary activities. At the Yamen's request, the court sent this circular to leading provincial officials on October 12, 1867 for comment in order to achieve the benefit of collective thinking. The Yamen's opinion on the dispatch of envoys appeared as follows:

> Discussion of the sending of envoys: It has been the practice everywhere among the Western nations, after treaties are signed, to send envoys for mutual accreditation to carry on intercourse. But China has never undertaken such an action. The foreign ministers have repeatedly come to petition for the imperial appointment of [envoys] to go abroad. This Yamen has argued against it on the ground that the various nations that have come to China have mercantile and missionary matters to deal with, and therefore have a need to send envoys, whereas China, having no such business in foreign countries, need not send envoys.
>
> However, for more than ten years foreigners have thoroughly acquainted themselves with our points of weakness and power, while we are very vague about their conditions. The saying of the military strategist, "know others as oneself," [1] has not been considered at all. Moreover, when the envoys of the nations in question are perverse, headstrong and unreasonable, we can only restrain them with dignified words; we cannot

question their respective governments about it. This is the greatest [source] of all misunderstandings.

In regard to China's dispatch of envoys to foreign countries, there are two difficulties. First, most men fear and dislike moving far on big oceans, and the costs of sea and land travel and hotel bills are especially high. Moreover, with the accreditations scattered over many different places, financing them would not be easy. Secondly, the [foreign] written and spoken languages are not yet well understood, and it is still necessary to rely on translation, which inevitably makes difficulties. Furthermore, men who are equally good at initiating and maintaining things, and who have the ability to handle situations independently are always difficult to find. When the wrong men are sent, they may be slighted and insulted, thus leaving an unexpected legacy of shame in foreign lands to the detriment of our [national] affairs. If the envoys are carelessly sent, we cannot but worry about a misfortune such as that brought upon the Han [dynasty] by Chung-hsing Shu.[2]

Last year this Yamen memorialized for permission to send Pin-ch'un with the students Feng-i and others on a sea voyage to various places in the West, and to make a preliminary study of customs and attitudes there. This is different from sending envoys and cannot be repeated. Hereafter, the issue of the dispatch of envoys must be an important concern [of ours], and cannot be regarded as subject to further delay. As to how this is to be done, we hope it will be decided after collective deliberation.[3]

Recognition of the need for diplomatic representation was thus apparent. The Yamen needed the support of important officials in the nation to initiate such a novel step in order to avoid the conservatives' accusation that the ancestral regulations on foreign relations were being broken. Some eighteen provincial grandees were asked to express their views on this issue, and their replies fall into three groups: some favored the new move, some did not, but most of them were rather noncommittal. It is interesting that the more outspoken ones were all Chinese; the Manchus merely elaborated the ideas already existing in the circular or in the edict, without suggesting anything new.

Those in favor regarded diplomatic representation abroad as a good way to end the haughty pretension and annoying maneuvers of foreign diplomats in Peking. Li Hung-chang, viceroy of Hu-kuang, took the lead in expounding this line of thought. Since he felt somewhat unqualified to speak on foreign affairs, having left the post of superintendent of trade for the Southern Ports, Li expressed his views only upon the repeated urgings of the Yamen.[4] He favored the dispatch of envoys on the grounds that they could reach the ears of foreign rulers and check the foreign diplomats in China. They could also learn the secrets of Western prowess and prosperity and so destroy the Western monopoly of Nature's mysteries. He was pessimistic about the prospect of finding suitable native diplomats; yet he opposed the continued employment of foreigners as envoys.[5]

Tso Tsung-t'ang, viceroy of Shen-Kan, who agreed with Li, suggested that China first send able men from the coastal areas to travel in foreign countries and acquaint themselves with foreign conditions. From these men, the court might later select the outstanding ones to be envoys to the West for a term of five years.[6] Tseng Kuo-fan, viceroy of Nanking, expressed similar but more restrained views: "China and foreign countries having already maintained friendly relations, mutual communication is a normal affair. . . . With the right men on hand we will send envoys; without them we will not send them. The decision rests with us; foreigners surely will not start a war simply because we have not kept our promise to send [envoys]."[7]

Strangely, the strongest opposition came not from Wo-jen, the archconservative, or his followers, but from Shen Pao-chen, superintendent of the Foochow Dockyard and a supporter of "foreign matters." He cogently argued:

"Foreigners say that the sending of envoys will be of great benefit to China. This is absurd. They control our life and death through their military power and wealth, and not through their resident ministers in Peking. In spying out our solidarity or hollowness, they rely on their merchants and missionaries, who are scattered all over the interior and are in daily contact with our officials and people. They do not rely solely on their resident ministers in the capital. The unrestrained and impudent behavior of the merchants and missionaries has been personally witnessed by their foreign ministers, who nevertheless protect them in many ways. Is it possible to say that the [foreign] rulers will not defend their own ministers' unreasonable actions, simply because they listen to our envoys' complaints?"[8]

Shen would, however, consent to dispatch of temporary missions as measures of expediency in given situations: "Your minister is of the opinion that this proposition [of sending regular embassies] should be rejected if possible; if not, then a temporary makeshift arrangement might be adopted. But this is not to be regarded as the key to peace."[9] His opposition was seconded by Ma Hsin-i, governor of Chekiang, who reiterated his old fallacious argument that, if the

Chinese envoys were given the nominal status of "power-wielder" by foreign governments, Western diplomats in Peking would claim a similar status for themselves and attempt to influence Chinese politics in gross violation of the rules of propriety. To avoid such an eventuality, China must not send envoys herself.[10]

The Manchus on the whole offered very few constructive opinions. More politicians than statesmen, they followed the old Chinese saying, *k'an-feng chuan-to*, "watch for the wind before turning the rudder." Ch'ung-hou, minister-superintendent of trade for the Three Northern Ports, who previously had responded favorably to the Wade memorandum, now changed his position. Although he continued to believe that the foreigners were asking China to send diplomatic missions abroad out of a genuine desire for equality with her, he nevertheless opposed the immediate dispatch of envoys because China had no business in foreign countries for the time being and the problem of ceremonies in the presentation of the credentials to foreign rulers had not been solved.[11] Jui-lin, viceroy of Canton, repeated the common opinion that China might send envoys when she had the right men.[12] Kuan-wen, viceroy of Chihli, after quoting the Yamen's views at length, expressed doubts as to whether Chinese envoys could influence foreign rulers against their own ministers.[13] Most of the other memorialists suggested delaying the dispatch of permanent missions but were agreeable to a temporary one, like Pin-ch'un's to satisfy the foreigners for the moment.

The attention that the officials gave to treaty revision and diplomatic representation indicated the anxiety, fear, and tenseness that prevailed among the Ch'ing officialdom in 1867. Yet such worries, in retrospect, were unwarranted. The Old China Hands in Shanghai and London were clamoring for an aggressive policy to open more of China and hasten her modernization, even at the risk of precipitating a dynastic collapse, but the British government considered such a policy not worth the risk involved.[14] It wanted a policy that would preserve peace for a long time. Lord Stanley, the Foreign Secretary, informed Alcock, British minister in China, on August 17, 1867 of his disinclination to push modernization in China with undue haste: "We must not expect the Chinese, either the Government or the people, at once to see things in the same light as we see them; we must bear in mind that we have obtained our knowledge by experience extending over many years, and we must lead and not force the Chinese to the adoption of a better system. We must reconcile ourselves to waiting for the gradual development of that system, and content ourselves with reserving for revision at a future period, as in the case before us, any new arrangement which we may come to in 1868." [15] The British position was further elucidated by Louis Mallet, permanent under-secretary of the Board of Trade, when he stated that the "safe course" for the British government to follow in the treaty revision was to devote its efforts "to the consolidation of the position already obtained, by patient, moderate, and gradual negotiation, and by bringing to bear as much as possible the moral influences derived from the principles of international equity which regulate and control the intercourse of civilized nations." [16] The Foreign Office told Alcock to be guided by Mallet's statement in his negotiations with the Chinese.[17]

Alcock himself was not in favor of the foreign merchants' aggressive attitude in China. In fact, in his years as envoy in China, he had become Sinicized to some degree and had developed a sympathetic understanding of the Chinese position. He warned his countrymen and government against promoting a dismemberment of China unless foreign powers were prepared to take over the nation and turn it into a protectorate. "But it is difficult to see to what uses, political, military, or commercial, any portion of China could be applied by European Powers." [18] Clarendon, Foreign Secretary after Stanley, was in full accord with this view. The "soft" policy of Alcock and Clarendon exasperated the Old China Hands, who now accused Alcock of mandarin-mindedness and suggested his replacement by someone fresh from the "political life of Europe." [19] As to Clarendon, they went so far as to suggest a civil service examination for all secretaries of the Foreign, Colonial, and Indian Offices, to make sure that they had "full knowledge of the people and countries they are called on to have dealings with." [20]

b. The First Missions to the West, 1868–1870

Of course, China had no knowledge of the moderate policy of the British government in London, and still less inkling of the conflict between the Foreign Office and the Old China Hands. Nonetheless, if the mandarins lacked the diplomatic intelligence to exploit this situation to their advantage, they were ingenious enough to use one barbarian to check another. Even amidst the heated national discussion of treaty revision in 1867, the Yamen saw fit to appoint Anson Burlingame, the retiring American minister, as China's roving ambassador to the West to persuade the powers not to force modernization in China.

Recent research reveals that Burlingame actually suggested the idea of a Chinese assignment for himself.[21] Prince Kung's memorial on the subject records that Burlingame, in grateful acknowledgment of Chinese hospitality at a lavish farewell party, "declared of his own accord that in any future dispute with foreign countries, [China] could count on him to exert his utmost [on her behalf] as if he were China's envoy." Prince Kung went on: "Your ministers have been troubled precisely by the lack of [suitable] men to go abroad. Now that Burlingame intends to make a name for himself, readily taking the task upon himself, we believe his sentiments to be not superficial or untrue."[22] Wen-hsiang, the pillar of the Yamen, then exploited the happy social occasion to the full by playfully asking Burlingame: "Why will you not represent us officially?"[23] Burlingame reported to the Department of State that he did not take the Chinese suggestions seriously until they were followed by several formal conversations culminating in the official offer of a roving ambassadorship to the West. Then, with great eloquence that calls to mind Churchillian rhetoric, Burlingame declared: "When the oldest nation in the world, containing one-third of the human race, seeks, for the first time, to come into relations with the West, and requests the youngest nation, through its representative, to act as the medium of such change, the mission is one not to be solicited or rejected."[24] To give the mission a Chinese appearance, a Manchu, Chih-kang, and a Chinese, Sung Chia-ku, were appointed co-envoys at the suggestion of Robert Hart.

The mission left Shanghai on February 25, 1868, reaching San Francisco in May. The governor of California enthusiastically greeted Burlingame as "Our guest, the son of the youngest, and representative of the oldest, government." Burlingame, a born orator, was carried away by the grand welcome, responding that "the hour has struck, the day has come" when China was ready to extend her "arms towards the shining banners of Western civilization." The same rhetoric was exhibited in New York a month later when he declared that China wanted to invite the missionaries to "plant the shining cross on every hill and every valley." His eloquence captivated the

American public and government alike, and President Andrew Johnson accorded the mission a flattering reception. Actually, Burlingame had been instructed by the Chinese government before his departure not to seek audiences with foreign heads of state, lest Western diplomats in Peking should demand reciprocal treatment even during Emperor T'ung-chih's minority. However, the Chinese government conceded that if audiences with foreign chiefs were unavoidable, Burlingame was to make it clear that he did so in accordance with the Western, and not Chinese, manner, so as to avoid foreign accusation of Chinese unwillingness to reciprocate their courtesy.

The audience with the President was followed by conclusion of a treaty between Secretary Seward and Burlingame, on July 28, 1868, stipulating the sending of Chinese consuls and laborers to the United States, reciprocal rights of residence, religion, travel, and access to schools in either country, and freedom from interference in the development of China. Burlingame had signed this treaty entirely on his own initiative and was not authorized by either his instructions or the Chinese government. Apparently he planned to explain his action to the Chinese after his return but he never had the chance. The Chinese government, on the other hand, was too grateful for his services to disown his commitments.

The mission then proceeded to England and was received by Queen Victoria on November 20. Burlingame succeeded in committing the British government to a policy of moderation toward China. Lord Clarendon declared on December 28, 1868, that the British government would not pressure China "to advance more rapidly than was consistent with safety and with due and reasonable regard for the feelings of her subjects," and that it would deprecate any European pressure to force China into adopting new systems.[25] He authorized Alcock on June 4, 1869, to accept any arrangements satisfactory to the Chinese in treaty revision.[26]

The mission then visited Paris, Stockholm, Copenhagen, the Hague, and Berlin, where Burlingame succeeded in persuading Bismarck to issue a statement that the North German Confederation was ready to deal with the central government of China in whatever manner the latter considered to be in its best interest. The mission next moved to St. Petersburg, where, after an audience with the Tsar, Burlingame contracted pneumonia and died on February 23.

The two co-envoys carried the mission to a close after visiting Brussels and Rome on their own and returned to China in October 1870.[27]

This first Chinese diplomatic mission was undoubtedly a great success insofar as its immediate objectives were concerned. The leading Western nations were now committed to a policy of restraint in treaty revision, and this was all the Chinese government wanted at the moment.

In the actual negotiation over treaty revision, however, the issue of Chinese diplomatic representation abroad was not even touched upon. The chief concern of the British traders was to get more profit and concrete gains such as greater trade opportunities, more modernized foreign enterprises, and lower taxes and transit dues. It mattered little to them whether or not China had a diplomatic agent in London. The British government, although it would have liked to see China move in the direction of progress, did not feel called upon to make an issue of the question of diplomatic representation. Victorian pride was not hurt by the absence of a Chinese ambassador at the Court of St. James. The only group of foreigners anxious to see Chinese envoys abroad were a few individuals who regarded themselves as friends of China, such as Hart, Wade, Alcock, Martin, and Burlingame. Their well-intentioned advice was misinterpreted by the mandarins as a bad omen of future foreign demands; hence the panic before treaty revision.

Of the treaty revision itself and the resultant Alcock Convention of 1869,[28] we need only say here that the terms — such as the qualified most-favored-nation treatment, the right to have a Chinese consul in Hongkong, and the fixing of the combined tariff and transit dues at 7.5 per cent *ad valorem* — were so repugnant to the British merchants that they mobilized all their power to block its ratification. In this they succeeded, and the first equal treaty between Britain and China was shelved.

The weathering of the storm of treaty revision in China and the success of Burlingame's mission abroad at a cost of 160,000 taels [29] gave the Ch'ing court a feeling of confidence. The thought arose that foreigners after all could be "managed" at a price. Complacency now replaced the fear and anxiety that had characterized the previous year, and the court was quick to sink into another respite of inaction. This self-confidence and complacency may have indirectly

encouraged the resurgence of anti-foreignism and general conservatism in the 1870's. The two co-envoys in Burlingame's mission fared
badly after their return to China. Chih-kang was sent to a post in
Mongolia, and Sung Chia-ku to an obscure part of West China, as
if they had been contaminated by their Western trip. The suggestion of Ting Pao-chen, governor of Shantung, to follow the Burlingame mission with another, was conveniently ignored,[30] and the
envoy issue was not raised until the Formosa Incident of 1874.

Between the Burlingame mission and the Formosa Incident,
several events took place which in themselves may not have exerted
a decisive influence on the permanent legations issue, but which
familiarized the Chinese with the process of sending missions
abroad. These were the dispatch of Ch'ung-hou on an apology
mission to France after the Tientsin Massacre in 1870, the educational mission to the United States in 1872, and the participation in
the International Exhibition at Vienna in 1873.[31] Of these activities,
the Ch'ung-hou mission had the most direct bearing on the envoy
issue. It left China on October 28, 1870 with two French employees
of the Chinese customs service, Messrs. Novion and Imbert, and an
Englishman, Mr. Brown. France, then fighting a losing war with
Prussia, was in no mood for this apology mission. Official reception
was continuously denied to Ch'ung-hou on the pretext that China
had not yet reciprocated to the French minister in Peking the
courtesy Napoleon III showed to Burlingame in 1869. In this situation, the Tsungli Yamen ordered Ch'ung-hou to dispense with the
personal presentation of the Letter of Apology to the French ruler.
He started his homeward journey by way of the United States when
suddenly, in New York, he received a summons to go back to France.
An official reception was finally accorded to him by the provisional
president, M. Thiers, at Versailles on November 23, 1871. The
French chief of state accepted the Chinese Letter of Apology and
hoped that China could establish a permanent legation in Paris. The
mission of apology thus came to an end. Doubtless, these foreign
experiences increasingly drew China into the stream of world affairs,
and it became all too clear that international living could not be
rejected for long.

It must also be noted here that the Chinese had undergone
significant changes in their attitude toward their overseas population. The old disdain toward Chinese subjects abroad, seen in the

conversations between William B. Reed and T'an Ting-hsiang quoted above, slowly gave way to a new concern for them. In this the Chinese were doubtless influenced by the Western practice of protecting overseas citizens, but they were also motivated by the thought that the dynasty might enlist the services of those Chinese overseas who had learned the secrets of Western power through long association. This changing attitude can be detected in the long secret memorial of the Tsungli Yamen quoted above. Article three of Burlingame's Supplementary Treaty to the Sino-American Treaty of 1868 and Article two of the Anglo-Chinese Supplementary Convention of 1869 stipulated that China could send consuls to the United States and England to protect her overseas subjects. Similar provisions appeared in the Sino-Japanese treaty of commerce and friendship in 1871.

c. *The Japanese Treaty of 1871 and the Formosa Incident of 1874*

In 1870 Yanagihara Sakimitsu of the Japanese Foreign Office arrived in China to seek a commercial treaty similar to China's treaties with the Western nations. Ying-han, the ultraconservative governor of Anhui, asked the court to reject the Japanese request because Japan was a former tributary of China known as the "Dwarf Nation," which had engaged in piracy along the China coast during the Ming period. The very fact that she came seeking a commercial treaty amidst the Tientsin Massacre crisis proved that she was opportunistic and eager to fish in the troubled waters of China. Japan, he asserted, was in an entirely different category from the great Western states of England and France, and China should not deal with her in the same way. To do so would set a bad example for other tributaries like Annam and Korea.[32]

The court referred the issue to Li Hung-chang, now viceroy of Chihli. Li repudiated Ying-han's argument on the basis that Japan, which was not a dependency of China, was totally different from Korea and Annam. That she had come to request trade without first seeking support from any Western powers showed her independence and good will. If China refused her this time, her friendship would be lost and she might even seek Western intervention on her behalf, in which case it would be difficult for China to refuse again. An antagonized Japan could be an even greater source of trouble than the Western nations because of her geographical proximity. It was therefore in China's interest to treat Japan on a friendly and equal basis and send commissioners to Japan who could look after the Chinese there, watch the movements of the Japanese government, and cultivate harmonious relations between the two states.[33] Tseng Kuo-fan, viceroy of Nanking, also favored treaty relations with Japan, noting that the commercial relations between the two nations were mutual, not unilateral, as they were between China and the West. He favored treating Japan in the same way as the Western nations, but withholding the most-favored-nation treatment.[34]

The court accepted these suggestions and signed a commercial treaty with Japan in 1871. Articles four and eight provided for the exchange of envoys and consuls respectively, but China did not put them into practice. The ills of this omission were keenly felt during the Formosa Incident of 1874. It may be recalled here briefly that Japan sent a military expedition to Formosa in 1874 to punish the aborigines for killing some shipwrecked Ryūkyūan sailors. Peking hastily charged Shen Pao-chen, superintendent of the Foochow Dockyard, with the defense of the island. Careful examination revealed that effective defense of Formosa, let alone the winning of a war, was impossible.[35] The guns cast by Dr. Halliday Macartney of the Nanking arsenal could fire nothing but salutes; real cannon-fire would burst the guns and kill the gunners rather than the enemy. Li Hung-chang, who was quite aware of this, agreed with Shen's evaluation and was disinclined to fight the invader. Through the good offices of Sir Thomas Wade, the British minister, China was able to forestall a conflict by paying half a million taels to the aggressor. Prince Kung, terrified by China's weakness after more than a decade of self-strengthening, bitterly remarked that such a glaring exposure of unpreparedness to a small country like Japan would certainly invite cupidity from larger Western states.[36] The court was shocked and astounded; it hastily instructed the viceroys and governors of the whole nation to study the problem of maritime defense. In the course of the ensuing national debate the envoy issue was reopened.

Li Hung-chang, whose proposal to send commissioners to Japan had gone unheeded three years ago, now advised the throne, in a restrained yet rueful tone, that if his earlier suggestion had been followed, the Formosan situation could not have deteriorated so hopelessly. The Chinese commissioners would have attempted to stop the Japanese expedition in the first place; at the very least they

would have warned the Chinese government of the Japanese movement in time to allow preparation. Even if hostilities had broken out,
Li stated, it would still have been more advantageous to negotiate
in Tokyo than in Peking. To avoid similar mistakes, he recommended
the immediate dispatch of envoys and consuls to Japan for the express purpose of observing Japan's situation, cultivating her friendship, and protecting the Chinese subjects there.[37] This memorial was
received at court on December 12, 1874, and on the same day Li
wrote to the Tsungli Yamen: "It appears that the issue of sending
envoys to Japan cannot be further delayed. To the various big nations of the West we should also accredit a roving ambassador so
that China may communicate her feelings to foreign nations. Envoys from the little state of Japan have been on their way to Europe
continuously. Although China need not be so anxious to please, it is
not good to over-limit ourselves. The expenses are small but the benefits are great. I humbly pray that you consider it." [38]

While the emphasis in the national debate was on maritime defense, a few memorials from the viceroys and governors touched on
the envoy issue. Wang K'ai-t'ai, governor of Fukien, stated that hitherto foreigners had come to China but no Chinese had gone to the
West. "With only coming and no going, we are like those who wish
to see well with their faces set against a wall and those who wish to
hear well with their ears covered." [39] Foreigners had been urging
China to send envoys. Why shouldn't she comply with their request
for her own good? The problem of finding suitable men would not
be insoluble, for only a limited number were needed to fill the leading posts in England, Franch, the United States, Russia and Japan.[40]
Similar views were expressed by Li Tsung-hsi, now viceroy of Nanking, who regarded diplomatic representation abroad as a convenient way to learn about new inventions in the West and arrange for
their purchase. He deplored the fact that the missions of Pin-ch'un
and Burlingame had not been followed by similar ones and asserted
that in this age of world-wide communication it was more necessary
than ever to send missions abroad. China must face this new situation with new arrangements.[41]

Ting Jih-ch'ang, ex-governor of Kiangsu, in his masterly "Itemized
discussion of maritime defense" (*Hai-fang t'iao-i*) stressed the importance of both admirals and ambassadors in the self-strengthening movement. The government, he said, should select envoys from

among the ambitious and highly qualified officials in the capital, who need not have had previous experience in foreign affairs. Scholars and merchants in coastal areas might also be considered, since ability and willingness to accept the difficult foreign assignment were more important than formal qualifications and social background. Sir Rutherford Alcock's background as a medical doctor was cited to support his argument. He recommended sending men of tested courage and eloquence as envoys to England, Russia, France, the United States, and the Papal State.[42]

These memorials, though influential and convincing, did not receive the immediate attention of the court, which was preoccupied with the serious illness of Emperor T'ung-chih, who died on January 12, 1875. The whole issue was not reopened until two months later when Li Hung-chang's long memorial was again presented. Apparently it had been studied seriously by the council of princes called to select a new emperor.[43]

To prepare the way for sending embassies, W. A. P. Martin had specially prepared a dozen essays on the rights and duties of ambassadors and consuls.[44] Meanwhile in response to an imperial call for suggestions and collective thinking, Hsüeh Fu-ch'eng, magistrate of an independent department, submitted in March 1875 a secret memorial on national policies, which was later said to have been instrumental in persuading the council of princes to approve the dispatch of envoys.[45] In this ten-point state paper, Hsüeh stressed the use of diplomacy as an instrument of foreign policy and the desirability of instituting a special government examination for the selection of envoys. Ever since the opening of China, he stated, no decent men had stooped to study foreign affairs. When incidents occurred, the Chinese were as lost as the blind. The self-styled foreign affairs experts were usually poor material, with nothing but profit in mind. It was necessary to create a new line of civil service examinations in foreign subjects to spur desirable men on to a study of foreign affairs and enterprises. With competent men in charge of diplomacy, China could negotiate and stand with the more peace-minded nations, like the United States, to counter the designs of other nations.[46]

The court received these suggestions with interest and passed them on to various important quarters for comment. Li Hung-chang and Shen Pao-chen, superintendents of trade for the Northern and Southern Ports respectively, responded favorably to Hsüeh's ideas.

Prince Li and Prince Ch'un, however, rejected the suggestion of a new governmental examination, although they approved the general principle of diplomatic representation abroad.[47] The Tsungli Yamen was in general accord with Hsüeh's ideas but considered the new civil service examination too slow a procedure to serve the immediate needs. It suggested that the court direct provincial authorities to recommend competent men for the position of envoy. On May 30, 1875, the court approved in principle the dispatch of diplomatic missions abroad and ordered the recommendation of suitable men. On June 17, the Yamen took the lead in recommending nine men.[48]

Benjamin P. Avery, American minister in Peking, commented that the Chinese had finally "realized how inconvenient it is for their country, while receiving a large body of ministers and consuls from abroad, who subject her to a constant sharp criticism before the world, to have no representative of her own, who can speak for and defend her." [49] The stage was set at long last, and the Margary murder in 1875 provided the spark that set things in motion.

d. *The Margary Incident, 1875–1876*

Prince Kung's fear that the unpreparedness and weakness, revealed by China in the Formosa Incident, might invite new trouble turned out to be warranted. Sir Thomas Wade had in fact been waiting anxiously for a chance to extend the scope of China trade, to relieve the depressed English economy brought about by the European tariff war. If China was "willing to pay for being invaded" in Formosa,[50] how much more would she pay for the loss of a British life?

In 1874 the Chinese court granted permission to a British trade expedition from Burma to explore the mineral resources of Yünnan province. Passports were issued by the Tsungli Yamen to the expedition leader, Colonel H. A. Browne, and a party of two hundred. Augustus R. Margary, a twenty-eight-year-old consular officer in China, was assigned as Browne's interpreter and guide because of his previous traveling experience in the Burma-Yünnan area, and was given permission by the Yamen to travel from China to meet the expeditionary mission. Early in 1875 it was learned that the Yünnanese were hostile to the expedition. Unimpressed, Margary volunteered to prepare the way for Colonel Browne; he was murdered by native tribesmen after crossing the Burmese border. Although international law holds no one responsible for the life of one who exposes himself to danger, the Margary incident was too good an opportunity for Wade to ignore. As was to be expected, he demanded an investigation and an indemnity for the bereaved family as well as the right to send another expedition to Yünnan from India. But he went further and exploited the occasion to the full by making many extraneous demands relevant to audience procedure, transit dues, settlement of claim cases, better diplomatic etiquette in Peking, an apology mission to England, and the trial of Ts'en Yü-ying, acting viceroy of Yün-Kuei, within whose jurisdiction the unfortunate murder had occurred.

The Chinese government readily agreed to the proposed payment and an investigation, having become accustomed to paying high fees for foreign heads. But they looked askance at the extraneous demands. Wade, whose impetuosity had been little tempered by his advancing years, petulantly withdrew his legation from Peking to Shanghai, believing that such a move would threaten Peking into submission. Indeed, Peking was terrified by the prospect of a diplomatic impasse; it was further dumbfounded by the rumor that Wade had entered into a secret agreement with the Russian minister, by which England would advance an army from India to Yünnan while Russia sent another from Ili.[51] Facing this supposed Anglo-Russian duplicity, the harassed court instructed the Tsungli Yamen to avoid a rupture at all costs, and as a first step to ease the tension it acceded to Wade's demand for an apology mission to England. On August 29, 1875 an edict was issued: "Let Kuo Sung-t'ao, expectant vice-president of a Board, and Hsü Ch'ien-shen, expectant *taotai* on the staff of the Province of Chihli, fill the posts of imperial commissioners on a mission to England. At the same time, we confer upon Hsü Ch'ien-shen the official button of the second rank."[52] Although pleased with the choice of Kuo as chief of the mission, Wade requested a delay in its dispatch while negotiations were going on in China.[53] Obviously he feared that Kuo's mission might settle the case directly in London, thereby reducing the luster of his own work.

If Wade was known for his irascibility, Hart was no less famous for his tact. As a second step to save the situation, Peking sent this devoted foreign employee to Shanghai to persuade Wade to reopen the negotiations. On his way to Shanghai Hart met with Li Hung-chang at Tientsin, proposing that if his mediatory mission failed,

China should at once send the apology mission to England and negotiate directly with the London government, in which case he would be glad to accompany Kuo.[54] Li doubted whether this apology mission could reach England in time to stop the rumored English expedition, and the Tsungli Yamen feared that Hart would dominate the mission if he went along with it.[55] Moreover, the Chinese had some misgivings that England might detain Kuo as a hostage or refuse to receive him just as the French authorities had continuously refused to receive Ch'ung-hou in 1870. After consultation with the Russian minister Butzow, Li Hung-chang assured the Yamen that international law would not allow England to detain a foreign envoy as hostage or to refuse to receive a foreign negotiator, and that the present English situation was different from that of wartime France in 1870.[56] Its fears thus dispelled, the Yamen was prepared to send the mission at the first opportune moment.

In Shanghai, Hart tactfully intimated to Wade that if they failed to reach a compromise, the Chinese would send Kuo to England. Wade, ostensibly unimpressed, replied that he did not believe such a mission could settle the Yünnan case in London.[57] Hart, however, was convinced that while the success of Kuo's mission could not be vouched for in advance, it could still do China no harm. "If China had always had a resident minister in England," he wrote to Li Hung-chang, "the Yünnan case definitely could not have deteriorated to the present state." [58] As the situation now stood, he proposed that Li save Wade's face by meeting with him at the summer resort of Chefoo. Li went there. After exchanging views with the foreign ministers than vacationing in Chefoo, Li wrote to the Yamen on September 1, 1876: "The foreign ministers of the various nations all say that in not sending our envoy to England last fall, we were tricked by Minister Wade. If we do it now, it is still not too late." [59]

Furious at Hart's efforts on China's behalf, Wade snubbed his old friend by refusing to see him or answer his letters any more. Piqued by this open insult, Hart even more emphatically urged direct negotiations with London. "The officials at the English court," he declared, "certainly will not be so intransigent as Minister Wade. I volunteer to go with the [Chinese] envoy and assist him!" [60]

In Chefoo, Li's diplomacy reached a new high. On the occasion of the Empress Dowager's birthday on August 30, 1876, he invited all the foreign diplomats in Chefoo to a party and spared no efforts to cultivate their sympathy for China and mobilize public opinion against Wade. Feeling isolated, Wade softened his stand and told Li after the party: "Your Excellency has come here to settle business. It is necessary to decide speedily and not to temporize. Now the officials of the various nations are all in Chefoo, of whom Your Excellency knows many. Today someone may offer an idea, and tomorrow another offer another, while in reality none of them can interfere with this case. Only Your Excellency and I myself can decide the issue. I pray that you do not listen to them so that the important thing may not be spoiled." [61]

With both sides willing to negotiate, the famous Chefoo Convention was promptly concluded on September 13, 1876. It was arranged in three sections: (1) relative to the settlement of the Margary Affair, including the payment of 200,000 taels and the dispatch of an apology mission to England, (2) relative to the drawing up of a new code of etiquette between the Chinese and foreign diplomats, and (3) relative to trade. [62]

After the signing of the Convention, Li Hung-chang considered it necessary also to send envoys to countries other than England. He wrote to the Tsungli Yamen: "In regard to the sending of envoys, the five big nations — England, France, Russia, Germany, the United States — and Japan are all indispensable . . . . In future, after our envoys have departed for England and the United States, it is hard to believe that ministers of other nations will not come to inquire and press for [similar arrangements]. But competent men for this type of work are hard to find. Only by sending men of relatively high and substantive position to the various big nations will they not be slighted. But I do not feel free to recommend rashly." [63] He was sufficiently clever and careful to leave the touchy problem of personnel to the Yamen, knowing full well that nobody enjoyed going abroad.

The Margary Affair was a lesson to the Chinese. They learned once more that diplomatic representation was more to their own advantage than to anyone else's. The Chefoo Convention precipitated a long-delayed measure, which in principle had been approved by the court before the Yünnan case.

CHAPTER 12

Legations Abroad as Permanent Institutions

Kuo Sung-t'ao (1818–1891), chief of the apology mission, was a proud product of Old China, learned, incorruptible, loyal, straightforward, and a bit stubborn. He had served under Tseng Kuo-fan during the campaigns against the Taipings, and had collaborated with the famous Mongolian general, Prince Seng-ko-lin-ch'in in the defense of Taku against Lord Elgin in 1859–1860. At that time, because he was not in favor of military measures against the foreigners, he had advised the general: "The foreigners' first principle is to trade. We should look for a way to deal with them accordingly, and not confront them with an army. Maritime defense will leave you neither success to speak of nor merits to record. You should not engage in it." [1] However, Seng-ko-lin-ch'in was determined to inflict punishment on the advancing enemy. Seventeen times Kuo wrote him to advise against easy recourse to war, suggesting instead "talking sense" to the foreigners. The iron-willed Mongolian soldier was unmoved by his persistent pleas, and ordered the bombardment of the Anglo-French army according to plan. The result was his disastrous defeat near Pei-t'ang,[2] which made Kuo the more confident of his own judgment on foreign affairs. Later, when the enemy was marching on to Peking in 1860, he declared openly at a social gathering that the barbarian problem could be solved by proper management but never by fighting. A long silence ensued among the audience, followed by the quiet but obvious departure of one guest after another. His friend Ch'en Chih-ho [En-fu], president of the Board of War, sympathetically warned him that such an utterance should only be made in private if he was not to invite public persecution and condemnation.[3] But Kuo did not care too much about the warning.

With the return of peace after the Convention of Peking in 1860, Kuo embarked upon an intensive study of the barbarian problem in Chinese history, from very early times to the present. He came to the conclusion that there had never before been any barbarian tribe which was even remotely similar to the barbarians of his time. The only way to deal with these new barbarians was to treat them with sincerity and not to discriminate against them.[4] During his term as acting governor of Kwangtung in the early sixties, he befriended foreigners so as to study them at first hand. Henri Cordier wrote of him: "Il est certainement l'un des hauts fonctionnaires chinois que j'ai connus avec lequel j'ai les plus agréables relations."[5] Even Li Hung-chang paid tribute to his insight into the barbarian problem.[6]

Kuo's basic philosophy for the solution of the barbarian problem was quite simple and to the point: in dealing with foreign nations, China must rely on international law and the treaty system, and in dealing with foreign individuals, Chinese officials must administer justice and not exercise emotion.[7] He never urged the rattling of the sword to ward off foreigners, but consistently expounded the wisdom of meeting each situation as it arose, for he realized that China had no chance of victory in a military contest. His indifference to military preparation was criticized by some of his contemporary foreign-affairs experts as indicative of an incomplete understanding of the West, which always used military power to support its diplomacy.[8]

a. *The Apology Mission and the First Legation, 1876–1877*

At the time of his appointment to the apology mission, Kuo was sixty years old and a judge in Fukien. Many of his friends persuaded him to spurn the foreign assignment, which they regarded as a political dead end. He accepted the post nevertheless, after a few futile attempts to decline it. His pride in his knowledge of foreign affairs led him to believe that no one else could discharge the duties as well as he.[9] It was said that because of this foreign assignment he missed the governorship of Fukien.

Prior to Kuo's appointment, Li Hung-chang was approached by the Tsungli Yamen to assess his fitness. Li declined to commit himself, conscious of the general apathy toward foreign assignments. The appointment nevertheless came through. Fearing that Kuo might impute this to his recommendation, Li wrote to him three days after his appointment was announced: "I truly know of your lack of interest in making a long trip late in life. Therefore, when the Yamen first consulted me about [the appointment], I dared not make any gratuitous comment." [10] He surmised that the Empress Dowager herself must have made the selection and urged Kuo to exercise self-denial in the interest of the state.[11]

Kuo came to Peking to accept the assignment, but the mission was delayed on Wade's request. Kuo was temporarily made a vice-president of the Board of War in December 1875, and, shortly afterward, a minister of the Tsungli Yamen, to further his acquaintance with the more recent foreign affairs.[12]

Prior to this Kuo had secretly memorialized for the impeachment of Governor Ts'en Yü-ying of Yünnan, on charges that he had failed to take precautionary measures against the Margary murder and had permitted the trouble to arise.[13] While this impeachment looked on the surface like an appeasement of Wade at the expense of an unfortunate loyal official, in whose jurisdiction a foreign exploiter happened to have been killed, Kuo's real motive was to save Governor Ts'en by a light charge of dereliction of duty and so avoid the alternative heavy charge of having instigated and connived in the murder. His secret motive was not detected by the literati, who now rallied to Ts'en's defense and condemned Kuo as a traitor and an enemy of the nation. In deep disappointment and distress, Kuo sighed: "Nowadays, [in ordinary cases] a single impeachment may remove a viceroy or governor, but in the murder case of a foreigner, not even a slight charge is allowed. Yet we can present no argument to convince the foreigners. With men of this type [in the government], how is it possible to avoid misguidance of the state and the suffering of the people?" [14]

Kuo's impeachment of Ts'en was referred by the court to Viceroy Li Han-chang, brother of Li Hung-chang, now in charge of the investigation of the Margary case in Yünnan. On April 20, 1876, Li's verdict arrived at the court: "Vice-President of the Board Kuo Sung-t'ao has impeached Ts'en Yü-ying on the charge of allowing trouble to grow, etc. He based [his charge] on distant hearsay and is therefore out of order. However, Ts'en Yü-ying, having failed to settle the case speedily, ought to be punished." [15]

The literati's attack on Kuo continued to mount until it virtually assumed the proportions of a campaign of defamation. The indiscriminate public was quick to follow. When a Catholic cathedral was built in 1876 by some foreigners in Changsha, Kuo's native place, the local gentry and populace rose to charge Kuo with instigating the foreign move and threatened to destroy his residence.[16] The great Hunanese scholar, Wang K'ai-yün, wrote in his famous *Diary of the Hsiang-i-lou*: "Hunanese feel most ashamed of association with Kuo."[17] A pair of sarcastic scrolls also appeared to satirize Kuo's mission to England:

> Outstanding among his associates,
> Elevated above his peers,
> Yet ostracized in the nation of Yao and Shun.

> Unable to serve men,
> Why able to serve devils?
> Of what use to leave his fatherland and mother country![18]

Kuo countered the slanderous attack with a loud charge that the literati were following the unworthy trend of the Southern Sung (1127–1280 A.D.) in denouncing peace and glorifying war, not knowing the historical fact that China had always been cautious with foreign tribes before the Northern Sung (960–1127 A.D.). War had been waged then only as a last resort. Kuo asserted that to attack foreigners without first knowing them was to lead the nation into disaster. He felt it his duty to point this out even at the risk of sacrificing his personal reputation.[19]

However, Kuo found the social pressure intolerable. He begged the court to permit his resignation from the foreign mission "so as to exonerate him from the public condemnation."[20] He argued that diplomatic representation abroad was not absolutely necessary except in the United States, Peru, and Cuba, where numerous Chinese overseas subjects resided and needed protection. To other foreign countries where China had no concrete interests at the moment, envoys were not really needed. Kuo doubted whether any definite results could come from using Chinese diplomats at a distance to argue cases with foreign governments. Moreover, he entertained misgivings that an inaccurate or unskillful presentation of facts to a foreign government might damage China's position and bring ridicule and disgrace on the envoy. However able the envoy might be, he would be a useful man wasted in a useless place. Only after the Chinese had gone abroad to trade and travel in large numbers would it be justifiable to send ministers and consuls to foreign countries. To prepare for such a day, Kuo suggested that the Board of Ceremonies select officials under fifty years of age for training in foreign affairs.[21]

The court did not allow him to resign, and he had to go to England. Well-intentioned friends hoped that his exit would quiet the literati's outcry against him, but it soon became clear that although out of their sight he was not out of their minds.

As the negotiations for the Chefoo Convention came to an end in 1876, Thomas Wade emphatically urged the early departure of the mission.[22] The ordeal of slander at home and the ominous prospect of begging pardon for his country in England made Kuo's departure anything but a happy occasion. His heart was indeed heavy, and Li Hung-chang could not help writing sympathetically, "Old Kuo is quite noble in making this trip of 30,000 *li.*"[23] On December 1, 1876 the mission sailed from Shanghai with a retinue of fifteen men, including Liu Hsi-hung, who had replaced the original associate envoy Hsü Ch'ien-shen, and two foreign secretaries, Dr. Halliday Macartney and W. C. Hillier.[24] It arrived in London on January 21, 1877, and on February 8, Kuo presented to Queen Victoria the Chinese emperor's Letter of Apology, which read in part:

> That Margary, while traveling under passport within the frontiers of Yünnan, should lamentably have been murdered, is a fact that not only involves [a loss of] life, but also has come close to disturbing our relations of amity and concord. I profoundly regret and lament it. I have now made special appointment of Kuo Sung-t'ao, acting senior vice-president of the Board of Ceremonies and a minister of the Office of Foreign Affairs, as imperial commissioner to proceed to Your Majesty's country to express the sentiments of my heart, as a proof of my genuine desire for amity and concord.
>
> I know that Kuo Sung-t'ao is capable, experienced, loyal, truthful, amicable and just, and highly intelligent. He is quite familiar with the procedures of Chinese and foreign affairs. I pray that sincere confidence be reposed in him so that the blessings of friendly relations may be forever maintained, and that all alike may enjoy the happiness of a state of rising peace. This, I presume, will be greatly to [Your Majesty's] satisfaction.[25]

After the presentation of the Letter of Apology, Lord Derby of the Foreign Office notified Kuo that his continued stay in England as a resident minister would necessitate additional credentials, and that the name of the associate envoy, which was not mentioned in the Letter of Apology, must also be included in the new credentials in order to give him official status.[26] While this was duly reported to the court, Kuo reiterated his view that permanent accreditation to England at the moment was not a *sine qua non.* Liu Hsi-hung, exasperated by the reluctance of the British government to recognize his official status, memorialized separately for permission to return home.[27]

Their memorials were referred to the Tsungli Yamen, which hastily defended its negligence in not preparing the regular credentials for Kuo on the ground that no such documents had ever been issued to the earlier missions of Burlingame and Ch'ung-hou. The presence of a resident minister in England was strongly urged upon the court by the Yamen in view of the increasing transaction of business between the two states. It also suggested that Liu's request to return home be granted. The court approved the issuance of new credentials to Kuo, but did not recall Liu, who was instead transferred to Berlin as the first Chinese envoy to Germany. The post of associate envoy in England was abolished on May 12, 1877.[28]

b. *Other Legations, 1875–1880*

The need for diplomatic representation in other countries was also keenly felt. Even before Wade's demand for an apology mission to England, Li Hung-chang had vigorously urged the court to send envoys to Peru and Cuba to protect the Chinese there. On December 11, 1875, the court appointed Ch'en Lan-pin, a senior secretary of the Board of Punishments, and Yung Hung [Yung Wing], a brevet subprefect and a graduate of Yale College in 1854, as envoys to the United States, Spain, and Peru. Both men had been in the United States as superintendents of the Chinese Educational Mission at Hartford, Connecticut, and had also made trips to Cuba to investigate the coolie trade. At the time of their appointment as envoys, Yung Wing was still in the United States superintending the educational mission; Ch'en Lan-pin was in Peking. Ch'en's credentials had first been translated by the American legation in Peking which wanted to make sure that they were not so "presumptuous" as those of Burlingame in 1869. Of Ch'en the American minister, George Seward, wrote to the Department of State quite favorably: "He appears well informed, and while complaisant in his manner, seems to have decided opinions. He is . . . a fair representative of the Chinese official class." [29] Ch'en reached Washington on September 19, 1878, and presented his credentials to President Hayes on September 29. With Yung Wing in charge of the legation in Washington, Ch'en proceeded first to Spain, where he presented his credentials on May 24, 1879, then to Peru, where he presented the credentials on April 17, 1880.[30]

On September 30, 1876, Hsü Ch'ien-shen, who had originally been designated associate envoy to England, was made envoy to Japan, and Ho Ju-chang, a Hanlin editor, was made associate envoy to Japan. But before leaving for Tokyo, Hsü was again transferred to the directorship of the Foochow Dockyard. Ho Ju-chang became the regular envoy to Japan, and Chang Ssu-kuei, who had written a foreword to Martin's translation of Wheaton, was appointed associate envoy. They left China on November 21, 1878, and presented their credentials to the Japanese emperor on December 17. The legation in Germany was set up by Liu Hsi-hung, who presented his credentials to the Kaiser in late November 1877. On February 22, 1878, the court in Peking made the envoy to England concurrently envoy to France. Kuo Sung-t'ao proceeded to Paris to present his credentials on May 6, 1878. Finally, Ch'ung-hou was appointed envoy to the Court of St. Petersburg on July 20, 1878 and concurrently imperial commissioner of the first class to negotiate with the Russians for the return of Ili. He presented his credentials to the Tsar on January 20, 1879. With the establishment of these legations, China at long last took her place in the family of nations.[31]

Not all of these legations rested on the same legal basis. Those in London, Paris, and Tokyo were established on a treaty basis; those in Washington and St. Petersburg were not. It may be recalled that the British and French Treaties of Tientsin of 1858 and the Japanese Treaty of Commerce and Friendship of 1871 all provided for the mutual exchange of envoys with China, whereas the American and Russian Treaties of Tientsin merely stipulated the right of these two countries to establish legations in China, without giving China the right to reciprocate. Thus the Chinese legations in the United States and Russia rested not on a treaty basis but on the general principles of international law. However, since Secretary Seward of the United States had formally invited China to send a diplomat to Washington in 1865,[32] the Chinese legation in Washington may also be considered as having been established by invitation.

c. *The Plight of Kuo Sung-t'ao*

The external relations of the Chinese legation in London were marked by cordiality and tact, under the wise management of Minister Kuo and his English secretary, Dr. Halliday Macartney.[33] Kuo's urbanity and stateliness made him very much in demand in the salons of London and Paris, and his courtesy was taken by most foreigners for *politesse de coeur*. He participated in the sixth meeting of the Association for the Reform and Codification of the Law of Nations in 1878, and assisted in the Universal Exposition in France in 1878.[34]

But conditions within the legation were not nearly so harmonious. Liu Hsi-hung bore a grudge against Kuo from the very beginning. When the mission of apology was first organized, Liu, who was not a friend of Kuo's, had asked to go along as an attaché. Kuo was disinclined to accept him because of his inexperience in foreign affairs and his known prejudice against foreigners. Yet through his connections in the Grand Council Liu managed to go over Kuo's head and secure appointment as associate envoy.[35] This initial political maneuver sowed the seed of dissension and foreshadowed their subsequent disagreeable relationship. In London Liu made no secret of his proud association with a certain grand councillor to impress, and indeed he overwhelmed the legation staff with his importance. It was heartbreaking for Kuo to find these men, supposedly his personal staff, turning away from him in attempts to ingratiate themselves with Liu, under whose secret encouragement some of them even began to neglect Kuo's assignments. At times Liu succeeded in embarrassing Kuo by taking all the legation members for a walk or a visit, leaving an empty embassy for Kuo to guard.[36] Life in the embassy was difficult for Kuo.

Liu was a xenophobe *par excellence*. His anti-foreign sentiments were intensified by the British refusal to recognize his status as associate envoy, and from then on everything English became distasteful to him. England was the inverted image of China, and everything in England was abnormal: England's days were China's nights; Englishmen wrote from the left, Chinese from the right; England honored women, China honored men; England was governed by people's representatives, while China was ruled by a supreme emperor. For this "topsy-turvy" situation in England Liu had an explanation to offer: "It is because their country is situated under the axis of the earth. Their heaven, which is above them, is actually under our ground. Hence their customs and institutions are all upside down." [37] He was mortally shocked at the sight of a formal dance in the Court of St. James, where women danced in evening gowns "half-naked" and men in skin-colored tight trousers. He exclaimed: "From a distance, it looks as if his lower body were bare. Most disgraceful to look at!" [38]

Liu's feud with Kuo did not end with his transfer to Germany. He continued to send home malicious news about Kuo to inflame the literati.[39] Deeply harassed, Kuo sent a number of dispatches in self-defense, in which his temper was visibly heightened. In this excited mood, he expressed his views on foreign affairs even more bluntly than before. While sympathetic with his plight, Li Hung-chang nevertheless advised him to speak in a more restrained manner and not to burden the high Peking circles with overly long and unsolicited writings.[40] Quite frankly he informed Kuo in December, 1877: "Henceforth this kind of writing need not be undertaken. I have heard that friends in the Grand Council and Tsungli Yamen all feel that writings from your place have been too numerous. Straightforward expression of opinions has not been appreciated for a long time!" [41]

Meanwhile, complaints from legation members about Liu's strange behavior in Berlin had also come to Li Hung-chang's attention. He tactfully intimated to the Tsungli Yamen that, since Liu was not representing China well in Germany but busying himself in a personal conflict with Kuo across the continent, he was a nuisance and a laughing stock to foreigners. Li suggested that the Yamen take proper measures to rectify the situation. The Yamen's response was noncommittal.[42]

Kuo Sung-t'ao suffered another misfortune when, in accordance with instructions, he sent home his diary, entitled "A record of my mission to the West" (*Shih-hsi chi-ch'eng*), which was published by the Yamen without his knowledge. In that work he lauded the Western nations as having a civilization of two thousand years' antiquity and being totally different from the ephemeral, powerful barbarian tribes known in Chinese history.[43] The literati, seizing upon this occasion to blacken his name further, cited this passage as evidence of his traitorous character, and insisted vehemently that the diary should be banned and the printing plates destroyed. Ho Chin-shou, a Hanlin editor, impeached Kuo for his heretical views, and Chang P'ei-lun, a subreader in the Hanlin Academy and son-in-law of Li Hung-chang, demanded his recall.[44] Yielding to the force of "public opinion," the court ordered the destruction of Kuo's diary. Li Hung-chang could not help expressing his sympathy for Kuo when he wrote to a friend on July 23, 1877: "Kuo was indeed a bit too stubborn, yet his grasp of foreign affairs is truly remarkable. I had not expected that he would be slandered to such an extent. If high officials and valuable men all become scared of [foreign affairs], China will never witness a day of strength and prosperity; perhaps she will not even find a way to survive. My heart is really cold." [45]

Caught between the slanderous attack by the literati in China and Liu Hsi-hung's defamation campaign abroad, Kuo became utterly discouraged in his service to the state. He repeatedly asked permission to resign on grounds of age and illness, but was persuaded by Li Hung-chang to serve out his three-year term.[46] In late 1878 the court finally found a successor in Tseng Chi-tse, better known as the Marquis Tseng. Probably realizing that he might inherit Kuo's misfortune as China's envoy, Tseng took the precaution of begging the Empress Dowager, during an audience, for her indulgence in the future treatment of Kuo, to which she yielded a ready assent.[47] An excerpt from their conversation is presented here:

Tseng: "Kuo Sung-t'ao is certainly an upright and straightforward person. This time he again risked damage to his reputation in order to manage affairs for the nation. In the future it is hoped that the special grace of the Empresses and the Emperor will protect him in every respect."

Dowager: "We thoroughly understand. Kuo Sung-t'ao is a good man. Since his mission abroad he has managed many affairs but he has also received plenty of scolding from people."

Tseng: ". . . . Fortunately the Empresses Dowager and the Emperor understand him. Even though he has lost his reputation in the fight, still it is worthwhile."

Dowager: "We all know him. The princes and great ministers also understand him." [48]

Having thus insured Kuo's safety as well as his own, Tseng set out for Europe. Of course Kuo had no way of knowing of this conversation. He was so fearful of persecution in the capital that upon his return to China he dared not go to Peking but proceeded directly to his home in Hunan. He gave up the plough of the state for that of the farm, and lived out his life in relative obscurity.

Kuo spent his later life on the frontier of two worlds, repudiated by the old but not wholly accepted by the new. His statesmanship, surpassing that of many of his contemporaries, was somewhat obscured by his want of tact, which often produced results opposite to his aims. A modest posthumous honor was arranged in 1891 by his old friend Li Hung-chang when the latter succeeded in having his name entered in the Bureau of National History.[49]

d. *Organization and Finance*

The organization of Chinese legations abroad was governed by twelve regulations promulgated on October 18, 1876, which were drawn up partly on the model of Western legations in Peking.[50] Significant differences were to be noticed, however. In line with the domestic practice, the term of an envoy and his staff was uniformly three years. The envoys, known as imperial commissioners, were divided into three classes. Only the second-class imperial commissioners were sent out at first. Every legation member was instructed to keep a diary, and accounts of travel and of impressions of foreign customs, to be sent to the Tsungli Yamen for the benefit of home officers and future diplomats.[51]

A legation was made up, in order, of minister, counsellor, interpreter, and attaché, but the number of incumbents for each post was left unfixed, so that the envoy might decide this for himself according to need. Kuo Sung-t'ao brought to England, apart from the associate envoy, a retinue of fifteen men and a few cooks and servants; his successor, the Marquis Tseng, brought an entourage of nineteen men.[52] It was not until 1888 that the Tsungli Yamen succeeded in fixing the legation personnel at seven or eight: two counsellors or secretaries, two or three interpreters, a general-affairs officer, a military attaché, and a medical officer. If the envoy was accredited to more than one country, he was permitted to maintain an additional secretary, interpreter, and general-affairs officer in his second legation.[53] This new limitation on personnel, however, was not always observed by the envoys, who had become used to the practice of bringing large personal staffs. Attempts to reform the foreign service in the 1890's met with little success, and it was not until 1907 that the Foreign Office was able to limit the six big legations in England, France, Germany, the United States, Russia, and Japan to seven members each: a second counsellor, a third counsellor, a first secretary, a second secretary, a second interpreter, a third interpreter, and a commercial attaché. In a case of extreme necessity, a medical officer and a general-affairs manager might be added.[54]

The legation organization had many interesting and unique features. The appointment of an envoy and an associate envoy reflected the old tributary practice of sending two emissaries on each mission. When Kuo Sung-t'ao and Liu Hsi-hung were sent to London, the British government, as we have seen, found it hard to appreciate the peculiar Chinese practice and made no secret of its reluctance to acknowledge Liu's status. Peking, when apprised of this situation, abolished the post of associate envoy in England on May 12, 1877, and transferred Liu to Germany as envoy. However, the post of associate envoy in the United States, filled by Yung Wing, a Yale graduate, was not objected to by the United States government, and it continued to exist.

It is to be noted that almost all early envoys were accredited to more than one country, except those in Tokyo, who were accredited exclusively to Japan.[55] All the envoys held the rank of second class imperial commissioner, which was more or less equivalent to the rank of minister in the Western system. Throughout the late Ch'ing period there was only one exception to this general rule: the appointment of Ch'ung-hou in 1878 as first class imperial commissioner (corresponding to ambassador) to Russia to negotiate the return of Ili.

These envoys, while abroad, retained their home positions, just as an imperial commissioner in China kept his original appointment. The envoys' double status was deliberately planned for the purposes of showing their ranks at home to the foreigners and keeping a basis for their future promotion within the domestic hierarchy. This practice created no problem at first, when only a few envoys were sent out, but when China later maintained legations and consulates over most of the world, the absentee posts in Peking became so numerous as to form a vacuum in the civil service.[56] In 1895 Censor Ch'en Ch'i-chang suggested to the court that, since Western diplomats in China held no concurrent positions at home, Chinese envoys should not be given real domestic posts but only brevet titles, because their foreign assignments were their posts.[57] But this suggestion was not acted upon by the court.

An envoy was empowered to select his entourage. The Tsungli Yamen, which generally approved his selections as a formality, justified granting him this extraordinary power with the explanation that the attachés must be known and acceptable to the envoy in order to win his trust and confidence in a foreign land, and that a congenial atmosphere in the legation could help to expedite the discharge of official duties. A stranger in the embassy, on the other hand, might inhibit such harmonious companionship, and might even obstruct the free exchange of ideas.[58] The traditional Confucian emphasis on personal relationship was amply reflected here. When Liu Hsi-hung, as envoy to Germany, asked the Tsungli Yamen in 1877 to transfer two students of the German language from the T'ung-wen kuan to his legation, the Yamen hesitated at first because these students were not ready for service, but it yielded on second thought in view of the established principle that the legation members must be acceptable and congenial to the envoy.[59] The suggestion of Censor Yang Ch'en in 1889 to select embassy members from among the Yamen secretaries and well-known foreign affairs experts in the provinces was also rejected by the Yamen on the same grounds.[60]

The envoy could not only choose his own assistants but also designate their total number. It is said that at one point a certain envoy brought with him as many as thirty attachés, whereas the powerful British legation in China had only seven or eight members.[61] Moreover, the Chinese legation staff, though officially appointed for a three-year term, could be dismissed at will by the envoy, who reigned supreme in the legation. When an envoy returned home, whether or not he had served out his complete term, a large part of the legation staff usually returned with him, and the new envoy reserved the right to keep or dismiss whoever remained. The rate of personnel turnover was thus quite high in the legations, and needless to say, stability and continuity were proportionally low.

The salaries of the legation members, although fixed by official regulations, were also subject to control by the envoy, who could reduce or increase them at will. It was said that in the legations in London and Washington, the unusually large staffs made it difficult for the envoys to meet the budget while paying them full salaries. As a result, salaries were cut at one point to only 40 per cent of the regular emoluments. Yet the legation members dared not complain, because they were the "personal" staff of the envoy, in whose hands their future lay.[62] In 1895 Censor Ch'en Ch'i-chang proposed to the court that the envoy should cut the number of sinecure holders rather than the salaries of useful staff, whose emoluments should be kept at 90 per cent of the fixed pay. Yüan Shih-k'ai, governor of Shangtung, in 1901 also suggested that the British Foreign Service should be imitated and the envoy's right to appoint his own staff retracted.[63] But these suggestions were not accepted by the government until 1907 when the new Ministry of Foreign Affairs revamped the whole foreign service.[64]

A most peculiar feature of the legation was its triangular relationship with the emperor and the Tsungli Yamen. The envoy memorialized directly to the court on important matters and the court issued him instructions without going through the Tsungli Yamen, which was allowed to concern itself only with the routine business of the legations.[65] Kuo Sung-t'ao's dispatches were sent to the court through his special agent in the China Merchants Steam Navigation Company in Shanghai, and the court's orders, prepared by the Grand Council, were sent by the Board of War to Li Hung-chang, viceroy of Chihli, for transmittal to Kuo.[66] In both cases the Yamen was bypassed.

The transmission of dispatches from the envoys is a matter of some interest. Kuo Sung-t'ao appointed his personal friend, Major Huang Hui-ho of the China Merchants Steam Navigation Company, to handle his dispatches on the legation payroll. Other envoys followed this personal approach. Liu Hsi-hung trusted his correspondence to the Shanghai Customs commissioner; the envoys in Japan appointed their friend Wang Sung-sen of the China Merchants Steam Navigation Company to manage their correspondence. The inconveniences of this decentralized, personal management of official communications were soon discovered, and in 1878 the government instituted a centralized Office for the Transmission of Government Correspondence within the China Merchants Steam Navigation Company, under the general management of Major Huang Hui-ho.[67]

In theory the Tsungli Yamen had no way of knowing the contents of the communications between the court and the legations, unless the court referred to it a matter at issue. The envoy was not responsible to the Yamen but to the throne directly, as was the Yamen. The envoys and the Yamen were parallel organizations of the state, one outside China, one inside; neither enjoyed hierarchical superiority over the other.[68] The Yamen could not instruct the envoy directly; it could merely request the court to instruct him. This practice was in glaring contrast to the Western system, whereby the foreign office, under the sovereign, was usually the supreme organ of the state in diplomatic transactions. All envoys were responsible to it and sent dispatches to it alone. Cabinet decisions were transmitted to envoys, when necessary, through the foreign office, and the envoys' official communications to any other organ of the government must first go to the foreign office.[69]

The inadequacy of the Chinese practice was soon realized. In 1877 the envoys were instructed by the court to report monthly to the Tsungli Yamen. But since they were used to the old practice, the new order was honored more in the breach than in the observance. Minister Yang Ju in Washington, for example, reported to the Yamen only once or twice a year, and Minister Kung Chao-yuan in London and Paris never bothered to report to it at all.[70] On the other hand, most envoys kept some contact with Li Hung-chang, the venerable viceroy of Chihli and superintendent of trade for the Northern Ports, who maintained what might be called his own "little court" in Tientsin. They dared not neglect to furnish him with information on the latest models of guns and ships, new inventions, and political developments in the West. The Tsungli Yamen was helplessly eclipsed by Li.

As soon as the policy of sending permanent missions abroad was decided upon in 1875, the Tsungli Yamen set about to find ways and means of financing them, and in this it was quite successful. Temporary missions in the past, like Pin-ch'un's and Burlingame's, were first financed by Robert Hart from the Customs funds. These funds were later repaid by the Yamen from its own budget, which came from thirty per cent of the ship tonnage dues. Ch'ung-hou's apology mission in 1870 was financed by the Tientsin Customs.[71] But permanent legations required a standing fund. Prince Kung had his eye set on the foreign customs dues, 40 per cent of which had hitherto been assigned to the Board of Revenue and 60 per cent to some unfixed purposes such as reparations, foreign debts, or purchase of ships for the Pei-yang and Nan-yang fleets. Prince Kung now secured permission to use one-tenth of this unfixed portion (i.e. six per cent of the total foreign dues) as legation funds. The Shanghai Customs was assigned to assemble the allotted percentage of dues from the various local customs for remittance to the legations. Later, this six-per-cent sum, which was inadequate to the increasing legation expenditures, was increased to nine per cent, to which was added the ship tonnage dues of the China Merchants Company that were held by the Customs.[72]

The total income from these sources amounted to about a million taels annually, and after 1905 to about 1.8 million. The total expenditures of the legations averaged slightly over half a million taels per annum.[73] The legation funds actually exceeded the expenses. Why then did the Yamen repeatedly urge frugality and cut the salaries of embassy members by twenty per cent in 1887? The answer lay in the numerous extraneous uses to which the legation funds were put by the court, such as 400,000 taels for ships for the Nan-yang fleet in 1880, a certain sum in partial payment of the indemnity for the return of Ili in 1882, 50,000 taels for the laying of telegraph lines in Amur province, and 180,000 taels for British guns.[74] In name these funds were "borrowed," but they were never returned. From 1883 to 1885, more than 2.2 million taels was used for purposes other than the support of legations. It is small wonder that the legations often found themselves in the red.

There were no budgetary restrictions on the legations, however, until 1902, when the legation in the United States was limited to 200,000 taels per annum; that in England to 120,000; Japan, 70,000; France, 60,000; Russia, 60,000; Germany, 60,000; Korea, 50,000; and the commercial attaché's office in Vladivostok to 20,000, totaling 640,000 taels.[75] Salaries constituted the largest single expense item, amounting to nearly fifty per cent of the total. A detailed breakdown is presented in the accompanying table.[76]

Salaries paid in Chinese legations in 1876 and 1907 (taels per month)

POSITIONS	SALARIES (1876 SCALE)	SALARIES (1907)
First class envoy (ambassador)	1,400	1,400
Second class envoy (minister)	1,200	1,000
Third class envoy — third grade	1,000	800
Third class envoy — fourth grade	800	—
Acting envoy	600	—
Consul general	600	500
Consul	500	400
Vice consul	400	300
Acting consul	400	—
First counsellor	500	500
Second counsellor	400	400
Third counsellor	300	300
First class interpreter	400	400

Salaries paid in Chinese legations in 1876 and 1907 (taels per month)
(continued)

POSITIONS	SALARIES (1876 SCALE)	SALARIES (1907)
Second class interpreter	300	300
Third class interpreter	200	240
Interpreter in consulate	300	—
Commercial attaché	—	240
First class secretary	—	300
Second class secretary	—	240
Third class secretary	—	200
Attaché, doctor	200	—

The envoys were given quite liberal salaries on both scales, which compared favorably with the salaries of Board presidents, vice-presidents, and governors at home. For instance, a second class envoy on the 1876 scale received a salary of 14,400 taels per annum, as compared to the anti-corruption fee of 10,000 for Board presidents, 8,000 for vice-presidents, and 15,000 for governors.[77] Needless to say, high domestic offices offered many other attractions that were unavailable to envoys, but on the surface the financial aspect of service as an envoy was not unattractive.

The principal functions of a regular Western diplomat are to transact official business, protect the lives, interests, and properties of any of his countrymen resident in his accredited state, and report on the political and other conditions. The main occupations of the early Chinese envoys, however, were limited to protection of the interests of overseas subjects and the collection of information on foreign nations. There was no attempt to improve China's international status through active diplomacy; formal negotiations of importance were conducted mostly in Peking, rather than by Chinese legations abroad. A few notable exceptions were Kuo Sung-t'ao's negotiations with the British government on the establishment of a Chinese consulate in Singapore in 1878, and Tseng Chi-tse's successful negotiations with the Russians in 1880 over the return of Ili.

If the early envoys were not very active in international diplomacy, they were certainly active in keeping diaries and various accounts of foreign countries. The man was rare who went abroad and did not come back with some sort of report. But these reports seldom went beyond superficial descriptions of trips, impressions of foreign customs, visits to historical spots, and inspections of shipyards and munitions factories. A sound penetrating study of Western civilization and its political systems was yet to be made. But too much should not be expected of these pioneer diplomats, since the Ch'ing government did not require them to engage in active diplomacy or profound studies of foreign subjects. The 1899 edition of the *Collected Statutes of the Great Ch'ing Empire* (*Ta-Ch'ing hui-tien*) lists the functions of envoys as: [78]

1. To conduct important negotiations with "full powers."
2. To dismiss or impeach subordinates.
3. To supervise Chinese students and visitors.
4. To control Chinese consuls or nominate them from among their own legation members.
5. To protect and supervise Chinese overseas.
6. To control the budget and expenditures of the legation.

Not included in this list, was the very important additional duty of purchasing guns, ships, and machinery for the government or for Viceroy Li Hung-chang. For instance, Li Feng-pao, supervisor of Chinese naval students in England and France in 1876–1877, was also a purchasing agent for Li Hung-chang. He retained this lucrative position while an envoy in Germany until he was dismissed on a charge of embezzling over a million taels.[79] The collected works of Hsü Ching-ch'eng, envoy to Germany in 1884, are replete with accounts of purchasing gun-boats, visits to shipyards, railway factories, and munitions factories, munitions price lists, and his estimates of the naval strengths of different nations.[80]

The preoccupation with gun-purchasing and diary writing, coupled with the language difficulty and inexperience in international affairs, made it difficult for the early envoys to engage in active diplomacy. Li Feng-pao was said never to have seen Bismarck during his term as envoy in Berlin. Writers and publicists at home frequently suggested that these envoys and their staffs should be required to employ their time to better advantage by translating foreign books and journals for the benefit of their countrymen.[81]

Judged by the standards of their Western contemporaries, the early Chinese envoys certainly had a rather mediocre record. A happy exception was the famous Marquis Tseng, who could probably compare favorably with many of his Western contemporaries. Kuo Sung-t'ao and Hsüeh Fu-ch'eng, envoys to Britain before and after the Marquis Tseng, must also be considered remarkable in their own way. Other envoys may be said to have been able legation administrators rather than active diplomats. All in all, as pioneers in the nascent diplomatic service of China, they succeeded more in introducing the West to the Chinese than in elevating China's international position. Their diaries and travel writings have been a source of inspiration for many generations.

CHAPTER 13

Epilogue: The Imperial Chinese Tradition in the Modern World

Fifteen years elapsed after the establishment of foreign legations in Peking before China sent diplomatic missions abroad. Why did she delay so long? The stock explanation given by the mandarins was the unavailability of suitable men and concern over the expenses involved. Yet the facts belied these explanations. Early envoys were readily chosen from the existing officialdom without special training in foreign affairs, and the early legation funds far exceeded the expenditures. The mandarins' explanations could only be accepted as excuses for inaction. What they really meant was that suitable men were not willing to be envoys, and the court was not willing to spend money in that way. The disinclination to accept diplomacy as a normal function of the state was rooted in Chinese institution and psychology. While closely interrelated, these two aspects may be usefully distinguished. The institutional barrier was the *t'i-chih*, which has been discussed in a previous chapter; the psychological barrier is studied here.

a. *The Ideological Opposition to Legations Abroad*

A state seldom initiates a new policy until it has recognized its necessity. It took the mandarins some fifteen years to appreciate the benefit of diplomatic representation abroad. This process involved a fundamental psychological transformation which by its very nature was slow and gradual. Several stages can be observed. The initial reaction to the idea of diplomatic representation was rejection, and the recommendations of Hart and Wade in 1865–1866 were regarded by the mandarins as veiled threats. The success of the Burlingame mission could not have failed to impress them with the usefulness of foreign missions, and the Formosa Incident of 1874 literally shocked the mandarins into realizing the stupidity of further delay. They came to see that diplomatic representation abroad would benefit China more than anyone else, and Wade's demand for a mission of apology in 1875 set off the long delayed move and brought China out of her shell. That this reorientation was so long delayed is attributable to the unfavorable intellectual milieu in which it was taking place.

The intellectual world of Imperial China was dominated by the literati, composed largely of censors, courtiers, writers, and gentry. Their utterances constituted "public opinion," which even the court dared not ignore. This type of "public opinion" was very different from that of the West. It was not *vox populi*, but the prevailing opinion of the educated few who were the articulate section of the society. It was not expressed through newspapers or public speaking, but through such media as official impeachments, social gatherings, poems, folk songs, scrolls, ballads, and gossip. In Chinese it is known as the *ch'ing-i*, meaning roughly "pure discussion" or "gossipy criticism," and implying an irresponsible attitude on the part of the critics. While it is hard to describe precisely this fluid term *ch'ing-i*, what eludes definition need not pass understanding. For the sake of simplicity, *ch'ing-i* may well be accepted as the Chinese counterpart of Western public opinion.

Ch'ing-i in the late Ch'ing period was molded by three main forces: the noisy accusations of the censors, the murmured gossip in the court, and the casual expressions of the literati. The censors were particularly vociferous. Known as the *yen-kuan*, or speech officials, they were first appointed by the Emperor Wu of the Liang dynasty (502–557 A.D.). During the T'ang (618–907) they were merely subordinates of the prime minister, but during the Sung they were promoted and became independent officials. In the wake of foreign incursions during the Southern Sung (1127–1280) they became unusually assertive and led the attacks on the prime ministers for having failed to take revenge on the enemy. Gradually they acquired a reputation as leaders of public sentiment. During the Ming and Ch'ing (1368–1911) they were made the "eyes and ears" of the court in order to ferret out secret opposition, and were given the privilege of attacking, impeaching, criticizing, or praising a man or a policy, openly or secretly as they saw fit, under no pain of penalty. Even high officials dreaded them. Robert Hart, in his memorandum of 1865 on modernization, sarcastically remarked that the censors were "the wrong eyes and ears for the throne, men who contributed to the corruption of officials and did not hear the people's anger." [1]

The Ch'ing censorate, headquarters of die-hards and ultra-conservatives, consisted of two Left Grand Censors, four Left Associate Censors and a large number of departmental and circuit censors.[2] Right Grand Censor was usually a brevet title to be conferred on worthy and meritorious viceroys and governors. The censors' institutional functions were to detect derelictions of duty by any official and to keep the emperor informed on all important matters. Although they were not supposed to concern themselves with governmental policies, yet through their watchful supervision of the execution of such policies and their constant readiness to impeach the officials in charge, they actually exerted a considerable influence on both the administration of current policies and the formulation of future ones. Moreover, they considered themselves loyal defenders of the Chinese heritage and jealous guardians of the principle of *li*, which was "the unwritten constitution of the state and the moral code of soicety." [3] Any un-Chinese activity was condemned by them as traitorous to the national tradition and unfilial to the ancestors. They freely described the actions of members of the Tsungli Yamen, advocates of Westernization, and envoys to the West, in such offensive terms as "ingratiating themselves with foreigners," "serving the barbarians," or "having clandestine relations with the enemy." [4] Their fierce accusations usually produced quick results. A typical example was the destruction of Kuo Sung-t'ao's diary.

In parallel existence with the censorate were the conservative courtiers, the Hanlin scholars, and the headstrong literati. Steeped in tradition and secure in vested interests, they spent their days in political maneuvering or reading old books, and their nights in idyllic idleness or metaphysical contemplation. Externally they advocated a get-tough policy toward foreigners, and internally they adopted an attitude of *quieta non movere*, opposing any changes that threatened their comfortable and privileged position. They announced that they had heard of transforming the barbarians by the Chinese way of life, but never of changing the Chinese with barbarian ways. Texts from the classics were carefully chosen to disarm opposition, and the failures of Shang Yang and Wang An-shih were often cited as proofs of the evils of reform. Boldly they dared anyone to try to change

China; those who accepted their challenge were quickly condemned as "sinners against the Confucian heritage." [5] Kuo Sung-t'ao, for one, was ruined by their defamatory campaign against him. They ridiculed him for having left his fatherland to serve the foreign devils, and his diary was derided by the great Hunanese scholar Wang K'ai-yün as a product of "foreign poison." [6] Wang also offered a piece of advice to the Marquis Tseng in 1877 on foreign affairs: "To advocate war is good for you both from the private and public standpoints." [7]

The literati had extensive roots in both the metropolis and the countryside. Local gentry usually echoed their views, and opportunists and social climbers, craving fame at all costs, were anxious to be associated with them. They also found a ready following in disgruntled men who had themselves failed to find positions in foreign affairs and, out of jealousy, attacked those who had succeeded. [8] The censors, courtiers, literati, gentry, opportunists, and petty men together created a powerful anti-foreign atmosphere, which was most unfavorable to the growth of progressive ideas and novel undertakings. Their anti-foreignism, in the view of Communist writers today, did not stem from a realization of the dangers of foreign imperialism, but from a feeling of insecurity about their privileged position in a society under the disrupting influence of foreign forces. [9]

These anti-foreign elements successfully created the impression that foreign affairs was a dangerous subject and to associate with it was to betray one's decency. When Grand Secretary Yen Ching-ming was asked, "Who among men of rectitude today excel in foreign affairs?", he snapped back: "Do men of rectitude care to engage in foreign affairs?" [10] To serve as an envoy was described by the obscurantists as particularly degrading because it implied begging peace from barbarian rulers. No man would volunteer to exile himself to a far, outlandish nation. Li Hung-chang continually declined Yamen's requests for recommendations of competent men to serve as envoys, mainly because he was afraid of offending the men he thus recommended. He wrote: "Men all seek after governmental positions, but not envoyships. I am afraid that those who are willing to be envoys are not too reliable." [11] Liu Hsi-hung told Li: "The envoy of today is the hostage of the past." [12] Even a liberal like Kuo Sung-t'ao could not help conceding: "Being an envoy abroad is looked down upon by men today. It is what people do not care to be." [13]

A general impression prevailed over the nation that to be an envoy was even worse than to be banished, for it meant a term of exile in a foreign land plus a dark future after returning to China. People recalled that one of Burlingame's associates, Chih-kang, spent his life on the frontier of Mongolia, and the other, Sun Chia-ku, in an obscure part of West China.[14] Such was the misfortune of the early envoys that no man could think of foreign missions without a shudder; all wanted to avoid this fate. Even Kuo Sung-t'ao did not accept his foreign assignment willingly.

The principal targets of the censors and literati were the advocates of Westernization, better known as the *yang-wu* group. This group adopted "foreign matters" not out of love or admiration but out of a cold realization that it was the only way to survive. They understood, if the majority of the literati, censors, and Hanlin scholars did not, that the traditional view of foreign affairs must be rectified in the light of current circumstances and necessities. Alone in the sprawling hierarchy of the state, they saw in international living a way to survival in the new world that had been so rudely thrust upon China recently. In this they were at once very un-Confucian and very Confucian: un-Confucian in their willingness to adapt themselves to foreign ways, Confucian in their practical approach to the facts of life. Progressives by the standards of their time, they have been scorned in recent decades by many as forerunners of the compradores. Communist writers take the stand that these *yang-wu* men did not really want to create a progressive force in China but wanted merely to maintain the old, decadent social order with foreign help.[15]

The die-hard obscurantists spared no one. A man of Tseng Kuofan's stature enjoyed no exemption. His impartial report on the Tientsin Massacre in 1870 was vehemently attacked by the old guard and young politicians, some of whom made high-flown attacks in order to hurl themselves into national prominence overnight. The thought of their selfishness and misguidance of state affairs drove Tseng into "bitter cries and gushing tears." Unable to withstand the powerful force of "public opinion," he bowed out of the Tientsin scene.

Li Hung-chang succeeded Tseng as viceroy of Chihli. As the

central spirit of the modernization program, he was branded by the obscurantists as a traitor to traditionalism. Li in return ridiculed them as blind "bookworms," who wanted to cure all diseases with the same ancient prescription. He proudly announced: "Now is the right time to discuss 'foreign matters.' People fear and are loath to talk about them. When incidents occur, they become either lost or rash, and it is seldom that they do not misguide the nation. It may be all right for you people not to take an interest in [foreign matters], but if I too do not talk about them, by what method is the ship of state to be steered?" [16]

The one that suffered most at the hands of the censors and literati was also the one that criticized them the most. Kuo Sung-t'ao declared publicly that his study of history had revealed the amazing fact that censors were more harmful than beneficial to the state.[17] The institution of censors was not bad in itself, he stated, but when the censors became a privileged class after the Southern Sung and meddled in politics in attempts to influence national policies, they became a nuisance. "The trouble is not censors *per se*," he wrote, "but rather their unbridled interference in things outside their jurisdiction." [18] In the Southern Sung, when barbarian incursions were frequent, the generals and soldiers urged war against foreign tribes to efface the national humiliation, but during the Ming period, when the generals had become timid and dared not fight, the censors forced them into war. Thereafter the censors took on the new role of voicing "public opinion" and attempted to impose their will on policy makers. They had become so powerful that opportunists flocked to them as a sure way to win imperial attention and subsequent appointment. The court was thus led into the belief that it had the support of the public, when in fact the "support" consisted merely of empty arguments and verbal assurances. Kuo insisted that good government was impossible with these men in power.[19]

Caught between the horns of die-hard obscurantists and progressive modernizers was the court, which, in the last analysis, was the Empress Dowager Tz'u-hsi herself. Her miserable flight to Jehol in 1860 in the face of the advancing enemy under Lord Elgin was too painful an experience to forget. No less violently anti-foreign at heart than the censors and the literati, the Dowager nevertheless was bold enough to side with the progressive *yang-wu* group in many respects, as the price for building up defenses with which to erase the humiliation of 1860. In aim, she was at one with the conservatives. In method, she was with the modernizers.

The Dowager's political acumen was highest when she played the intricate game of the balance of weakness in domestic politics. She was so deeply apprehensive of things Western that she secretly feared the *yang-wu* advocates, especially when they were Chinese and not Manchu. Her attitude toward the powerful Li Hung-chang is a good case in point. She respected Li's unusual abilities as she feared his vast powers. Yet she was too clever to dismiss a man who had behind him a Huai army, a Pei-yang navy, and a coterie of enterprising compradores and able foreign advisers.[20] He must be humored by high positions but kept in check by some force. A balancing force was found in the violent accusations of the censors and the literati. The meaninglessness of the censors' hue and cry was only too obvious, yet she secretly fostered it, under the appealing pretexts of "opening the way for opinions" and "getting the benefits of collective thinking," thus creating a powerful force to checkmate the progressive *yang-wu* group. She dignified the nonsense of the old guard as "pure discussion" and "public opinion." In 1874 Li urged the construction of a railway, running from north to south, to facilitate transportation. Prince Kung approved the plan but hesitated to sponsor it. "I repeatedly requested him to speak to the two Dowagers at an opportune moment," Li wrote, "he said that even the two Dowagers could not decide upon such an important policy. Henceforth, I shut my mouth and spoke no more." [21] Undoubtedly the Dowager Tz'u-hsi pretended that she had to listen to the "public opinion" of the literati; it was her ingenious device to restrict Li's aggrandizement. Years later, when visiting Bismarck in Germany, Li asked him for the secrets of statesmanship, to which Bismarck replied that the first essential was to win control over the sovereign, but if the sovereign was a woman, it would be a different matter.[22] Li accepted the implication of the statement in deep silence.

By playing both sides the Dowager cleverly established a delicate balance, taking constant precaution that it not be tipped. She allowed Wo-jen and his associates to remain in high posts, despite their vicious attack on Western learning, while at the same time she allowed Prince Kung to launch the self-strengthening movement and expand the T'ung-wen kuan. When a magistrate of an independent department, Yang T'ing-hsi, suggested the abolition of the T'ung-wen kuan as a way to avert natural calamity, she reprimanded him for "murmuring a few thousand words" of nonsense.[23] On the other hand she acceded to the popular demand for the destruction of Kuo Sung-t'ao's diary.

The subject of diplomatic missions abroad was personally unpleasant to the Dowager, who understood the functions of envoys only from the past history of China. When China was strong, her envoys spread the prestige of the Son of Heaven to distant lands; when China was weak, they begged peace from foreign tribes. During the 1860's and 1870's China was undoubtedly weak. To send envoys would be humiliating, and to be forced to send them was even worse. Time and again she procrastinated, hoping to put off the evil day by delaying its coming. High officials joined her in the feeling that envoys should not be sent until China was relatively strong. Li Hung-chang felt it unwise to send envoys without an accompanying naval force, impressed as he was with the close coordination between the Western diplomats and their gunboats.[24] Pride and vanity thus were also deterrents.

In conclusion, one cannot escape the impression that under the secret patronage of the court an anti-foreign, anti-modernizing atmosphere prevailed over the nation. The feeble efforts of the *yang-wu* men met opposition everywhere, and the idea of permanent legations abroad lacked a fertile soil in which to grow. The Dowager feared for the future, and the future confirmed her fear. Ironically, the first permanent Chinese legation abroad had its origin in a mission of apology.

b. *Tradition within Change: China among the Nations*

China had no sooner firmly established her legations in the Western world than she was invited to participate in the sixth meeting of the Association for the Reform and Codification of the Law of Nations in 1878. This association, founded in Brussels in 1873, had exhibited a strong interest in extending international law to the Far East during its fourth and fifth meetings in 1876 and 1877, and a motion had been passed to invite China and Japan to participate in its future meetings. Kuo Sung-t'ao, China's first minister to England, accepted the invitation on China's behalf, and Ueno Kagenori, Japanese minister in London, accepted for his government. The presence of the two Far Eastern representatives lent much interest and color to the meeting of 1878, and the honorary international secretary of the association enthusiastically characterized their attendance as "a novel feature in the history of the Association and, indeed, in the history of European Congresses." [25] Kuo, on his part, paid high tribute to the association for its efforts to improve the law of nations "for the benefit of all governments and peoples." Politely he explained that although his country had not completely subscribed to the rules of international law because of her different cultural and political background, he was "very desirous of attaining a knowledge of the science, in the hope that it will be beneficial to my country." [26] In appreciation of China's new membership, the association elected Kuo honorary vice-president, and his name, for some mysterious reason, remained in every issue of the association's *Report* until 1922, some forty-five years after his retirement from his London post and some thirty-five years after his death!

Kuo's successor in London, the famous Marquis Tseng Chi-tse, was also elected to the same honorary post in the association. Versatile and familiar with Western diplomacy, while retaining the fundamental Confucian touch, Tseng attempted to blend the requirements of international law with the established Chinese practices of foreign intercourse. In a conversation with an English international jurist in 1879 he made it clear that in a country like China, where traditions and old standards abounded, time was needed to assimilate new ideas and values. Nonetheless, despite disagreements and divergent views on international law among Western writers themselves, which confounded its ready understanding by China, she had striven to make frequent references to it in her dealing with foreign powers. China was willing to take into consideration the Western methods of international relations without totally and unconditionally surrendering her own traditional practices, some of which, like the treatment of tributary states, Tseng pointed out, were far more benevolent than Western colonial practices.[27]

By 1880 China's international position had reached a point where she maintained legations in most of the leading Western states and Japan, kept membership in the leading international law association, and indicated her willingness to learn more about the new science of international law and make reference to it in conducting her foreign relations. So inextricably was she drawn into the stream of world affairs that it was a foregone conclusion that the age of her universal empire was far spent and the day of nation-statehood was at hand. Through increased contact with the outside world the statesmen of the T'ung-chih and Kuang-hsü periods discovered the stark fact that in a world of contending states, where social Darwinism was a dominant force, the only way to survive was to struggle for survival like anyone else. A universal state had no place in a family of nation-states. The myth of universal overlordship became untenable, especially when foreign diplomats in Peking did not *kowtow* to the T'ung-chih Emperor during the audience of 1873, and when China had to send missions of apology to France and Britain in 1870 and 1876 to ward off foreign punitive expeditions. The Son of Heaven had to descend from the apex of the Confucian world order to bow to foreign countries not one-tenth the size of China. Was there any doubt that the universal state was a sweet dream of yesteryear, a glory of the past, and a luxury that China could no longer afford? Adjustment had to be made to metamorphose the Confucian universal empire into a modern nation-state in order to survive in the new world.

To be sure, the metamorphosis was long, hard, and painful. Every step in the process was a struggle, and in the final analysis, an intellectual one. Strangely enough, the diplomatic phase of the battle was among the first to be won. As early as 1864, in a preface to W. A. P. Martin's translation of Wheaton, Chang Ssu-kuei, a member of the Tsungli Yamen and later associate envoy to Japan, risked the accusation of "heresy" by comparing the leading Western states — England, France, Russia, the United States, Austria, Prussia, and Italy — to the seven contending nations of the Warring States Period in ancient China. The comparison amounted to a brave admission of the existence of strong and independent states beyond China; it was in fact an indirect disavowal of the Chinese claim to universal overlordship.

There was an increasing sense of urgency among the more enlightened elements in Confucian officialdom with respect to China's greatly changed position vis-à-vis the rest of the world. Li Hung-chang cogently told his countrymen that China's precarious status was such as she had never known in the past three thousand years. His powerful advocacy of diplomatic representation abroad had a decisive effect on the court, and once the missions were sent, increased understanding of the outside world followed. From Kuo Sung-t'ao came the daring revelation that the West had a civilization of two thousand years, and from the Marquis Tseng came the open admission that the modern Western nations were truly different from the historical barbarian tribes that had disturbed China from time to time. There was no mistake that the fictitious belief of China's unrivalled excellence and universal overlordship was disintegrating into the oblivion of history.

By 1880 China had realistically, if also painfully, assumed her place in the world community of nations. Forty years had elapsed since the Opium War and the opening of China, and some twenty years had passed since the appearance of the foreign diplomatic corps in Peking. Yet the diplomatic phase of China's response to the Western challenge, slow as it was, was much faster than many of the other phases. It came about in the wake of military modernization and was among the first measures adopted in the self-strengthening movement, probably because of its immediately discernible beneficial effects on China. A modernized foreign service enabled China not only to get along better with foreign diplomats, but also to bypass them when they proved headstrong and unyielding. With her own legations abroad, China could present her views directly to the foreign governments, which, far away from the China scene and hence less likely to be excited over local occurrences, could receive Chinese representations with broader perspective and greater objectivity. They were therefore more prone to peaceful settlement of disputes than their overseas servants.

The awareness of these tangible advantages to be gained from entering the Western world, added to the fact that such an awareness could be translated into reality by a few powerful officials from above without the support of the masses, largely accounted for the early completion of the diplomatic metamorphosis. Nationalism was not involved in the process. But after China's entrance into the family of nations, her new position gave rise to a new sense of national entity; hence it helped to stimulate the growth of nationalism in the long run.

When China accepted the fact that it was more profitable to act like a nation-state than a universal empire, she in fact subscribed to what had been the Western view since before the Opium War. The Western nations had always approached China as an incipient nation-state, and treaties with her were all drawn up on a bilateral nation-to-nation basis.[28] To the Westerner it was only a matter of time until China would accept this fact and emerge as a modern sovereign state in the family of nations. This wish was realized around 1880. The world community was enriched by the addition of the hitherto unaccounted one-fifth humanity, and China stood to gain new experiences and an enlarged world view from international living. Chinese history began to merge with world history.

But it was only through necessity, not free choice, that China had entered the world community. The old dream of universal empire, the glory of being the Middle Kingdom in East Asia, and the prestige of the tributary system still lingered in the Chinese mind, and their residual effects were clearly discernible. The nostalgia for the past generated a burning hope and even a strong conviction that some day China would again become strong and reassert her rightful place under the sun. If universal Confucianism could not attain such an objective, perhaps some other system could. A century of trial and error, and decades of groping in the dark led to the discovery that international communism, which envisages an ultimate universal classless society, might be the new vehicle for the fulfillment of the old dream. With the rise of Communist China as the most powerful nation in East Asia, with its growing influence in northern Korea, northern Vietnam and other peripheral states, and with the constant flow of peace delegations to Peking from East European and Asian states, one wonders whether the "universal" state and the tributary system of the past have not been revived in a modern form.

APPENDIXES

APPENDIX A. *Major Foreign Diplomatic Representatives in China during the Nineteenth Century* (with their Chinese names)

This chart is made from a variety of sources, including the *Ch'ing-shih-kao* (Draft history of Ch'ing), "Table on Foreign Intercourse"; H. B. Morse, *International Relations of the Chinese Empire*, vol. III, Appendix H, pp. 486–492; Tyler Dennett, *Americans in Eastern Asia*, Appendix. Minor inaccuracies are to be expected because of (1) discrepancy between the dates of appointment and actual arrival for duty, and (2) sick or business leave, or furlough, of the ministers while still officially holding office. If more than one minister was appointed to the same post within a year, the one that served longest appears in this chart.

Year	England	France	United States	Russia	Germany	Japan
1861–2	Frederick Bruce 卜魯斯	Bourboulon 布爾布隆	Anson Burlingame 蒲安仁	L. de Balluzeck 把留提克	......	......
1863	"	Berthemy 柏爾德密	"	A. Vlangaly 倭良嘎哩	......	......
1864	"	"	"	"	von Rehfues 李福斯	......
1865–6	Rutherford Alcock 阿禮國	"	"	"	"	......
1867	"	de Lallemand 喇明	"	"	"	......
1868	"	"	J. Ross Browne 勞文羅斯	"	"	......
1869	"	de Rochechouart 羅淑亞	"	"	"	......
1870–71	Thomas F. Wade 威妥瑪	"	Frederick F. Low 鏤斐迪	"	"	......

1872-3	" ,	de Geofroy 熱福理	"	"	"	......
1874	"	"	Benjamin P. Avery 米畯	Eugène de Butzow 布策	"	Yamagiwara Sakimitsu 柳原前光
1875	"	de Rochechouart	"	"	von Brandt 巴蘭德	Mori Arinori 森有禮
1876-8	"	Brenier de Montmorand 卜羅呪	George F. Seward 西華	"	"	"
1879	"	"	"	"	"	Shishido Tamaki 宍戸璣
1880-1	"	Bourée 寶海	James B. Angell 安吉立	"	"	"
1882	"	"	John R. Young 楊約翰	"	"	Enomoto Takeaki 榎本武揚
1883	Harry S. Parkes 巴夏禮	Tricou 德理國	"	S. Popoff 博博	"	"
1884-5	"	Patenôtre 巴特納	"	"	"	"

Foreign Diplomatic Representatives in China (continued)

Year	England	France	United States	Russia	Germany	Japan
1886	John Walsham 李喃身	G. Cogordan & Constans 戈可當	Charles Denby 田貝	"	"	Shioda Saburo 鹽田三郎
1887–8	"	Constans & Lemaire 恭思當	"	Alexis Coumany 庫滿	"	"
1889–90	"	Lemaire 李梅	"	"	"	Otori Keisuke 大鳥圭介
1891	"	"	"	A. P. Cassini 喀希尼	"	"
1892	Nicholas R. O'Conor 歐格訥	"	"	"	"	"
1893	"	"	"	"	Freiherr Schenk zu Schweinsberg 紳珂阿	"

Year	Japan	Germany	Russia	U.S.	France	Britain
1894	Komura Jutaro 小村壽太郎	"	"	"	Gérard 施阿蘭	"
1895	Hayashi Tadasu 林董	"	"	"	"	Claude M. MacDonald 竇訥樂
1896	"	von Heyking 海靖	"	"	"	"
1897	Yano Fumio 矢野文雄	"	"	"	"	"
1898	"	"	M. N. de Giers 格爾思	Edwin H. Conger 康格	Pichon 畢盛	"
1899	Nishio Tokujiro 西德二郎	von Ketteler 克林德	"	"	"	"
1900	"	(killed May)	"	"	"	Ernest M. Satow 薩道義

APPENDIX B. Chinese Diplomatic Representatives in Major Foreign Countries during the Nineteenth Century

This chart is made, with slight modifications, from Ch'en Wen-chin, "Ch'ing-chi ch'u-shih ko-kuo shih-ling ching-fei, 1875–1911" (The expenditures of the Chinese legations in foreign countries at the end of the "Tsing Dynasty") in *Chung-kuo chin-tai ching-chi-shih yen-chiu chi-k'an* (*Studies in modern economic history of China*), vol. I, no. 2 (May 1933), p. 275.

Year	England	U.S., Spain, Peru	Japan	Germany	France	Russia	Italy
1875	Kuo Sung-t'ao 郭嵩燾	Ch'en Lan-pin 陳蘭彬	......	......	......	......	......
1876	"	"	Hsü Ch'ien-shen 許鈐身	......	......	......	......
1877	"	"	Ho Ju-chang 何汝璋	Liu Hsi-hung 劉錫鴻	......	......	......
1878	"	"	"	Li Feng-pao 李鳳苞	Tseng Chi-tse 曾紀澤	Ch'ung-hou 崇厚	......
1879	Tseng Chi-tse	"	"	"	"	Shao Yu-lien 邵友濂	......
1880	"	Cheng Tsao-ju 鄭藻如	Hsü Ching-ch'eng 許景澄	"	"	Tseng Chi-tse	......
1881–3	"	"	Li Shu-ch'ang 黎庶昌	"	"	"	Li Feng-pao
1884	"	"	Hsü Ch'eng-tsu 徐承祖	"	"	"	"
1885–6	"	Chang Yin-huan 張蔭桓		Hsü Ching-ch'eng	Hsü Ching-ch'eng	"	Hsü Ching-ch'eng

Year							
1887	"	"	Li Shu-ch'ang	"	"	"	"
1888	Liu Hsi-hung	"	"	"	Liu Hsi-hung	"	Liu Hsi-hung
1889	"	Hung Chün	"	Hung Chün	Ts'ui Kuo-en 崔國恩	"	Hsüeh Fu-ch'eng 薛福成
1890–2	Hsüeh Fu-ch'eng	Hsü Ching-ch'eng	Li Ching-fang 李經方	Hsü Ching-ch'eng	"	Li Ching-fang 李經方	"
1893	"	Wang Feng-tsao 汪鳳藻	Hung Chün	Hsü Ching-ch'eng	"	"	"
1894–5	Kung Chao-yüan	Kung Chao-yüan	Yang Ju 楊儒	"	"	Yang Ju 楊儒	Kung Chao-yüan 龔照瑗
1896	"	"	Yü Keng 裕庚	"	"	"	"
1897	Lo Feng-lu	Yang Ju	Ch'ing-ch'ang 慶長	Lü Hai-huan 呂海寰	Lo Feng-lu	Wu T'ing-fang 伍廷芳	Lo Feng-lu 羅豐祿
1898–9	"	"	Li Sheng-to 李盛鐸	"	"	Li Sheng-to 李盛鐸	"
1900	"	Yü Keng	"	Yü Keng	"	"	"

APPENDIX C. Funds Supplied to Chinese Legations in Major Foreign Countries (in taels)

Year	U.S., Peru, Spain	England	France	Japan	Germany	Russia	Korea	Italy	Belgium, Holland	Austria	Total
1878	*	61,886	20,030	82,460	54,984	—					*
1879	200,000	51,992	36,617	80,000	48,348	120,000					536,947
1880	*	43,763	36,466	50,000	93,445	31,156					*
1881		50,466	30,000	*	*	111,915					*
1882	*	80,528	80,000	60,000	36,264	59,167					*
1883	*	41,216	47,256	60,000	40,835	52,474					*
1884	100,000	92,436	49,744	60,877	*	47,256					374,209
1885	100,000	55,529	40,000	78,725	54,929	45,026					*
1886	314,798	22,130	*	40,313	47,050	67,187					*
1887	185,471	98,480	40,000	80,173	40,000	*					548,946
1888	174,528	60,441	40,000	66,227	162,270	45,480					*
1889	192,000	64,774	16,640		20,000	40,000					484,550
1890	170,000	130,550	60,000	60,000	20,000	44,000					*
1891	100,000	59,591	40,840	*	66,000	80,000					388,390
1892	140,000	83,390	25,000	60,000	40,000	40,000					*
1893	260,000	68,274	*	60,000	50,000	40,000					*
1894	300,000	141,409		80,000	40,000	40,000					*
1895	300,000	58,293	50,000	80,000	*	60,000					*
1896	100,000	199,184	54,813	—	40,000	42,452					*
1897	293,000	149,525	51,170	—	55,000	82,193					715,888
1898	200,000	128,231	73,011	85,000	160,000	*	40,000				*
1899	260,000	98,306	125,000	50,000	80,000	120,000	40,000		20,000		803,306
1900	290,000	*		60,000	70,000	140,000	80,000		11,805		*
1901	180,000		80,000	110,000	100,430	*	60,000				*
1902	*	41,606	90,000		*		50,000	20,000	*		*
1903	180,000	85,788	80,000	65,000	40,000	80,000	61,000	40,000	40,000	40,000	726,788
1904	213,309	99,720	90,720	80,000	60,000	109,332	45,429	40,250	30,000	41,908	800,668
1905	195,475	91,000	80,000	70,000	61,444	113,924	63,500	40,000	40,068	46,710	812,127
1906	227,770	94,600	104,840	80,000		114,221		48,039	91,345	23,702	*
1907	212,400	21,650	*	86,000	60,050			40,360	93,998	43,300	*
1908	206,680	75,040	91,050	61,126	67,040	91,739		48,480	86,480	50,480	822,381
1909	206,680	75,040	102,600	105,392	67,040	101,568		48,480	104,790	50,480	869,670
1910	206,680	75,040	102,600	112,992	67,040	*		48,480	106,388	50,480	*
1911	206,680	75,040	102,600	105,392	67,040			48,480	106,388	50,480	*

APPENDIX D. Expenditures of Chinese Legations in Major Foreign Countries (in taels)

Year	U.S., Peru, Spain	England	France	Japan	Germany	Russia	Korea	Italy	Belgium, Holland	Austria	Total
1878	*	47,091	15,243	76,458	46,949	—	—	—	—	—	*
1879	161,491	80,589	42,775	68,378	27,957	86,152	—	—	—	—	467,342
1880	*	53,049	37,766	57,443	42,482	38,702	—	—	—	—	*
1881	*	57,034	34,383	*	*	92,060	—	—	—	—	*
1882	*	64,209	43,768	51,772	45,261	61,100	—	—	—	—	*
1883	*	68,545	79,850	53,733	40,352	86,101	—	—	—	—	*
1884	165,136	72,794	44,896	58,459	*	61,182	—	—	—	—	*
1885	151,553	61,275	*	59,674	59,232	51,843	—	—	—	—	*
1886	270,685	131,596	*	62,212	57,316	56,180	—	—	—	—	*
1887	204,759	68,335	59,716	71,399	42,216	*	—	—	—	—	562,400
1888	206,817	92,337	52,510	70,157	102,132	38,447	—	—	—	—	*
1889	*	70,426	43,704	*	45,512	42,733	—	—	—	—	487,244
1890	147,153	108,746	44,745	79,886	41,098	65,616	—	—	—	—	*
1891	138,882	70,479	43,640	*	81,586	73,131	—	—	—	—	420,492
1892	142,948	77,991	48,771	60,091	45,809	44,882	—	—	—	—	*
1893	295,916	72,851	*	82,300	49,560	47,840	—	—	—	—	*
1894	273,903	165,120	*	117,854	37,711	46,050	—	—	—	—	*
1895	302,163	111,192	54,656	—	37,008	70,300	—	—	—	—	*
1896	242,247	144,153	61,326	—	42,155	43,642	—	—	—	—	*
1897	265,581	178,958	66,500	87,961	71,292	81,595	—	—	—	—	751,887
1898	258,784	112,057	71,079	119,143	140,664	27,645	25,990	—	—	—	*
1899	255,183	103,903	135,076	75,747	79,964	88,525	51,597	—	—	—	*
1900	263,144	*	*	71,851	78,888	125,464	64,117	—	19,681	—	*
1901	207,311	*	80,701	103,150	100,886	50,150	62,930	—	*	—	*
1902	*	87,568	81,850	77,479	76,953	19,893	56,913	—	—	—	*
1903	216,572	98,489	93,995	84,466	66,692	108,010	58,649	46,799	39,171	43,980	856,823
1904	207,060	99,728	96,743	78,686	58,332	106,458	61,878	41,079	40,846	45,035	835,845
1905	199,549	89,936	90,113	81,373	*	116,595	71,125	40,663	37,876	49,790	*
1906	235,756	90,941	96,153	85,452	*	101,735	—	42,146	94,924	*	*
1907	210,182	*	*	*	*	81,910	—	42,457	67,664	42,376	*
1908	*	*	93,682	*	*	25,665	—	*	47,829	*	*
1909	*	*	*	*	*	37,612	—	*	31,281	*	*

* Taken from Ch'en Wen-chin, 297–298.

NOTES

INDEX

ABBREVIATIONS USED IN THE NOTES

BPP: British Parliamentary Papers.

CSL: Ta-Ch'ing li-ch'ao shih-lu (Veritable records of successive reigns of the Ch'ing dynasty).

CSK: Ch'ing-shih kao (Draft history of the Ch'ing).

CSPSR: The Chinese Social and Political Science Review.

HJAS: Harvard Journal of Asiatic Studies.

IWSM: Ch'ou-pan i-wu shih-mo (The complete account of the management of barbarian affairs).

Sen. Exec. Doc.: The Executive Documents, the Senate of the United States.

THL: Tung-hua lu (Tung-hua records).

THHL: Tung-hua hsü-lu (Tung-hua records continued).

USFR: Foreign Relations of the United States.

WCSL: Ch'ing-chi wai-chiao shih-liao (Historical materials concerning foreign relations in the late Ch'ing period; 1875–1911).

Unless otherwise indicated, all translations from the Chinese are mine.

CHAPTER 1. PROLOGUE: THE MEETING OF THE WESTERN
AND EASTERN FAMILIES OF NATIONS.

1. George McCune, "The Exchange of Envoys between Korea and Japan during the Tokugawa Period," *The Far Eastern Quarterly*, 5:308 (May 1946). Both terms may be found in *Mencius*.

2. J. K. Fairbank and S. Y. Teng, "On the Ch'ing Tributary System," *HJAS*, 6.2:175–176 (June 1941).

3. Lo Meng-ts'e, *Chung-kuo lun* (On China; Chungking, 1943), pp. 84–85. See also Ch'en Fang-chih, *Ch'ing-tai pien-chih shu-lüeh* (A brief account of the border institutions in the Ch'ing period), *Yen-ching hsüeh-pao* ("Yenching Journal of Chinese Studies"), 34:134 (June 1947).

4. Ueda Tōshio, *Tōyō gaikōshi gaisetsu* (A survey of Far Eastern diplomatic history; Tokyo, 1948), pp. 217–218.

5. John King Fairbank, *Trade and Diplomacy on the China Coast: The Opening of the Treaty Ports, 1842–1854* (Cambridge, Mass., 1953), I, 14.

6. *Book of Odes*, "Hsiao-ya: Pei-shan" chapter II. James Legge's translation of these passages is somewhat different and probably less literal than mine. Cf. J. Legge, *The Chinese Classics*, IV, Part II, p. 360.

7. Lo Meng-ts'e, p. 52.

8. Pan Ku, The *History of Han*, "Chapter on the Hsiung-nu," quoted in Shigematsu Toshiaki, "Kanjin no gaikō shisō ni tsuite" (On the Chinese idea of diplomacy), *Rekishi chiri* (History and geography), 29.2:162 (February 1917).

9. *Ibid.*, p. 165.

10. Translation taken from Legge, *Chinese Classics*, III, *The Shoo King*, p. 42.

11. *Ibid.*, p. 55.

12. Legge, *Chinese Classics*, IV, 346.

13. Hsiao Kung-ch'üan, *Chung-kuo cheng-chih ssu-hsiang shih* (A history of Chinese political thought; Shanghai, 1947), I, 56.

14. Translation taken from Legge, *Chinese Classics*, I, *The Confucian Analects*, p. 156.

15. Legge, *Chinese Classics*, IV, Part II, "The She King," p. 626.

16. Quoted in Shigematsu, p. 159.

17. *Ibid.*, p. 161. Exceptions of course can readily be found to this ideal of nonintervention and nonexploitation: such as Chinese "colonization" in Mongolia and pressing the Miao tribes into uplands.

18. In practice, there was much barbarian mixture with the Chinese.

19. Shigematsu, p. 163.

20. *Ibid.*, p. 167.

21. Wang T'ung-ling, *Han-T'ang chih ho-ch'in cheng-ts'e* (The policy of diplomacy by marriage during the Han and T'ang periods), *Shih-hsüeh nien-pao* ("Historical Annual"), No. 1 (July 1929), pp. 9–10.

22. Nieh Ch'ung-ch'i, *Sung-Liao chiao-p'ing k'ao* ("Embassies between Liao and Sung"), *Yen-ching hsüeh-pao* ("Yenching Journal of Chinese Studies"), No. 27 (June 1940), pp. 3–5, 24, 37–38.

23. Yano Jinichi, *Kindai Shina ron* (On modern China; Tokyo, 1927), pp. 24–25.

24. *Ibid., passim*, pp. 3, 4, 24–26, 114.

25. John King Fairbank, "Synarchy under the Treaties," in Fairbank, ed., *Chinese Thought and Institutions* (Chicago, 1957), p. 208.

26. Information in the above two paragraphs is drawn from Ch'en T'i-ch'iang, *Chung-kuo wai-chiao hsing-cheng* (China's administration of foreign affairs; Chungking, 1943), pp. 16–17.

27. Ch'en Fu-kuang, *Yu-Ch'ing i-tai chih Chung-O kuan-hsi* (Sino-Russian relations during the Ch'ing period exclusively; Yunnan, 1947), pp. 43–44.

28. Information on China's administration of foreign affairs before and after the Opium War is drawn from two succinct articles by Chang Chung-fu: "Ya-p'ien-chan ch'ien Ch'ing-t'ing pan-li wai-chiao chih chi-kuan yü shou-hsü" ("The office and procedure for dealing with diplomatic affairs of the Ch'ing dynasty before the Opium War"), *Wai-chiao yüeh-pao* ("Foreign Affairs"), 2.2:1–7 (1933); and "Tzu Ya-p'ien chan-cheng chih Ying-Fa lien-chün ch'i-chung Ch'ing-t'ing pan-li wai-chiao chih chi-kuan yü shou-hsü" ("The office and procedure for dealing with diplomatic affairs of the Ch'ing dynasty during the period between the First and Second Anglo-Chinese Wars"), *Wai-chiao yüeh-pao*, 2.5:43–51 (1933).

29. Horatio N. Lay, *Note on the Opium Question and Brief Survey of Our Relations with China* (London, 1893), p. 3.

30. *North China Herald*, No. 501 (March 3, 1860) p. 35, col. 3–4. An essay on Hsien-feng.

CHAPTER 2. THE RESIDENT MINISTER ISSUE: THE
DIPLOMATIC PRELUDE

1. D. Bonner-Smith and E. W. R. Lumby, eds., *The Second China War, 1856–1860*, Publications for the Navy Records Society, XCV (1954), Introduction, xxi.

2. *Hansard's Parliamentary Debates*, 144:1155–63, 1215, 1397 (1857).

3. *Ibid.*, p. 1401.

4. *Ibid.*, p. 1417.

5. *Ibid.*, p. 1802.

6. Bonner-Smith and Lumby, p. 157.

7. J. L. Morison, *The Eighth Earl of Elgin* (1928), p. 194.

8. China: *Dispatches*, Vol. 16, Doc. 13, Reed to Cass, April 10, 1858 (National Archives, Washington, D.C.).

9. Bonner-Smith and Lumby, p. 159.

10. *Ibid.*, p. 240.

11. *Record of Occurrences in China* (Royal Asiatic Society, North China Branch), Old series, 1:143 (June 1858) — hereafter cited as *Occurrences*. On the Canton episode, see Huang Yen-yü, "Viceroy Yeh Ming-ch'en and the Canton Episode (1856–1861)," *HJAS*, 6.1:37–127 (March 1941). This study is based on a translation of Hsüeh Fu-ch'eng, "Shu Han-yang Yeh-hsiang Kuang-chou chih pien" (On Viceroy Yeh of Han-yang and the Canton Incident), in Tso Shun-sheng, *Chung-kuo chin-pai-nien shih tzu-liao* (Materials relating to Chinese history of the last hundred years; Shanghai, 1928), I, pp. 51–63.

12. *Occurrences*, p. 143.

13. Stanley Lane-Poole and Frederick V. Dickins, *The Life of Sir Harry Parkes* (London, 1894), I, 339; Alexander Michie, *The Englishman in China during the Victorian Era* (London, 1900), I, 323.

14. *IWSM*, Hsien-feng period, 18:19–22.

15. *BPP*, 33 (2571), *Correspondence Relative to the Earl of Elgin's Special Mission to China and Japan, 1857–1859*, pp. 228–229; also *IWSM*, 18:17–18, 26b–33b.

16. *BPP*, 33:242; *IWSM*, 18:34b.

17. *IWSM*, 18:34b.

18. *BPP*, 33:257.

19. *Ibid.*, p. 266.

20. *Ibid.*, p. 2.

21. *Ibid.*

22. *Ibid.*, pp. 2–3.

23. *Ibid.*, p. 3.

24. *Ibid.*, p. 4.

25. Bonner-Smith and Lumby, Doc. 126, pp. 176–177.

26. *Ibid.*, Doc. 127, p. 180.

27. W. C. Costin, *Great Britain and China, 1833–1860* (Oxford, 1937), p. 345.

28. Henri Cordier, *L'expédition de Chine de 1857–58, Histoire diplomatique, notes et documents* (Paris, 1905), p. 97.

29. *Ibid.*, p. 98.

30. *Ibid.*, p. 148.

31. John F. Cady, *The Roots of French Imperialism in Eastern Asia* (1954), p. 183.

32. *Sen. Exec. Doc.*, 36th Cong., 1st Session (1859–60), 10.30:4.

33. *Sen. Exec. Doc.*, 35th Cong., 1st Session (1857–58), 12.47:7.

34. *Ibid.*, pp. 7–9. In point of fact, the President does have the right to order the navy into action but did not choose to do so in this case.

35. *Sen. Exec. Doc.*, 36th Cong., 10.30:6.

36. *Ibid.*, p. 8.

37. *Ibid.*, p. 220.

38. China: *Instructions*, I, 171 (National Archives, Washington, D.C.).

39. *Sen. Exec. Doc.*, 35th Cong., 12.47:2–4.

40. Baron A. Buksgevden (Buxhöwden), *Russkiĭ Kitaĭ: Ocherki diplomaticheskikh snosheniĭ Rossiĭ s Kitaem — Pekinskiĭ dogovor 1860 g.* (Russia's China: An account of the diplomatic relations between Russia and China — the Treaty of Peking, 1860; Port Arthur, 1902), p. 1.

41. Petr Shumakher, "K istorie priobrateniya Amura, snosheniya s Kitaem s 1848 po 1860 god" (Toward a history of appropriating the Amur — relations with China from 1848 to 1860), *Russkiĭ Arkhiv* (Russian Archives), No. 3 (1878), p. 287.

42. A. Popov, "Tsarskaya diplomatiya v epokhu Taĭpinskogo vosstaniya" (Tsarist diplomacy during the Taiping Rebellion), *Krasnyi Arkhiv* (Red Archives), 21:190 (1927). My translation here is taken from Leonid S. Rubinchek, *A Digest of the Krasnyi Arkhiv*, Part I (Cleveland, 1947), p. 246.

43. *Krasnyi Arkhiv*, pp. 188–189. Translation, with minor modifications, from Rubinchek, p. 246.

44. *Krasnyi Arkhiv*, p. 195.

45. Buksgevden, p. 51.

46. Cady, p. 196.

47. *BPP*, 33:254.

48. Joseph L. Sullivan, "Count N. N. Muraviev-Amursky," Ph.D. thesis (Harvard, 1955), pp. 198, 224. Thanks are due the author for permission to use this work.

49. T. C. Lin, "The Amur Frontier Question between China and Russia, 1850–60," *Pacific Historical Review*, 3:14 (1934).

50. *Ibid.*, p. 17.

51. Frederick W. Williams, ed., "The Journal of S. Wells Williams, LL.D.," *Journal of the North-China Branch of the Royal Asiatic Society*, 42:10 (1911).

52. Marquis de Moges, *Recollections of Baron Gros's Embassy to China and Japan in 1857–58* (the authorized translation of Gros's *Souvenirs d'une Ambassade en Chine et au Japon en 1857 et 1858* [Paris, 1860]; London, 1860), p. 200.

53. *BPP*, 33:299; *IWSM*, 21:26–b, 31. Text of Ch'i-ying's full powers in *BPP*, 33:301. For Pottinger's argument with Ch'i-ying on the full powers, see John K. Fairbank, "Chinese Diplomacy and the Treaty of Nanking, 1842," *The Journal of Modern History*, 12.1:19–22 (March 1940).

54. *BPP*, 33:304–305; H. B. Morse, *The International Relations of the Chinese Empire* (London, 1910), I, 515.

55. *BPP*, 33:305; *IWSM*, 21:26b.

56. *BPP*, 33:303, 307; Williams, p. 17.

57. *Sen. Exec. Doc.*, 36th Cong., 10.30:274.

58. *IWSM*, 21:13b–15.

59. Williams, p. 17.

60. *Sen. Exec. Doc.*, 36th Cong., 10.30:260.

61. *Ibid.*, p. 282.

62. *Ibid.*, pp. 260–61.

63. *IWSM*, 21:29; *CSL*, 249:11.

64. *BPP*, 33:307.

65. *IWSM*, 23:34b; *CSL*, 251:38.

66. *BPP*, 33:316.

67. *BPP*, 33:318; *IWSM*, 24:19b–20.

68. *IWSM*, 23:35. My translation here is more literal than the one in *BPP*, 33:319. Italics mine. The Chinese text may also be found in *THHL*, 51:16b.

69. *BPP*, 33:319, footnote by Wade.

70. Morse, p. 519.

71. *BPP*, 33:318, Elgin to Malmesbury, June 12, 1858.

72. *IWSM*, 23:34b.

73. *BPP*, 33:318.

74. *BPP*, 33:331; *CSL*, 252:24b.

75. *BPP*, 33:298, Elgin to Malmesbury, May 9, 1858. Ch'ung-lun's memorials on the subject had been found in Yeh's yamen and translated by Wade, see *Sen. Exec. Doc.*, 36th Cong., pp. 474 ff.

76. Laurence Oliphant, *Narrative of the Earl of Elgin's Mission to China and Japan in the Years 1857, '58, '59* (London, 1859), I, 342.

77. Reed described Elgin as taking the full powers of a minister as "evidence of an ability to bind the sovereign." See *Sen. Exec. Doc.*, 36th Cong., p. 298.

78. L. Oppenheim, *International Law*, ed. H. Lauterpacht, 7th ed. (London, 1948), I, 818, 787, n. 2.

79. J. Mervyn Jones, "The Retroactive Effects of the Ratification of Treaties," *American Journal of International Law*, 29:54–55, 64–65 (1935).

80. *Sen. Exec. Doc.*, 36th Cong., p. 298.

81. John King Fairbank, *Trade and Diplomacy*, I, 96.

82. T. F. Tsiang, "Notes and Suggestions: Origins of the Tsungli Yamen," *CSPSR*, 15.1:92 (April 1931); Banno Masataka, "Sōrigamon setsuritsu no haikei" ("Determining factors in the instituting of the Tsungli Yamen"), Part I, in *Kokusaihō gaikō zasshi*, 51.4:35, 38 (August 1952).

83. Chiang-shang-ch'ien-sou (Hsia Hsieh), *Chung-Hsi chi-shih* (A record of Sino-Western events; 1868), 14:2b.

84. *Sen. Exec. Doc.*, 36th Cong., p. 282.

85. *BPP*, 33:2.

86. *CSL*, 251:38.

87. *CSL*, 326:13.

88. Moges, pp. 232–233.

89. Oliphant, I, 356–357; Williams, p. 81; *North China Herald*, No. 413 (June 26, 1858), p. 190.

90. John K. Fairbank, "The Manchu Appeasement Policy of 1843," *Journal of the American Oriental Society*, 59.4:484 (December 1939). On Ch'i-ying's personality, earlier career, and foreign policy, see Fairbank, *Trade and Diplomacy*, I, 92–113.

91. Chiang-shang-ch'ien-sou, 14:2b.

92. *IWSM*, 24:1, 9b.

93. *IWSM*, 24:10.

94. *IWSM*, 24:11b.

95. *IWSM*, 24:16b–18b.

96. *IWSM*, 24:20b; *CSL*, 252:16.

97. *CSL*, 252:20a–b.

98. Miyazaki Ichisada, "Shinagawa shiryō yori mitaru Ei-Futsu rengōgun no Pekin shinnyū jiken, tokuni shusenron to waheiron" ("The incident of the intrusion into Peking of the Anglo-French allied force as viewed from the Chinese sources, with special reference to the arguments for war and peace"), *Tōa kenkyū shohō*, No. 24 (Oct. 1943), p. 856.

99. *IWSM*, 25:20a–b; *CSL*, 252:15–16.

100. *IWSM*, 24:38b; *CSL*, 252:27a–b.

101. *Sen. Exec. Doc.*, 36th Cong., p. 339, *BPP*, 33:321.

102. William B. Reed, "Private Diary" (July 5, 1857–April 13, 1859; MS., Library of Congress, Manuscript Division), II, 378, June 10, 1858.

103. *Sen. Exec. Doc.*, 36th Cong., p. 339.

104. *BPP*, 33:321–322.

105. Oliphant, pp. 359–366. A full translation of this document may be found in S. Y. Teng and John K. Fairbank, *China's Response to the West, A Documentary Survey, 1839–1923* (Cambridge, Mass., 1954), pp. 37–40. This was one of Ch'i-ying's less derogatory reports on barbarians. A more disparaging memorial may be found in *Shih-liao hsün-k'an* (Historical materials published every ten days), 35:295. The memorial Lay produced was written by Ch'i-ying in 1844, not 1850 as Morse and Lord Elgin mistakenly stated (Morse, I, 521; *BPP*, 33:334), probably owing to a misunderstanding of Wade's introductory note to his translation of the memorial: "The following memorial was found in a separate wrapper, of several folds, sealed with the Imperial Commissioner's

seal of the reign of Tau Kwang, which style ceased to be used at the end of the year 1850" (*BPP*, 33:175).

106. Teng and Fairbank, *China's Response*, pp. 38–40.
107. Oliphant, pp. 357, 359; Cordier, *L'expédition, 1857–58*, p. 387.
108. China: *Dispatches*, Vol. 17, Doc. 21, Reed to Cass, June 15, 1858.
109. Reed, "Private Diary," II, 379, 381.
110. William B. Reed, "The China Question," *North American Review*, No. 90 (1860), 162–164.
111. China: *Dispatches*, Vol. 17, Doc. 21, Reed to Cass, June 15, 1858.
112. *Ibid.*, enclosure 9.
113. Cady, p. 201.
114. *IWSM*, 25:17.
115. *IWSM*, 26:2a–b.
116. *IWSM*, 25:19a–b; 26:2b.
117. Banno, "Sōrigamon," Part III, in *Kokusaihō gaikō zasshi*, 52.3:100.
118. Miyazaki, p. 858.
119. *IWSM*, 25:20.
120. *IWSM*, 25:25.
121. Earl Swisher, *China's Management of the American Barbarians, A Study of Sino-American Relations, 1841–1861, with Documents* (New Haven, 1953), p. 502.
122. Texts of these three depositions are translated in *Ibid.*, pp. 498–501.
123. *IWSM*, 26:31a–b.
124. Miyazaki, pp. 864–865.
125. Swisher, pp. 506–507.
126. Complete text of the edict is translated in *Ibid.*, pp. 507–509.
127. Chiang-shang-ch'ien-sou, 14:3b.
128. *THL*, 51:2.
129. *CSK*, 376:6b. Fan Wen-lan, *Chung-kuo chin-tai shih* (Chinese modern history; Peking, 1949), I, 228.
Having read these Chinese documents, one must feel that Morse was very bold in stating: "We shall *never* know whether he [Ch'i-ying] had been brought forward by his government as an administrator who, having controlled the barbarian in the past, might again succeed in bringing them under his control; or whether he had volunteered his services as a means of using his past record in order to reestablish his position in the Chinese state" (Morse, I, 504).
130. Chiang-shang-ch'ien-sou, 14:4b–5.
131. Morse, I, 525.

CHAPTER 3. THE TIENTSIN NEGOTIATIONS.

1. Over such issues as Britain's harboring of Mazzini and Victor Hugo, both enemies of Louis Napoleon, and the fact that Felèco Orsini's plot to assassinate the French emperior was prepared in England. Cady, p. 195.
2. Cady, pp. 194–195.
3. Bonner-Smith and Lumby, Doc. 141, Elgin to Clarendon, July 2, 1857, p. 211.
4. *BPP*, 33:227.
5. Toshio Ueda, "Shina no kaikoku to kokusaihō" (The opening of China and international law), *Tōyō bunka kenkyū* 1.1:34 (October 1944); Oppenheim, I, 234–235.

6. *Sen. Exec. Doc.*, 36th Cong., p. 298.

7. *BPP*, 33:346.

8. Oliphant, p. 416.

9. China: *Dispatches*, Vol. 16, Doc. 13, Reed to Cass, April 10, 1858.

10. Theodore Walrond, *Letters and Journals of James, Eighth Earl of Elgin* (London, 1872), pp. 253–254, Elgin to Lady Elgin, June 12, 1858.

11. *BPP*, 33:346.

12. *Sen. Exec. Doc.*, 36th Cong., pp. 382–383, Reed to Cass, July 29, 1858.

13. China: *Dispatches*, Vol. 16, Doc. 13, Reed to Cass, April 10, 1858.

14. Stanley F. Wright, *Hart and the Chinese Customs* (Belfast, 1950), p. 139.

15. Lay, *Note*, p. 12.

16. Lay, *Our Interests in China* (London, 1864), p. 49.

17. *Ibid.*, p. 70.

18. Lay, *Note*, pp. 21–22.

19. S. Wright, *Hart*, p. 146: "He realized — if his employers did not — the real import of the claim for foreign representatives to reside at Peking, namely, the need of drawing China into the stream of the world's history, and of bringing her rulers into living touch with the governments of the other civilized nations of the earth."

20. China: *Dispatches*, Vol. 16, Doc. 13, Reed to Cass, April 10, 1858.

21. Reed, "The China Question," p. 173.

22. China: *Dispatches*, Vol. 17, Doc. 23, Reed to Cass, June 30, 1858.

23. *Sen. Exec. Doc.*, 36th Cong., p. 338, Reed to Cass, June 30, 1858.

24. China: *Dispatches*, Vol. 16, Doc. 13, Reed to Cass, April 10, 1858.

25. Cady, pp. 196, 200.

26. Bonner-Smith and Lumby, Doc. 185, p. 299.

27. *BPP*, 33:183.

28. *IWSM*, 21:42a–b.

29. *IWSM*, 22:8b.

30. *IWSM*, 22:9, 12b.

31. *IWSM*, 22:9, 10.

32. *IWSM*, 22:13b.

33. *IWSM*, 23:6b–7.

34. *IWSM*, 22:23a–b.

35. Biographies of both men may be found in A. W. Hummel, *Eminent Chinese of the Ch'ing period (1644–1912)* (Washington, 1943); also in Swisher, pp. 722, 728–729.

36. *Sen. Exec. Doc.*, 36th Cong., p. 336.

37. Williams, "Journal," p. 49.

38. *IWSM*, 24:19ff.

39. Wright, *Hart*, p. 121.

40. Chiang-shang-ch'ien-sou, 14:4; *CSK*, 160:7b.

41. *IWSM*, 24:27a–27b; *BPP*, 33:325–326.

42. *BPP*, 33:327; Lay, *Note*, p. 13. The pleading of *ad misericordiam* was one of the many tactics used by early Chinese barbarian managers. Other tactics included ambiguous promises, avoidance of issues, delay, personal friendship, etc. See Banno Masataka, "Gaikō kōshō ni okeru Shinmatsu kanjin no kōdō yoshiki" ("Behavior of the mandarins as diplomats late in the Ch'ing dynasty"), Part I, in *Kokusaihō gaikō zasshi*, Vol. 48, No. 4 (Oct. 1949). There is a summary of this article in Fairbank, *Trade and Diplomacy*, p. 102, n.

43. Lay, *Note*, p. 13.
44. *IWSM*, 24:27, received at court June 7, 1858.
45. *IWSM*, 24:28b–29.
46. *IWSM*, 24:34a–b, received at court June 9, 1858.
47. *IWSM*, 24:37–38, received June 10.
48. Reed, "The China Question," 165–167.
49. Reed, "Private Diary," II, 380.
50. Lay, *Note*, p. 13.
51. *BPP*, 33:407.
52. *BPP*, 33:327.
53. *BPP*, 33:330.
54. *IWSM*, 35:4, received at court June 12, 1858.
55. *IWSM*, 25:16b–17, received June 14.
56. *IWSM*, 25:7, 17b–18.
57. *IWSM*, 25:28.
58. *BPP*, 33:332.
59. Henri Cordier, *L'expédition de Chine de 1860, Histoire diplomatique, notes et documents* (Paris, 1906), p. 2.
60. Cady, p. 201.
61. *IWSM*, 25:37–38.
62. *IWSM*, 25:38a–b.
63. *IWSM*, 26:8, received at court June 22, 1858.
64. *IWSM*, 25:40.
65. *IWSM*, 25:40b.
66. Yin Keng-yün, *Hsin-pai-shih-chai chi* (Collection of the Hsin-pai-shih Study; 1885), 1:1–17b.
67. *Ibid.*, 1:9b; *IWSM*, 25:9b.
68. Wang Chih-ch'un, *Kuo-ch'ao jou-yüan chi* (An account of our imperial dynasty's benevolence toward men from afar; 1896), 13:13b–16.
69. Wang Mao-yin, *Wang-shih-lang tsou-i* (Memorials of Vice-President Wang; 1887), 9:18a–b.
70. Shen Chao-lin, *Shen-wen-chung-kung chi* (Collection of Shen Chao-lin; 1869), 1:15–16b.
71. Miyazaki, pp. 877–878.
72. *IWSM*, 26:11–12b.
73. *IWSM*, 26:18–19.
74. *IWSM*, 26:20.
75. *IWSM*, 26:22b–23b.
76. *IWSM*, 26:13–15b.
77. *IWSM*, 26:20b.
78. Chiang-shang-ch'ien-sou, 12:3–4b, 12.
79. *IWSM*, 26:15b–17.
80. *IWSM*, 26:24b; Yin Keng-yün, 3:15b.
81. Banno, "Sōrigamon," Part III, p. 95.
82. *IWSM*, 23:36; 24:4b.
83. Yin Keng-yün, 3:15b–18.
84. *Ibid.*, 1:12b.
85. *Ibid.*, 16b.
86. Banno, "Sōrigamon," Part III, p. 96.
87. *Ibid.*, Part II, pp. 79–83; Part III, p. 96. Mr. Banno is preparing an English version of these articles, part of which he has kindly shown me.

88. Morse, I, 599.
89. *IWSM*, 26:25a–b.
90. *IWSM*, 26:25b–26b.
91. *IWSM*, 26:28b.
92. *IWSM*, 26:29.
93. Reed, "Private Diary," II, 399–400.
94. *Ibid.*, p. 402.
95. *BPP*, 33:339.
96. *IWSM*, 27:2a–b.
97. *IWSM*, 27:2b–3.
98. *IWSM*, 28:4; *BPP*, 33:340, 342–345. A writer, Wei-tai Shen, has held that "the Emperor ratified the treaties of Tientsin *under duress*. It was only because the Allies had occupied Tientsin and threatened Peking that he gave his consent to the treaties." See his *China's Foreign Policy, 1839–1860* (New York, 1932), p. 165. It appears that the term "under duress" is misused here. "Under duress" in international law applies to a threat to the life of the delegate, and not to the state. Kuei-liang and the emperor were not threatened by Elgin insofar as their personal lives were concerned; the state was threatened.
99. *Treaties, Conventions, etc., between China and Foreign States* (Shanghai: Statistical Department of the Inspectorate General of Customs, 1917), p. 405.
100. Moges, pp. 238–239.
101. *BPP*, 33:345–346.
102. Oliphant, pp. 434 ff; Morison, p. 226. Other reasons: forces needed in the south to protect Hongkong against a rumored massacre; cold weather coming, etc.
103. *Sen. Exec. Doc.*, 36th Cong., p. 434, Reed to Cass, Sept. 4, 1858.
104. China: *Instructions*, Vol. I, Doc. 15, Cass to Reed, Oct. 16, 1858.

CHAPTER 4. THE SHANGHAI TARIFF CONFERENCE.

1. *IWSM*, 29:8, 9b.
2. *CSK*, "Biographies," 175:2. For a summary account of this secret plan see T. F. Tsiang, "The Secret Plan of 1858," *CSPSR*, 15.2:291–299 (July 1931).
3. *IWSM*, 31:35b–36, received at court Oct. 19, 1858.
4. *IWSM*, 30:11b, received at court August 18, 1858.
5. *IWSM*, 30:28, Sept. 12, 1858.
6. *IWSM*, 30:29b–30.
7. *IWSM*, 30:31, Sept. 14, 1858.
8. *IWSM*, 30:38b–39, Sept. 29, 1858.
9. *IWSM*, 30:40a–b.
10. *IWSM*, 30:42a–b, 43.
11. *IWSM*, 30:44–46, received Oct. 5; 31:18–19, Oct. 9.
12. *IWSM*, 30:46b.
13. *IWSM*, 31:21b–22b.
14. *IWSM*, 31:29b–31.
15. *IWSM*, 31:36, 41b–42, received Oct. 21, 1858.
16. *IWSM*, 31:44, received at court Oct. 27, 1858.
17. Michie, p. 341.
18. *IWSM*, 31:49–51.
19. *BPP*, 33:409; *IWSM*, 31:49–50; Oliphant, p. 476.

20. *BPP*, p. 409; Oliphant, p. 478.
21. *BPP*, 33:410; *IWSM*, 31:49b.
22. *IWSM*, 31:50. Lay was not an official British negotiator but an observer at the Shanghai Tariff Conference. Morse, I, p. 533.
23. *BPP*, 33:411.
24. *BPP*, 33:406.
25. *BPP*, 33:407.
26. Cady, p. 194.
27. *Ibid.*, p. 205; Costin, p. 277.
28. *BPP*, 33:407–408.
29. China: *Dispatches*, Vol. 17, Doc. 35, Reed to Cass, Nov. 5, 1858.
30. *BPP*, 33:408.
31. Reed, "The China Question," p. 173.
32. Morse, I, 536; China: *Dispatches*, Vol. 17, Doc. 35.
33. *BPP*, 33:412; Oliphant, p. 483.
34. Lay, *Note*, p. 15.
35. Quoted in Michie, p. 336.
36. Michie, pp. 346, 337.
37. *BPP*, 33:414.
38. China: *Dispatches*, Vol. 17, Doc. 35, Reed to Cass, Nov. 5, 1858.
39. *IWSM*, 32:3a–b; *CSL*, 266:4a–b.
40. *IWSM*, 32:9b.
41. *IWSM*, 33:9, received at court Dec. 15, 1858.
42. *IWSM*, 33:10b–11.
43. *IWSM*, 33:32b.
44. *CSL*, 272:35b.
45. *IWSM*, 23:20b.
46. *IWSM*, 35:14–17, received at court March 15, 1859.
47. Banno Masataka, "Tenshin jōyaku (1858-nen) chōin go ni okeru Shin-koku gaisei kikō no dōyō (I)" ("Institutional development in the Chinese conduct of foreign affairs after the signing of the Tientsin treaties in 1858"), *Kokusaihō gaikō zasshi*, 55.6:12 (March, 1957).
48. *Ibid.*, p. 9.
49. *IWSM*, 35:19a–b, March 15, 1858.
50. *BPP*, 33:482, Elgin to Malmesbury, Feb. 26, 1859.
51. *BPP*, 33:484–485.
52. *BPP*, 33:482.
53. *BPP*, 33:484–485.
54. *Ibid.*
55. *IWSM*, 36:17a–b.
56. *IWSM*, 36:13b.
57. *BPP*, 33:488; Morison, pp. 243, 295.

CHAPTER 5. PERSONALITY AND DIPLOMACY: A STUDY IN LEADERSHIP.

1. Walrond, p. 213, Elgin to Lady Elgin, Dec. 22, 1857.
2. Morison, pp. 202, 212.
3. *Ibid.*, p. 212.
4. Walrond, pp. 212–213, 252–253, Elgin to Lady Elgin, Dec. 22, 1857 and June 12, 1858.

5. Morison, pp. 202, 258; George Wrong, *The Earl of Elgin* (London, 1905), p. 105.
6. Morison, p. 213.
7. Lane-Poole and Dickins, pp. 283, 339.
8. *North China Herald*, No. 384 (Nov. 14, 1857), p. 62.
9. Nathan A. Pelcovits, *Old China Hands and the Foreign Office* (New York, 1948), p. 17.
10. *Ibid.*, p. 18.
11. Walrond, p. 305.
12. *Ibid.*, p. 238, undated.
13. Bonner-Smith and Lumby, Doc. 198, p. 313; Doc. 203, pp. 319, 324.
14. *Ibid.*, pp. 329–330, 331, Elgin to Malmesbury, May 15, 1858.
15. *Ibid.*, p. 361, n., Seymour to Admiralty, Sept. 27, 1858.
16. Hansard, 156:935, 948 (1860).
17. *Ibid.*, p. 1465.
18. Cady, pp. 181–182.
19. *Ibid.*, p. 193.
20. Williams, "Journal," p. 81.
21. *North China Herald*, No. 406 (May 8, 1858), p. 162.
22. *Ibid.*, No. 413 (June 26, 1858), p. 190.
23. *Sen. Exec. Doc.*, 36th Congr., 1st Session, No. 30, pp. 438–439, Reed to Cass, Oct. 21, 1858.
24. *Ibid.*, p. 257; China: *Dispatches*, Vol. 15, Doc. 36, Reed to Cass, Dec. 15, 1857.
25. China: *Dispatches*, Vol. 15, Doc. 36.
26. China: *Dispatches*, Vol. 17, Doc. 23, Reed to Cass, June 30, 1858.
27. *BPP*, 33:345, Elgin to Malmesbury, July 12, 1858.
28. Walrond, pp. 253–254, Elgin to Lady Elgin, June 29, 1858.
29. China: *Dispatches*, Vol. 16, Doc. 9, Reed to Cass, Feb. 13, 1858.
30. Reed, "The China Question," p. 172.
31. Miyazaki, pp. 862–863; Banno, "Sōrigamon," Part III, pp. 90–91. These two Japanese scholars seem to suggest that Prince Kung's anti-foreign stand was not his real attitude but a tactic to test the court's attitude, and that he, basically inclined toward peace, was a secret supporter of Kuei-liang, his father-in-law. However, I cannot find evidence to corroborate their suggestion.
32. *BPP*, 33:328.
33. *IWSM*, 24:29b, received at court, June 7, 1858. For a complete story of Mr. Chang's services to the Allied armies, see Ting Yün-shu, Ch'en Shih-hsün and Ko Yü-ch'i, eds., *Chang-kung hsiang-li chün-wu chi-lüeh* (A brief record of Squire Chang's contributions to the military affairs), 6 *chüan*.

CHAPTER 6. THE RESIDENT MINISTER ISSUE AFTER TAKU.

1. *IWSM*, 35:38b, received at court March 26, 1859; 36:38b–39, April 30.
2. *IWSM*, 35:40b; 36:14b, 40.
3. *IWSM*, 37:9b, received at court May 20, 1859.
4. *IWSM*, 36:16a–b.
5. *BPP*, 62 (2587):1–3, *Correspondence with Mr. Bruce, 1860*.
6. *Ibid.*, pp. 4–6.
7. *Ibid.*, p. 13.
8. *Ibid.*, p. 23, Bruce to Malmesbury, July 13, 1859.

234 Notes to Chapter 6

9. *IWSM*, 38:13–15b, 21a–b.

10. The British government later thanked the United States for Tatnall's service. See China: *Instructions*, Vol. I, Doc. 10, Cass to Reed, Nov. 28, 1859.

11. Hansard, 157:1597–98.

12. Costin, p. 294.

13. Hansard, 157:1601.

14. *Ibid.*, 156:940.

15. Quoted in Cady, p. 229.

16. *BPP*, 69 (2587):39.

17. *BPP*, 69 (2606):5.

18. *BPP*, 69 (2641):1.

19. Costin, p. 300.

20. Hansard, 157:790.

21. Quoted in Costin, pp. 298–299.

22. *BPP*, 69 (2606):4.

23. Hansard, 156:1463–64.

24. Hansard, 156:920–930.

25. Hansard, 157:788.

26. Hansard, 157:780–781.

27. Hansard, 157:1608.

28. Hansard, 156:1463–64.

29. *Ibid.*

30. Hansard, 157:1605.

31. Hansard, 157:807.

32. Hansard, 159:1910.

33. Hansard, 159:1905–06.

34. Hansard, 156:946 (1860).

35. Hansard, 157:722–723.

36. Hansard, 156:946.

37. Hansard, 159:1880–86.

38. Hansard, 159:1886–87.

39. *BPP*, 66 (2754):12.

40. *BPP*, 69 (2677):5–7.

41. *CSL*, 309:28b.

42. *BPP*, 66 (2754):53.

43. *BPP*, 66 (2754):29–30.

44. Hansard, 157:790, 1603; Walrond, pp. 325, 327.

45. Walrond, pp. 257, 328.

46. Bonner-Smith and Lumby, p. 391.

47. Lane-Poole and Dickins, p. 340.

48. *CSL*, 318:31a–b.

49. *IWSM*, 54:25b.

50. *CSL*, 321:37b.

51. *CSL*, 321:38.

52. *IWSM*, 55:22b, 30b.

53. Ward himself and the United States government did not think the reception was unsatisfactory. For an account of Ward's visit, see S. W. Williams, "Narrative of the American Embassy to Peking," *Journal of the North-China Branch of the Royal Asiatic Society*, No. 3 (Dec. 1859), pp. 315–349.

54. *IWSM*, 59:9b; Lane-Poole and Dickins, p. 343.

55. *IWSM*, 59:17b–18.

56. *CSL*, 326:10b; *IWSM*, 59:12; 60:7.
57. *IWSM*, 59:18b.
58. *IWSM*, 59:19b.
59. *CSL*, 326:15a–b.
60. *IWSM*, 60:13b; *BPP*, 66 (2754):172.
61. *BPP*, 66:165.
62. *IWSM*, 61:24b.
63. *BPP*, 66:227.
64. *BPP*, 66:229.
65. Chiang-shang-ch'ien-sou, 15:4b–5; *IWSM*, 62:14, 18; Yano Jinichi, *Kinsei Shina gaikō shi* (Modern Chinese diplomatic history; Tokyo, 1935), p. 580.
66. *Ibid.*
67. Parkes' own account of his arrest and prison life appear in *BPP*, 66: 226–244.
68. *CSL*, 327:8.
69. *IWSM*, 63:23. For details of the emperor's exile, see Chiang-sheng-ch'ien-sou, 15:6b; on the occupation of Peking, see Wu K'o-tu, "Ying-fa lien-chün shih-tai chih Pei-ching ching-hsiang" (Situations in Peking during the time of the Anglo-French campaign), in Tso Shun-sheng, *Chung-kuo chin-pai-nien shih tzu-liao hsü-pien* (Materials relating to the Chinese history of the recent hundred years, Supplementary volume; Shanghai, 1933), pp. 125–132. For a record of the Anglo-French army's entry into Peking, see Meng Sen, "Ch'ing Hsien-feng shih-nien yang-ping ju-ching chih jih-chi" (A diary concerning the entry of foreign soldiers into Peking in 1860), *Shih-hsüeh chi-k'an* ("Historical Journal"; Peking), No. 2 (Oct. 1936), pp. 179–193.
70. Buksgevden, pp. 6–7.
71. *Ibid.*, pp. 10, 50.
72. Petr Shumakher, p. 304.
73. For a succinct account of Ignatiev's mission, see Mark Mancall, "Major-General Ignatiev's Mission to Peking, 1859–1860," *Papers on China* (Harvard University, Center for East Asian Studies), 10:55–96 (1956).
74. Buksgevden, pp. 53–54.
75. Popov, 21:199 (1927).
76. For details see Mancall; also Chiang T'ing-fu (T. F. Tsiang), *Chin-tai Chung-kuo wai-chiao shih tzu-liao chi-yao* ("A collection of essential sources of Chinese modern diplomatic history"; Shanghai, 1931), 1:295–322.
77. General Sir Hope Grant, *Incidents in the China War of 1860* (London, 1875), pp. 37, 136.
78. *IWSM*, 65:22b.
79. *IWSM*, 65:31b–32; *CSL*, 330:15b.
80. Buksgevden, p. 207.
81. *IWSM*, 67:8.
82. China: *Dispatches*, Vol. 19, Doc. 26, Ward to Cass, Nov. 28, 1860.
83. Ch'en Fu-kuang, p. 132.
84. Michie, p. 354.
85. Lane-Poole and Dickins, pp. 402–404.
86. Buksgevden, p. 213.
87. Henri Cordier, *Histoire des relations de la Chine avec les puissances occidentales 1860–1900* (Paris, 1901), I, 44–45.
88. *BPP*, 66:254.
89. Ch'en Fu-kuang, pp. 132–134; Chiang T'ing-fu (T. F. Tsiang), "Tsui-

chin san-pai-nien Tung-Pei wai-chiao-shih" (Diplomatic history of Manchuria in the last three hundred years), *The Tsing Hua Journal*, 8.1:62 (1932).

90. Quoted in Ch'en Fu-kuang, p. 132.
91. *BPP*, 66:204–205.
92. *Ibid.*
93. *BPP*, 66:252.
94. *IWSM*, 68:4b.
95. *IWSM*, 68:2b.
96. *IWSM*, 68:3b.
97. *Wen-hsien ts'ung-pien* (Collectanea from the Historical Record Office), 23:8.
98. *IWSM*, 70:2.
99. Yano Jinichi, p. 634.
100. *IWSM*, 70:33–34.
101. Cordier, *Histoire des relations*, p. 113.
102. Tyler Dennett, *Americans in Eastern Asia* (New York, 1941), p. 343.
103. Cordier, *Histoire des relations*, p. 112.
104. *Ibid.*, pp. 113–114.
105. *Ibid.*, p. 115.
106. *IWSM*, T'ung-chih period, 7:51b.
107. Two excellent studies of the Tsungli Yamen are: Meng Ssu-ming, "The Organization and Functions of the Tsungli Yamen" (Ph.D. thesis, Harvard, 1949); Banno, "Sōrigamon," Parts I, II, III.
108. *IWSM*, 71:27, Jan. 12, 1861.
109. *CSL*, 342:20a–b.
110. Lay, *Interests*, p. 58.
111. *Ibid.*, p. 59.
112. *Ibid.*, p. 55.
113. For a study of China's position in the modern world, see T. F. Tsiang, "Chung-kuo yü chin-tai shih-chieh ti ta-pien-chü" (China and the great changes of the modern world), *The Tsing-hua Journal*, 9.4:783–828 (Oct. 1934).

CHAPTER 7. THE IDEOLOGICAL ISSUE: DIPLOMATIC
REPRESENTATION VS. T'I-CHIH.

1. Oppenheim, I, 700.
2. R. R. Foulke, *A Treatise on International Law* (Philadelphia, 1920), I, 184–185.
3. Fan Wen-lan, I, 197.
4. Hu Sheng, *Ti-kuo chu-i yü Chung-kuo cheng-chih* (Imperialism and Chinese politics; Peking, 1952), p. 47.
5. Hsiao Kung-ch'üan, I, 75 and 77.
6. On the tributary system, see J. K. Fairbank and S. Y. Teng, "On the Ch'ing Tributary System," *HJAS*, 6.2:135–246 (June 1941).
7. Ch'en Ch'iu, "Wu-hsü cheng-pien shih fan-pien-fa jen-wu chih cheng-chih ssu-hsiang" (Political thought of anti-reformers during the coup d'état of 1898), *Yen-ching hsü-pao* ("Yenching Journal of Chinese Studies"), 25:88 (June 1939); see also *Ch'ing-kung shih-lüeh* (Historical sketches of the Ch'ing palaces), p. 1. Upon the death of the Emperor Hsien-feng, his biographer praised him for "perfect reverence and emulation of his ancestors." See *CSL*, 356:19b–20.
8. Swisher, p. 13.

9. *IWSM*, 29:32b, received at court Aug. 2, 1858.
10. *IWSM*, Tung-chih period, 50:26.
11. Hua Kang, *Chung-hua min-tsu chieh-fang yün-tung-shih* (A history of the Chinese people's liberation movement; Shanghai, 1951), pp. 264–265.
12. *CSL*, 314:8a–b, 322:27b.
13. Wu Hsiang-hsiang, *Wan-Ch'ing kung-t'ing shih-chi* (Veritable accounts of the palaces in the late Ch'ing; Taipei, 1952), p. 15; Lo Tun-yung, "Ping-tui sui-pi" (Random notes after the guests are gone), *Yung-yen* ("The Justice"; Tientsin), 2.5:1.
14. Wu Hsiang-hsiang, p. 15.
15. T. F. Tsiang, "China and European Expansion," *Politica*, 2.5:3 (March 1936).
16. Ch'ing intellectual activities are discussed in Liang Ch'i-ch'ao, *Ch'ing-tai hsüeh-shu kai-lun* (A general survey of Ch'ing intellectual trends; Shanghai, 1921). This work has been translated by Immanuel C. Y. Hsü under the title *Intellectual Trends in the Ch'ing Period* (Cambridge, Mass., 1959).
17. On Chinese intellectual conservatism see Chap. 13 below.

CHAPTER 8. THE TRANSLATION OF INTERNATIONAL LAW INTO CHINESE.

1. Liu Shu-ping, *Wai-chiao kang-yao* (Essentials of diplomacy; Peking, 1915), preface. On China's ignorance of international law, see Ueda Toshio, "Shina no kaikoku to kokusaihō" (The opening of China and international law), *Tōyō bunka kenkyū*, 1.1:35–37, 41 (Oct. 1944).
2. Li Hung-chang, *Li-wen-chung-kung ch'üan-chi* (Complete works of Li Hung-chang; Shanghai, 1921), Series III, *Letters to the Tsungli Yamen*, 1:43b.
3. Hsüeh Fu-cheng, *Yung-an ch'üan-chi* (Complete works of Hsüeh Fu-ch'eng; Shanghai, 1897), Series II, Supplements, 1:1b.
4. Wang Chih-ch'un, Appendix, p. 14a–b; Wang T'ing-hsi and Wang Shu-min, eds., *Huang-ch'ao Tao-Hsien-T'ung-Kuang tsou-i* (Memorials of the Tao-kuang, Hsien-feng, T'ung-chih, and Kuang-hsü periods of our imperial Dynasty; Shanghai, 1902), 16:23b.
5. J. L. Brierly, *The Law of Nations* (Oxford University Press, 1949), pp. 58–59.
6. *Chinese Repository*, 8:634 (1840).
7. E. Vattel, *The Law of Nations* (New York, 1796), p. 97.
8. Wei Yüan, *Hai-kuo t'u-chih* (An illustrated gazetteer of the maritime countries; 1852), 83:18.
9. *Ibid.*, 83:18a–b.
10. Chang Hsi-t'ung, "The Earliest Phase of the Introduction of Western Political Science into China (1820–52)," *The Yenching Journal of Social Studies*, 5.1:13 (July 1950).
11. *Ibid.*, p. 14.
12. Wei Yüan, 83:20b–21. The original in Vattel, p. 359, is in much more elegant language.
13. Teng and Fairbank, *China's Response*, pp. 24–28.
14. *IWSM*, 27:25a–b. This memorial was received at court August 30, 1864.
15. W. A. P. Martin, *A Cycle of Cathay* (New York, 1897), p. 222.
16. Robert Hart, "Note on Chinese Matters" in appendix to Frederick W. Williams, *Anson Burlingame and the First Chinese Mission to Foreign Powers* (New York, 1912), p. 285. The part translated was Chapter 1 of Part III of

Henry Wheaton's *Elements of International Law* (Boston, 1855). Unfortunately Hart's translation cannot be found.

17. Martin, *Cycle*, p. 234.
18. *Ibid.*, p. 221.
19. *Ibid.*, p. 222.
20. M. E. Boggs, "William Alexander Parsons Martin, Missionary to China, 1850–1916," M.A. thesis (Presbyterian College of Education, Chicago, 1948), Appendix, p. 34.
21. W. A. P. Martin, *Wan-kuo kung-fa* (Public law of all nations; Peking, 1864), English preface, pp. 1, 2.
22. *Ibid.*, English preface, p. 3.
23. *Ibid.*
24. China: *Dispatches*, Vol. 15, Document 41, Reed to Cass, Dec. 31, 1857.
25. Martin, *Wan-kuo kung-fa*, Chinese preface.
26. China: *Dispatches*, Vol. 21, Doc. 52, Burlingame to William H. Seward, Oct. 30, 1863.
27. Martin, *Cycle*, p. 222.
28. W. A. P. Martin, "Journal of Removal to Peking," *Foreign Mission*, 22:228 (Feb. 1864), quoted, with permission, from Norma J. Burns, "W. A. P. Martin and the Westernization of China," M.A. thesis (Indiana University, March 1954), p. 125.
29. Martin, *Cycle*, p. 233.
30. *IWSM*, 27:25b, received at court August 30, 1864.
31. *IWSM*, 27:26.
32. *Ibid.* They were Ch'en Ch'in, Li Ch'ang-hua, Fang Chün-shih, and Mao Hung-t'u.
33. *IWSM*, 27:26b.
34. *Foreign Relations of the United States* (1865), pp. 438–439.
35. *Ibid.*
36. Ōhira Zengo, "Nihon no kokusai hō no juyō" (The reception of international law by Japan), Shōgaku Tōkyū, 4.3:309 (Dec. 1953).
37. Martin, *Wan-kuo kung-fa*, English preface, p. 3. Wheaton's sections 17, 18, 19 of Chapter 4, pp. 225–270, and Appendix, pp. 626–669, are omitted in Martin's translation.
38. *Ibid.*, Chinese preface.
39. In either the 1836 or the 1855 edition.
40. Hozumi Nobushige, *Hōsō yawa* (Nightly discourse on law; Tokyo, 1932), p. 179.
41. Henry Wheaton, *Elements of International Law*, p. 17.
42. Martin, *Wan-kuo kung-fa*, 1:11.
43. Osatake Takeru, *Kinsei Nippon no kokusai kannen no hattatsu* (The development of international ideas in modern Japan; Tokyo, 1932), p. 39.
44. Martin, *Wan-kuo kung-fa*, English preface, p. 3.

CHAPTER 9. SUCCESS AND FAILURE: CHINA'S LIMITED
APPLICATION OF INTERNATIONAL LAW.

1. T. F. Tsiang, "Bismarck and the Introduction of International Law into China," *CSPSR*, 15.1:100 (April, 1931).
2. *IWSM*, 27:25b–26, received at court August 30, 1864.
3. *IWSM*, 26:29b–30b, 31.

4. *IWSM*, 26:30.
5. *IWSM*, 26:30b.
6. Wheaton's "maritime territory" may be found in his *Elements*, p. 233, and Martin's translation of it in *Wan-kuo kung-fa*, 2:67a–b.
7. *IWSM*, 26:33.
8. *IWSM*, 26:31.
9. *Ibid.*
10. Boggs, Appendix, p. 41.
11. *IWSM*, 27:26a–b.
12. *IWSM*, 31:4, received at court Feb. 20, 1865.
13. *IWSM*, 31:4b–5; Martin, *Wan-kuo kung-fa*, Foreword.
14. Martin, *Wan-kuo kung-fa*, Foreword.
15. Wu Hsiang-hsiang, p. 123.
16. *IWSM*, 27:26b.
17. W. A. P. Martin, "Traces of International Law in Ancient China," *The Chinese Recorder*, 14.5:380 (Sept.–Oct. 1883).
18. Martin, *Wan-kuo kung-fa*, English preface, 1. Italics mine.
19. Foreign Mission Board of the Presbyterian Church File, *Letters and Papers, 1862–67*, reproduced in Boggs, p. 50.
20. Martin, *Cycle*, p. 234.
21. China: *Dispatches*, Vol. 21, Doc. 52.
22. China: *Dispatches*, Vol. 22, Doc. 104; China: *Instructions*, Vol. 1, No. 147, p. 361; Personal letter, p. 370; No. 149, pp. 363–364, Aug. 14, 1865.
23. *USFR* (1866), 1:485–486, Williams to Seward, Nov. 23, 1865.
24. *Ibid.*
25. *Ibid.*, p. 494, Seward to Williams, March 6, 1866.
26. *USFR* (1866), 1:487.
27. *Ibid.*, p. 492.
28. Martin, *Wan-kuo kung-fa*, 3:1a–b.
29. Anonymous, "The Life and Work of the Late Dr. W. A. P. Martin," *The Chinese Recorder*, 48.2:119 (Feb. 1917).
30. Martin, *Wan-kuo kung-fa*, English preface, pp. 2–3.
31. Martin, *Cycle*, p. 234.
32. *North China Herald*, No. 721 (May 21, 1864), p. 82.
33. F. C. Jones, *Extraterritoriality in Japan, And the Diplomatic Relations Resulting in Its Abolition, 1853–1899* (New Haven, 1931), pp. 2–3.
34. The T'ang, Sung, Ming and Ch'ing practices of non-interference in foreign communities are discussed in Hsiao I-shan, *Ch'ing-tai t'ung-shih* (A general history of the Ch'ing period; Peking), 4:292–293. The text of Article 10 of the Treaty of Kiakhta is in *Treaties, Conventions, etc. between China and Foreign States* (Shanghai, 1917), I, 29.
35. Chiang T'ing-fu, *Wai-chiao-shih*, 1:121.
36. Stanley F. Wright, *China's Struggle for Tariff Autonomy, 1843–1938* (Shanghai, 1938), pp. 2–3.
37. Chiang T'ing-fu, *Wai-chiao-shih*, 1:121.
38. Stanley Wright, *China's Struggle*, p. 15.
39. See T. F. Tsiang, "The Exension of Equal Commercial Privileges to Other Nations than the British after the Treaty of Nanking," *CSPSR*, 15:422–444; T. Kearny, "The Tsiang Documents, Elipoo, Keying, Pottinger and Kearny and the Most-favored-nation and Open Door Policy in China in 1842–44 — An American View," in *ibid.*, 16.1:75–104. Pottinger told the Manchu negotiator

in 1842: "The government of England has asked for no privileges or advantages with regard to trade and future intercourse with China that she will not be glad to see granted to other nations." Quoted in S. Wright, *China's Struggle*, p. 7. See also Fairbank, *Trade and Diplomacy*, I, 195–199.

40. *China Correspondence*, No. 1 (1870), p. 5, Alcock to Clarendon, Oct. 28, 1869.

41. The Alcock Convention is ably discussed in Mary Wright, *The Last Stand of Chinese Conservatism, the T'ung-chih Restoration 1862–74* (Stanford, 1957), pp. 287–291.

42. Ch'en Chih, *Yung-shu* (The book of utility), Wai-pien, 1:13b.

43. *IWSM*, 49:6.

44. Mary Wright, p. 232.

45. Feng Kuei-fen, *Chiao-pin-lu k'ang-i* (Protests from the Chiao-pin Studio), 2:45b.

46. *IWSM*, 49:6.

47. Tseng Chi-tse, *Tseng-hui-min-kung i-chi* (Collected works of Tseng Chi-tse), Series IV, *Diary*, 2:14b–15.

48. On "synarchy," see John K. Fairbank, "Synarchy under the Treaties," pp. 204–231.

49. *USFR* (1875), 1:251.

CHAPTER 10. EARLY APPROACHES TO THE PROBLEM.

1. Fang Pao, *Chou-kuan chi-chu* (Collected commentaries on the *Officials of Chou*), 10:13, 19b; also Ch'en Chih, *Yung-shu* (The book of utility), wai-pien, 2:9.

2. *The Confucian Analects*, Bk. 13, Chap. 20.

3. *Ibid.*, Bk. 13, Chap. 5, translation taken from Legge, *Chinese Classics*, I, 265.

4. *Ibid.*, Bk. 13, Chap. 20, verse 1; Legge, p. 271. The last word in this quotation, "scholar-official," is mine. Legge's rendition of "officer" seems too narrow.

5. Chang Hung, "Shih Mien lu" (My mission to Burma), in *Li-hsiang-chai ts'ung-shu* (Collected works of Li-hsiang-chai; 1833), pp. 1–3.

6. H. B. Morse, II, 186. For an account of these missions see Mark Mancall, "China's First Missions to Russia, 1729–1731," *Papers on China* (Harvard University, Center for East Asian Studies), 9:75–110 (1955).

7. Quoted in Ch'en Kung-lu, *Chung-kuo chin-tai shih* (Chinese modern history; Shanghai, 1935), p. 252.

8. Horatio N. Lay, *Note*, p. 11.

9. Oliphant, *Elgin's Mission*, I, 439.

10. *BPP*, 66(2754):273.

11. *USFR* (1868), Part I, p. 495.

12. Martin, *Wan-kuo kung-fa*, 3:1a–b; Wheaton, pp. 273–274.

13. *USFR* (1865), Part II, pp. 447–448.

14. Robert Hart, "Note on Chinese Matters," p. 285.

15. Martin, *Cycle*, p. 372; Morse, II, 190.

16. *IWSM*, Tung-chih period, 40:14.

17. *IWSM*, 40:16.

18. *IWSM*, 40:20a–b.

19. *IWSM*, 40:21b, 22.

20. *IWSM*, 40:10b. It has been reported that the Empress Dowager expressed her regret to Robert Hart in 1902 that his advice of 1865 had not been accepted. See Mary Wright, p. 268, n. x.

21. *IWSM*, 39:1a–b.

22. For a detailed account of this mission, see Knight Biggerstaff, "The First Chinese Mission of Investigation sent to Europe," *Pacific Historical Review*, 6.4:307–320 (Dec. 1937).

23. *IWSM*, 40:22b. The original English version of Wade's memorandum is not extant, but H. E. Wodehouse has made a free translation of it from the Chinese. See his "Mr. Wade on China," in *The China Review*, 1.1:38–44 (July–August, 1872) and 1.2:118–124 (Sept.–Oct. 1872).

24. *IWSM*, 40:23b. This is my own literal translation.

25. *IWSM*, 40:29a–b. This is my own literal translation.

26. *IWSM*, 40:30. My own translation.

27. *IWSM*, 40:30.

28. *IWSM*, 40:34–35b.

29. *IWSM*, 40:31b.

30. *IWSM*, 40:10b–11.

31. *IWSM*, 40:10b–11b.

32. *IWSM*, 40:12.

33. *IWSM*, 40:12b.

34. *IWSM*, 41:28a–b.

35. *IWSM*, 55:12b.

36. *IWSM*, 41:44b.

37. *IWSM*, 45:45–46. Apparently Ma mistook "full powers" and "plenipotentiary" for unlimited exercise of powers by an envoy.

38. *IWSM*, 41:41a–b.

39. *IWSM*, 42:46.

40. Ko Shih-chün, *Huang-ch'ao ching-shih-wen hsü-pien* (A supplementary compilation of noted writings of our imperial dynasty; 1888), 104:1b.

41. Hu Sheng, *Ti-kuo chu-i yü Chung-kuo cheng-chih* (Imperialism and Chinese politics; Peking, 1952), pp. 47, 53. Although this work is unscholarly, it reflects the Communist view and is therefore of interest.

42. Robert Hart, "Note on Chinese Matters," p. 286.

43. This is a famous phrase in the *Book of Changes*, Appendix III. Here the translation is not literal, but gives the general meaning. The translation is taken from James Legge, *The Sacred Books of China*, Part II, "The Yi King," p. 383. For a better understanding of this quotation, I quote the whole paragraph: "After the death of Shan-nang, there arose Huang Ti, Yao, and Shun. They carried through the (necessarily occurring) changes, so that the people did (what was required of them) without being wearied; yea, they exerted such a spirit-like transformation that the people felt constrained to approve their (ordinance) as right. When a series of changes has run all its course, another change ensues. When it obtains free course, it will continue long." (*Ibid.*, p. 383.)

44. Chou Chia-mei, *Ch'i-pu-fu-chai ch'üan-chi* (Complete work of the Ch'i-pu-fu Studio; 1895), Part I, "Political writings," 1:2–5b.

CHAPTER 11. THE ENVOY QUESTION AS A NATIONAL ISSUE.

1. This phrase, "to know others as oneself," is a simplified version of the common saying, "Know your enemy as yourself, a hundred victories out of a

hundred battles," which in turn is a corruption of the original statement in the famous military work, the *Sun-tze*: "Know your enemy as yourself, no danger in a hundred battles."

2. Chung-hsing Shuo, a eunuch in the court of Emperor Wen (179–156 B.C.) of the Former Han dynasty, was forcibly sent on a mission escorting a Han princess to the Hsiung-nu for marriage. His protest against this unpleasant and humiliating assignment having been ignored by the Han court, he surrendered to the Hsiung-nu out of vengeance and advised them to make trouble with the Han.

3. *IWSM*, 50:32a–b.

4. *IWSM*, 55:7.

5. *IWSM*, 55:12b.

6. *IWSM*, 51:21a–b.

7. *IWSM*, 54:3.

8. *IWSM*, 53:4b. This is my own translation after reference to Knight Biggerstaff, "The Change in the Attitude of the Chinese Government toward the Sending of Diplomatic Representatives, 1860–1880," Ph.D. thesis (Harvard, 1934), App. 16.

9. *IWSM*, 53:5.

10. *IWSM*, 55:27a–b.

11. *IWSM*, 54:17b–18b.

12. *IWSM*, 52:19b–20.

13. *IWSM*, 56:11a–b.

14. Pelcovits, *Old China Hands*, p. 36.

15. *Ibid.*, p. 38.

16. *Ibid.*, p. 68.

17. *Ibid.*

18. *Ibid.*, p. 42.

19. *Ibid.*, p. 48.

20. *Ibid.*, p. 58.

21. Mary Wright, p. 277.

22. *IWSM*, 51:27a–b.

23. *USFR* (1868), I, 494.

24. *Ibid.*

25. Pelcovits, p. 53.

26. *Ibid.*, p. 71.

27. For details of the Burlingame mission, see Frederick W. Williams, *Anson Burlingame and the First Chinese Mission to Foreign Powers* (New York, 1912); Knight Biggerstaff, "The Official Chinese Attitude toward the Burlingame Mission," *American Historical Review*, 41.4:682–702 (July 1936); "A Translation of Anson Burlingame's Instructions from the Chinese Foreign Office," *Far Eastern Quarterly*, 1.3:277–279 (May 1942). For a Chinese version of the mission, see Chih-kang, *Ch'u-shih t'ai-Hsi chi* (The first embassy to the West; 1890) 4 *chuan*.

28. For details see Alcock's report on the negotiations of the Convention in *China Correspondence*, 1870, No. 1; Pelcovits, pp. 32–97; Mary Wright, pp. 251–295.

29. Wu Ju-lun, *T'ung-ch'eng Wu-hsien-sheng jih-chi* (The diary of Mr. Wu of Tung-ch'eng; 1928), *chüan* 6, "Current Politics," p. 6b.

30. Ting Pao-chen, *Ting-wen-ch'eng-kung tsou-kao* (Memorials of Ting Pao-chen; 1896), 4:19b.

31. For details, see Knight Biggerstaff, "The Ch'ung-hou Mission to France, 1870–71," *Nankai Social and Economic Quarterly*, 8.3:633–647 (October 1935); T. E. LaFargue, *China's First Hundred* (Pullman, Washington, 1942); Stanley Wright, *Hart*, pp. 399–401.

32. *IWSM*, 79:7b–8b.

33. *IWSM*, 79:47b–49b. In fact, Japan did turn down an offer from Harry Parkes, British minister in Tokyo, to introduce her to China for treaty negotiations, because of national honor and her historical relations with China. See Tabohashi Kiyoshi, "Ni Shi shin kankei no seiritsu," (The establishment of new relations between Japan and China), *Shigaku zasshi* (Historical Review), 44.2:30 (Feb. 1933).

34. *IWSM*, 80:10b–11b.

35. *IWSM*, 98:19b.

36. *IWSM*, 98:20.

37. Li Hung-chang, *Ch'üan-chi*, Series I, "Memorials," 24:27a–b; *IWSM*, 99:33b.

38. Li Hung-chang, *Ch'üan-chi*, III, "Letters to the Tsungli Yamen," 2:58a–b.

39. *IWSM*, 99:48b–49.

40. A free translation of this memorial appears in *USFR* (1875), 1:379–380.

41. *IWSM*, 100:2a–b; 9b–10b.

42. Tso Hsi-chiu, ed., *Hai-fang yao-lan* (Essential writings on maritime defense; 1884), 1:22.

43. *WCSL*, 1:8b–10b.

44. Ko Shih-chün, 104:14ff; *chüan* 105; 106:1–19.

45. Hsüeh Fu-ch'eng, *Yung-an ch'üan-chi* (Complete works of Hsüeh Fu-ch'eng; Shanghai, 1897), Series I, "Literary works," 1:16b.

46. *Ibid.*, 1:12b–13.

47. *THHL*, 3:15.

48. *THHL*, 8:9b, 3:15b, 4:7a–b.

49. China: *Dispatches*, Vol. 38, Doc. 78, Benjamin P. Avery to Hamilton Fish, July 16, 1875.

50. These are the words of Harry Parkes, British minister in Japan; see S. T. Wang, *The Margary Affair and the Chefoo Agreement* (Oxford, 1940), p. 22.

51. *THHL*, 2:16.

52. *China Correspondence* (1876–84), China, No. 1, p. 73; *WSCL*, 3:15b.

53. *China Correspondence* (1876–84), No. 1, p. 98.

54. Li Hung-chang, *Ch'üan-chi*, III, 5:35b–36.

55. *Ibid.*, 5:36b.

56. *Ibid.*, 5:31b; 6:14b.

57. *Ibid.*, 5:36b.

58. *Ibid.*, 5:42b.

59. *Ibid.*, 6:14b.

60. *Ibid.*, 6:2.

61. *Ibid.*, 6:11b.

62. *China Correspondence*, No. 3 (1877), pp. 64–67; *WCSL*, 7:13b–18.

63. Li Hung-chang, *Ch'üan-chi*, III, 6:27b.

CHAPTER 12. LEGATIONS ABROAD AS PERMANENT INSTITUTIONS.

1. Kuo Sung-t'ao, *Yü-ch'ih lao-jen tzu-hsü* (Autobiography of Kuo Sung-t'ao; 1893), p. 8.
2. *Ibid.*, p. 8b.
3. *Ibid.*, p. 10b.
4. Kuo Sung-t'ao, *Yang-chih shu-wu ch'üan-chi* (Complete works of the Knowledge-cultivating Study), Series I, "Memorials," 12:7–9.
5. Henri Cordier, *Histoire des relations*, II, 133.
6. Li Hung-chang, *Ch'üan-chi*, Series II, "Letters to Friends and Colleagues," 17:15b.
7. Kuo Sung-t'ao, *Shih-Hsi chi-ch'eng* (A record of my mission to the West), in *Hsiao-fang-hu-chai yü-ti ts'ung-ch'ao* (A collection of geographical writings in the Hsiao-fang-hu-chai), Series 11, pp. 153, 158.
8. Hsü Ching-ch'eng, *Hsü-wen-su-kung wai-chi* (Collected works of Hsü Ching-ch'eng), Series II, "Letters," 1:3a–b.
9. Kuo Sung-t'ao, *Yü-ch'ih*, p. 23b.
10. Li Hung-chang, *Ch'üan-chi*, II, 15:25a–b. Li to Kuo, August 31, 1875.
11. *Ibid.*
12. Cordier, *Histoire des relations*, p. 111.
13. Kuo Sung-t'ao, *Yang-chih*, Series I, "Memorials," 12:1–2b.
14. *Ibid.*, 12:2b–3.
15. *CSL*, 28:10.
16. Chin Liang, *Chin-shih jen-wu chih* (Men of modern times; 1934), p. 129.
17. Wang K'ai-yün, *Hsiang-i-lou jih-chi* (Diary of the Hsiang-i Chamber; 1927), 5:6.
18. *Ibid.*
19. Kuo Sung-t'ao *Yang-chih*, I, 12:7–9.
20. *Ibid.*, 12:11b.
21. *Ibid.*, 12:10.
22. *China Correspondence*, No. 3 (1877), p. 80.
23. Quoted in Yü Ch'ang-ho, "Kuo Sung-t'ao yü Chung-kuo wai-chiao" (Kuo Sung-t'ao and Chinese diplomacy), *I-ching*, No. 31 (1937), p. 23.
24. Cordier, *Histoire des relations*, p. 112.
25. *WCSL*, 7:31b–32. My translation, after reference to that in *China Correspondence*, No. 3 (1877), p. 91.
26. *WCSL*, 9:22b.
27. *WCSL*, 9:23–24.
28. *WCSL*, 9:26b–27b; *THHL*, 15:11b.
29. China: *Dispatches*, Vol. 47, Doc. 420, George Seward to Williams M. Evarts, March 13, 1878.
30. The general information on the events in this paragraph may also be found in *CSL*, 21:13, and Knight Biggerstaff, "The Establishment of Permanent Chinese Diplomatic Missions abroad," *CSPSR*, 20.1:32–35 (April 1936).
31. The information in this paragraph may be found in *CSL*, 38:16b, 44:3; Biggerstaff, "Permanent Missions," p. 35; Cordier, *Histoire des relations*, p. 113; *WCSL*, 13:28b. For dates of the establishment of the legations see Ch'en T'i-ch'iang, p. 348.
32. *USFR* (1866), 1:487.

33. Demetrius C. Boulger, *The Life of Sir Halliday Macartney* (London, 1908), p. 282.

34. *Reports of Sixth Annual Conference* (Association for the Reform and Codification of the Law of Nations, Brussels, 1878), Preface; Cordier, *Histoire des relations*, p. 133.

35. Kuo Sung-t'ao, *Yü-ch'ih*, p. 31.

36. Chang Te-i, "Sui-shih jih-chi" (Diary of an attaché), in *Hsiao-fang-hu-chai yü-ti ts'ung-ch'ao*, Series 11, 3:265–266.

37. Liu Hsi-hung, "Ying-yao jih-chi" (Diary of Liu Hsi-hung), in *Hsiao-fang-hu-chai*, Series 11, p. 207b.

38. *Ibid.*, 11:191.

39. Kuo Sung-t'ao, *Yang-chih*, II, 13:30.

40. Li Hung-chang, *Ch'üan-chi*, II, 17:29.

41. *Ibid.*, 17:36.

42. Yü Ch'ang-ho, p. 23.

43. Kuo Sung-t'ao, *Shih-Hsi chi-ch'eng*, 11:153.

44. *WCSL*, 12:29; Chang P'ei-lun, *Chien-yü chi* (Collection of Chang P'ei-lun; 1918), 1:28a–b.

45. Li Hung-chang, *Ch'üan-chi*, II, 17:15b.

46. *Ibid.*, 17:29, 18:5b.

47. Tseng Chi-tse, Series IV, "Diary," 1:5b.

48. Taken, with minor changes, from Teng and Fairbank, *China's Response*, p. 106.

49. Li Hung-chang, *Ch'üan-chi*, I, 72:26.

50. *THHL*, 12:5a–b; for a free English translation see *USFR* (1887), pp. 85–86.

51. Hsüeh Fu-ch'eng, *Ch'u-shih kung-tu* (Official correspondence of envoys; 1897), 1:2b.

52. Chang Te-i, Series 11, 3:210: Kuo's mission consisted of a third councillor, three third-class interpreters, an English secretary, two attachés, an attaché-interpreter, five military attachés, an accountant, and a seal officer. Cordier, *Histoire des relations*, pp. 134–135: Tseng's mission consisted of two secretaries, three interpreters, seven attachés, four military attachés, and three others.

53. Ch'en Wen-chin, "Ch'ing-chi ch'u-shih ku-kuo shih-ling ching-fei, 1875–1911," ("The Expenditures of the Chinese Legations in Foreign Countries at the End of the Tsing Dynasty"), *Chung-kuo chin-tai ching-chi-shih yen-chiu chi-k'an* ("Studies in Modern Economic History of China"), 1.2:277 (May 1933).

54. *Ibid.*, pp. 278, 280.

55. Liu Chin-tsao, ed., *Huang-ch'ao hsü-wen-hsien t'ung-k'ao* (Supplementary encyclopedia of the imperial Ch'ing dynasty; 1905), 309:31b.

56. Ch'en T'i-ch'iang, p. 283.

57. Wang T'ing-hsi and Wang Shu-min, 19:6b.

58. Liu Chin-tsao, 309:27a–b.

59. Pei-yang yang-wu chü, ed., *Yüeh-chang ch'eng-an hui-lan* (A comprehensive guide to treaties, regulations, and precedents), Part II, 2:8b–9.

60. Liu Chin-tsao, 309:27a–b.

61. *Ibid.*, 309:33a–b

62. *Ibid.*, 309:33b–34.

63. Wang T'ing-hsi and Wang Shu-min, Part II, 6:4b–5.

64. Ch'en T'i-ch'iang, pp. 181–182.

65. Article 5 of the twelve regulations.
66. *THHL*, 12:21b–22.
67. *Yüeh-chang ch'eng-an*, 2:18–25b.
68. Ch'en T'i-ch'iang, p. 180.
69. *Ibid.*, p. 181.
70. Wang T'ing-hsi and Wang Shu-min, 19:6b.
71. Ch'en Wen-chin, p. 280.
72. *Ibid.*, p. 281.
73. *Ibid.*, pp. 287, 281.
74. *Ibid.*, p. 291.
75. *Ibid.*, p. 283.
76. *Ibid.*, p. 284; *THHL*, 11:8b–9.
77. Ch'en T'i-ch'iang, p. 321.
78. *Ch'in-ting Ta-Ch'ing hui-tien* (Collected statutes of the Great Ch'ing empire; 1899), 100:16b–17.
79. Liu Chin-tsao, 309:30a–b.
80. Hsü Ching-ch'eng, *Hsü-wen-su-kung i-kao* (Manuscripts of Hsü Ching-ch'eng, posthumous publication; n.p., n.d.).
81. Ch'en Chih, Part I, 1:4, 2:10a–b.

CHAPTER 13. EPILOGUE: THE IMPERIAL CHINESE TRADITION
IN THE MODERN WORLD.

1. Mary Wright, p. 264.
2. Edgar C. Tang, "The Censorial Institution in China, 1644–1911," Ph.D. thesis (Harvard, 1932), pp. 35, 69–72.
3. *Ibid.*, pp. 82–83.
4. Ch'en T'i-ch'iang, p. 26.
5. Wang Chih-ch'un, 19:6.
6. Wang K'ai-yün, 6:18.
7. *Ibid.*, 6:18.
8. Tseng Chi-tse, Series IV, "Diary," 1:15b.
9. Hu Sheng, pp. 61–63.
10. Quoted in Ch'en Kung-lu, p. 255.
11. Li Hung-chang, *Ch'üan-chi*, II, 16:2.
12. *Ibid.*, III, 8:6b.
13. Ch'en Kung-lu, pp. 252–253.
14. *THHL*, 1:7; Martin, *Cycle*, p. 379.
15. Hu Sheng, p. 63.
16. Li Hung-chang, *Ch'üan-chi*, II, 16:30a–b; I, 24:2b.
17. *San-hsing-shih shu-tu* (Correspondence of the three envoys; Shanghai, 1910), 1:8, 1:52.
18. Kuo Sung-t'ao, *Yang-chih*, I, 12:42.
19. *Ibid.*, 12:44a–b; 12:46.
20. Fan Wen-lan, p. 257.
21. Li Hung-chang, *Ch'üan-chi*, II, 17:13.
22. Liang Ch'i-ch'ao, "Chung-kuo ssu-shih-nien ta-shih-chi" (Major events in China during the last forty years), in *Yin-ping-shih ho-chih* (Collected works of the Ice-drinker's Study), *Chuan-chi* (Monographs), No. 3, p. 3.
23. *CSL*, T'ung-chih period, 204:30b.

24. Li Hung-chang, *Ch'üan-chi*, III, 4:24b.

25. *Reports of Sixth Annual Conference, 1878* (Association for the Reform and Codification of the Law of Nations), Preface.

26. *Ibid.*, p. 40.

27. Tseng chi-tse, Series IV, "Diary," 2:22b–23.

28. Fairbank, "Synarchy under the Treaties," p. 224.

Index

Adkin, Thomas, 105
Alcock, Sir Rutherford, 141, 156, 166, 167, 170
Alcock Convention of 1869, 141, 144, 170, 175
Amane, Nishi, 130
Amherst, Lord, 17
Amur, 30
Anglo-Chinese College, in Malacca, 124
Annam, 3, 4
Arrow War, The, 15, 21, 22, 36, 80, 84
Association for the Reform and Codification of the Law of Nations, 206, 207
Avery, Benjamin P., 145, 176
Ayuki, 15

Balluzeck, Colonel, 106, 137
Barbarians, 7, 8–9, 11, 15
Baring, T., 97
Bismarck, Otto von, 169
Bluntschli, Johann Kaspar, 138
Board of Ceremonies, 4, 5, 13, 14, 58, 183, 184
Board of Civil Office, 10
Book of Changes, 161
"Book of Chou," 8
Book of History, 7
Book of Odes, 6, 8
"Book of Yu," 7
Bourboulon, M. de, 18, 26, 106
Bowra, E. C., 156
Bowring, Sir John, 17, 21, 22, 26, 31, 33, 35
"Brief exposition of new ideas, A," 156
Brierly, J. L., 122
Bright, John, 96
British East India Company, 17
Brown, 171
Browne, Col. H. A., 176
Bruce, Frederick, 67, 92, 153; as minister, 93, 106, 156; repulse at Taku and its consequences, 94, 95, 97, 98, 99; and Martin, 137
Burlingame, Anson: as minister, 106, 127, 153–154; and Martin's translation, 127, 128, 136; as Chinese ambassador to the West, 168–169, 185; death, 169; mission analyzed, 170–172
Burma, 3, 4, 9, 150
Butzow, 178
Bynkershoek, 130

California, Chinese in, 137
Cambodia, 9
Campbell, James D., 143
"Canon of Shun," 7
Canton, 15, 17, 21, 23, 25, 26, 33, 35, 37, 47, 49, 55, 67, 68, 77, 78, 79, 81, 85, 86, 91, 108, 114, 123, 124, 140, 142
Canton Viceroy System, 16, 48, 68, 80
Cass, Lewis, 28
Censorate, The, 201
Champs, E. de, 156
Chang, Ch'ien, 9, 149
Chang, Chin-wen, 90
Chang, Hung, 150
Chang, I, 12
Chang, P'ei-lun, 188
Chang, Ssu-kuei, 134, 135, 186
Chang, Te-yi, 156
Changchow, 72
Changsha, 182
Chapdelaine, Abbé Auguste, 21
Chefoo, 178
Chefoo Convention, 184
Chen-tsung, Emperor of Sung, 11
Ch'en, Ch'i-chang, 191, 192
Ch'en, Chih-ho, 180
Ch'en, Ch'in, 134
Ch'en Lan-pin, 185
Ch'en, Su, 58
Cheng, Prince, 60, 61, 62, 63, 65, 66
Cheng, Ho, 9
Chi-mi, 142
Ch'i-shan, 15, 32, 80
Ch'i-ying: career of, 12, 15, 16, 37, 38, 53; powers granted to, 31–34; and Elgin, 37–40, 77, 90; Memorial of 1844, 41; arrest and death, 42, 43, 44, 65, 80, 89
Chia-ch'ing, 14
Ch'iang, 7
Chiang, Tun-fu, 160
Ch'ien, Pao-ching, 59, 63
Ch'ien-lung, Emperor, 13, 17, 113
Chih-kang, 168, 171, 203
Chin, An-ch'ing, 80
Ch'in-ch'ai ta-ch'en, 36
Ch'in unification of China, 6, 13, 149
China Merchant Steam Navigation Company, 193, 194
Chinese Educational Mission, 185
Chinese legations: establishment of, 185–

186, 199ff., 200; organization and finance, 190ff., 193–196; status of envoys, 191–192; relations with Tsungli Yamen, 193; functions of, 196–197; record of, 198

Ching-ch'ung-fu, 106

Ching-t'ien fa-tsu, 112

Ch'ing, 4, 7, 12, 13, 14, 15, 112, 113, 139, 141, 144, 151, 170, 200, 201

Ch'ing-i, 200

Chou dynasty, 6, 12, 13

Chou-kuan, 149

Chou Te-tse, 23

Chou, Tsu-p'ei, 58–59

Chü-wai p'ang-kuan lun, 154

Ch'üan-chow, 139

Chu-ch'üan, 130

Chü-wai, 129

Ch'un, Prince, 176

Chung-hsing, Shu, 164

Ch'ung, 7

Ch'ung-hou, 101; and Martin's translation, 127; and foreign missions, 159, 166, 185, 194; and France, 171, 178; and Russia, 186

Ch'ung-lun, 31, 32, 34

Chung-li, 129

Cicero, 130

Clarendon, Lord of, 23, 24–25, 95, 167, 169

Cobden, 22

Cochrane, Baillie, 96, 98

Collected Statutes of the Great Ch'ing Empire, 5, 14

Commission of Defence, 65

Commissioner of Guests, 13

Common Residence for Envoys, 13

Common Residence for Tributary Envoys, 13

Compulsory diplomatic relations, 109–111

Confucius, 6, 8, 10, 149

Convention of Peking, 104, 151, 153, 180

Cordier, Henri, on Kuo Sung-t'ao, 181

"Council of Prince," 65–66

Counsels of the Great Yü, 7

Court of Colonial Affairs, 14

Court of Sacrificial Worship, 13

Court of State Ceremonial, 13, 14

Crimean War, 21, 26

Culbertson, Dr., 126

Das moderne Völkerrecht, 138

De Republica, 130

Denmark, 132

Dent and Beale Company, 84

Derby, Lord, 184

Diary of the Hsiang-i-lou, 183

Diplomacy, as profession, 149–150, 152

Directors of State Ceremonies and Emissary Affairs, 13

Eastern Turkestan, 9

Elements of International Law, 126, 127, 153

Elgin, Lord, 180, 204; early career of, 22, 23, 24–25; and Tientsin negotiations, 18, 31, 33, 35, 46–48, 50, 68, 70, 76, 77–79, 82, 152–153; and Putiatin, 30; and Ch'i-ying, 38, 44–45; attitude toward British traders, 47, 84, 85; as imperial commissioner, 56, 81; and Kuei-liang, 77, 81–82, 95, 101; attitude toward Chinese, 83–85, 88; return to and reception in England, 82, 85–88, 95–97; second mission to China, 97, 98–102, 104–106, 110

Eliot, Charles, 13

Elliot, Captain, 15

Extraterritoriality, beginning of, 139

Fan, Wen-lan, 110

Fang, Chün-shih, 134

Feng, Kuei-fen, 142

Feng-i, 164

Flint, James, 17, 18

Foreign office, absence of, 13

Formosa Incident, 152, 172, 173, 176, 199

Foulke, R. R., 110

Fukien, 181

Gladstone, 22

Gorchakov, Prince, 29

Grand Council, 15, 23, 113

Grant, Sir Hope, 99, 103, 104

Great Learnnig, The, 6

Gros, Baron, 22, 23, 27, 49, 55, 69, 99, 105

Grotius, 130

Guide Diplomatique, 138

Gutzloff, Dr., 52

Hai-fang t'iao-i, 174

Hai-kuang Temple, 52

Hai-kuo t'u-chih, 123

Han, 6, 8, 11, 12, 149, 164

Hangchow, 93

Hanlin Academy, 13, 57, 64, 115, 128, 150, 186, 188, 203

Hart, Robert, 126, 128, 152–156, 168, 170, 177, 178, 194, 199, 200

Hayes, President, 185

Heng-ch'i, 101
Heng-fu, viceroy of Chihli, 100
Herbert, Sidney, 95, 96
Hideyoshi, invasion of Korea by, 4
Hillier, W. C., 184
History of Han, 7
Ho, Chin-shou, 188
Ho, Hsiu, on barbarians, 9
Ho, Ju-chang, 186
Ho, Kuei-ch'ing, viceroy of Nanking, 23, 24, 62, 71, 72–75, 79, 80–81, 98, 100, 114, 116, 117
Hongkong, 21, 23, 25, 74, 170
Hope, Admiral, 95
Hoppo, 15, 80
Hounds of Leu [Lu], 8
House of Commons, 22
House of Lords, 22
Howqua, 71, 73, 124
Hsiao-hsing-jen, 13, 149
Hsiao, Wang-chih, 9
Hsien-feng, Emperor, 38, 39, 44, 71–72, 79, 98, 102, 108, 112–114, 142
Hsien-liang Monastery, 106
Hsin-i lüeh-lun, 156
Hsing-yao chih-chang, 138
Hsiung-nu, 7, 9, 11
Hsü, Ch'ien-shen, 177, 184, 186
Hsü, Ching-ch'eng, 197
Hsü, P'eng-shou, 58
Hsüan-te, 10
Hsüeh, Fu-ch'eng, 121, 175, 198
Hsüeh, Huan, 74, 76, 100
Hsün-fang ch'u, 65
Hu, Sheng, 110
Hua-sha-na: and Elgin, 33–34, 50–55, 68; and Ch'i-ying, 41, 43; and Tientsin negotiations, 64, 68, 70, 117, 152–153; and Shanghai Tariff Conference, 71, 73
Hua-ta-erh. *See* Vattel
Huang, Hui-ho, 193
Huang, Tsung-han, 23, 81, 114
Hui, Prince (Mien-yü), 38, 43, 60, 61, 63, 65, 66, 74, 89
Hui-t'ung-kuan, 13, 106
Hui-t'ung ssu-i kuan, 13
Hung-lu ssu, 14
Huns, 7, 11, 149
Hunter, William C., 124

I, Prince, 60, 65, 66, 101, 102, 105–106
I-i chih-i, 11, 115
I-kuan lin-ch'en, 13
I-shan, 63
I-wu chi-mi, 57
Ignatiev, General Nikolai, 103, 104, 105

Ili, 80, 177, 186, 196
Ilipoo, 32, 140
Imbert, 171
Imperial University, in Peking, 136
Indoscythians, in Central Asia, 9
Industrial Revolution, 5, 17
International Law, 121, 122, 138ff., 145; Martin and, 123, 125, 126–131, 134
Introduction to the Study of International Law, 138

Jardine, Matheson and Company, 84
Java, 9
Jen, 111
Jesuit fathers, 16, 151
Johnson, Andrew, 169
Jui-lin, 166
Jungars, the, 151

K'an-feng chuan-to, 165
K'ang-hsi, Emperor, 14, 15, 112, 113, 140
K'ao-cheng hsüeh, 116
Kashgar, 103
Kiakhta, Treaty of, 14, 17, 139
Klecskowsky, M., 138
Ko-kuo lü-li, 123
Korea, 3, 4
Kovolevsky, Major General, 29
Kowtow, 4, 5, 11, 14, 17, 112, 139, 143, 208
Kuan-wen, 160, 166
Kuang-hsü, 208
Kung-fa chien-chang, 138
Kung-fa pien-lan, 138
Kuei-liang: and Tientsin negotiations, 33–35, 38, 39–41, 42–44, 64, 67–70, 114–115, 117; and Elgin, 50–55, 100–101, 152–153; and Ch'ien Pao-ching, 56–60; and Shanghai conference, 71–75, 76–79; analyzed as diplomat, 88–91, and arrival of Bruce, 92–94, 95
Kuo Sung-t'ao: and Su-shun, 115; and English mission, 177, 178, 181–185, 187, 196; career of, 180–185, 186, 188–190, 201–202, 204, 206; and Liu, 187, 188
Kung, Prince, 173, 194, 205; and Ch'i-ying, 38–39, 43–44; warlike tendencies of, 38–39, 58, 60, 64–65; and Kuei-liang, 89; and negotiations with Elgin, 102–104, 114; and legations, 106, 107–108; and Martin's translation, 125, 128, 132, 134; and missions abroad, 153, 156, 158
Kung, Chao-yuan, 194
Kuo-chi-fa, 129

Kyorin, 4

Law, Chinese idea of, 139
Laws and Regulations of All Nations, 134
Lay, George T., 40, 52
Lay, Horatio: and Ch'i-ying, 40–43; and resident-minister issue, 48–49, 107–108, 110; and Tientsin negotiations, 50–55, 67; and Shanghai conference, 76, 78
Leibnitz, 130
Li, 111, 112, 113, 116, 201
Li-fan-yüan, 14, 30, 103, 115, 124
Li-i, 129
Li, Ch'ang-hua, 134
Li, Feng-pao, 197
Li, Han-chang, 182
Li, Hsien, 10
Li, Hung-chang: role in government, 107, 152, 178–179, 181–182, 194, 202–204, 205, 208; feeling toward West, 121, 159, 164–165, 178; and treaties, 142, 172; and Japan, 172, 173–174, 175
Li, K'ai-fang, 57
Li, Prince, 176
Li, Tsung-hsi, 174
Liang Dynasty, 200
Liang, Duke of, 106
Liao, 11, 12
Lin, Feng-hsiang, 57
Lin, Tse-hsü, 15, 80, 123–125
Liu, Ching, 11
Liu-ch'iu, 4
Liu, Hsi-hung, 184, 185, 186, 192, 202
Liu, K'un-i, 159
Lowrie, Walter, 126, 133

Ma Hsin-i, 159, 165–166
Macao, 14, 17
Macartney, Halliday, 143, 173, 184, 187
Macartney, Lord, 5, 17
Magna Carta, 111
Mallet, Louis, 167
Malmesbury, Foreign Secretary, 46, 77, 94
Man, 7
Manchu, 30, 54, 55, 60, 61, 64, 65, 66, 104, 116, 117, 118, 139, 140, 151, 164, 166, 168, 205
Mandate of Heaven, 6
Manuel des lois de la guerre, Le, 138
Mao, Hung-t'u, 134
Marcy, W. L., 27, 28
Margary affair, the, 152, 176, 177, 179
Margary, Augustus R., 176, 182
Martens, George Friedrich de, 138
Martin, W. A. P., 123, 126–128, 129–131,

170, 175; reactions to his translation, 132–138
McCormick Seminary, 126
McLane, Robert M., 17, 31, 33, 35
Meiji, 113
Meritens, Baron de, 106
Middle Kingdom, 17, 151, 210
Ming, 4, 10, 13, 16, 106, 117, 139, 200, 204
Ming, Emperor, 9
Ming-shan, 72, 73
Modern Text School of classical learning, 9
Moncrieff Grove Company, 84
Mongolia, 103
Montaubon, General de, 99
Montesquieu, 130
Morse, H. B., 34, 66
Most-favored-nation treatment, Chinese idea of, 140
Mu-chang-a, 15
Muraviev, Governor, 30, 63

Nanking, 33, 39, 51, 62, 80, 93
Nanking, Treaty of, 15, 16, 17, 24, 39, 108, 121, 139, 140, 142
Nan-yang, 194
Napier, Lord, 27, 29
Napoleon III, 26, 27, 171
Napoleonic Wars, 5, 17
Nationalism, lack of, 13, 144, 145
Natural Law, 129
Neale, Colonel, 106
Neo-Confucianism, 115–116, 118
Nerchinsk, Treaty of, 14
Netherlands, 5
Newcastle, Duke of, 22
Newchwang, 69
Nicholaivich, Grand Duke Constantin, 29, 103
Ningpo, 126, 140
North China Herald, 84, 86, 87, 138
Northern Sung, 183
Novion, 171

"Observations by an outsider," 154
Office for the Transmission of Government Correspondence, 193
Officials of Chou, 149
Old China Hands, 110, 143, 166, 167
Oliphant, Lawrence, 23
Opium War, 13, 15, 16, 21, 36, 140
Ottoman Empire, 139

Pan, Ch'ao, 9
Pan, Ku, 7
Palmerston, 22, 96–97

P'an, Shih-ch'eng, 71
Papacy, 5
Paris, Treaty of, 3, 122
Parker, Peter, 27, 123–124
Parkes, Harry, 21, 22, 102, 105, 110, 143; and Elgin, 84, 100–101; and inspection trip, 100, 101
Peace Party, nonexistence of in 1858, 65
Peace Treaty of Ten Thousand Years, 142
Pearl River, 21
Pechili, Gulf of, 24
Peiho, 23, 24, 30, 94, 100
Pei-t'ang, 11, 94, 99, 100, 180
Pei-yang, 194
Peking, 4, 16, 17, 18, 24, 26, 27, 29, 30, 31, 33, 47, 48, 49, 50, 51, 52, 54, 55, 56, 57, 58, 59, 64, 72, 76, 80, 81, 87, 92, 93, 94, 95, 96, 97, 100, 101, 105, 106, 107, 108, 109, 110, 112, 114, 118, 121, 124, 126, 140, 142, 152, 163, 171, 174, 177, 180, 182, 185, 190, 191, 196, 209, 210
Peng, Yün-chang, 38
Peter the Great, 17
Pettlin, Ivashko, 16
Pin-ch'un, 156, 164, 166, 174, 194
P'ing t'ien-hsia, 6
Pires, Thome, 16
Portugal, 5, 16
Pottinger, Sir Henry, 12, 31, 40
Protective tariff, lack of the idea of, 140
Protests from the Chiao-pin Studio, 142
Prussia, 132
Putiatin, Admiral, 22, 24, 29–30, 49, 50, 103; and Elgin, 32, 42, 55, 67; and Lay, 41–42, 53–54

Reed, William B., 51, 127, 151, 172; as U.S. envoy in 1858, 22, 28–29; and Elgin and English, 32–33, 40, 41–42, 49, 53–54, 67, 78–79, 87 88; and resident-minister issue, 49; and Tientsin, 70
Rehfues, von, 133
Residence for Barbarian Envoys, 13
Resident-minister issue, the, 21; debate of June 23, 1858 on, 60–64; in the Treaty of Tientsin, 69; the consequence of the Taku repulse on, 95; Russell on, 97; barriers to, 111–112, 115–116; the affect of alien rule on, 117
Rinsho, Mitsukuri, 129
Roman Catholic School, in Penang, 124
Romance of Three Kingdoms, 58
Russell, Lord, 95, 97, 99, 105
Russia, Muscovite Empire of, 3, 5, 14, 15, 16

Russian religious mission in Peking, 14, 56, 106, 112

Sadae, 4
Savoy, 99
Scylla, 89
Scythians, 9
Sebastopol, 106
Secret Plan of 1858, 71–75, 113
Seng-ko-lin-ch'in, Prince, 39, 43, 57, 66, 67, 89, 92, 102, 180
Sepoy Mutiny, 23
Seward, Secretary of State, 136, 137
Seward, George, 127, 185
Shan-yüan, 11
Shang, Yang, 201
Shanghai Tariff Conference, 18, 70, 71, 75–76, 82, 83
Shannon, H.M.S., 23
Shen, Pao-chen, 165, 173, 175
Shih-Hsi chi-ch'eng, 188
Shih Mien lu, 150
Shih, Tsan-ch'ing, 102
Siam, 3, 4, 9
Sick Man of the East, 108
Sino-Japanese Treaty of 1871, 172–173
Son of Heaven, 4, 6, 8, 14, 74, 151, 206, 208
Southern Sung (1127–1280), 115, 183, 200, 204
Sponsio, 35
Spring and Autumn Annals, 10
Spring and Autumn Period, 149
Ssu-i-kuan, 13
Stanley, Lord, 166
Su, Ch'in, 12
Su, Prince of, 106
Su, Shih, 7, 10
Su-shun, 115
Su, Wu, 149
Summer Palace, burning of, 144
Sun, Chia-ku, 168, 171, 203
Sung, 7, 10, 11, 12, 139, 140, 200
Synarchy, 144

Ta-Ch'ing hui-tien, 111, 197
Ta-Ch'ing lü-li, 132
Ta-hsing-jen, 13, 149
Ta-hung-lu, 13
Ta-t'ung, 6
Taipings, 44, 55, 57, 62, 69, 78, 117, 152, 162, 180
Taku Forts, 24, 33, 51, 65, 67, 99, 113, 180
Taku Repulse, the, 94–95

T'an, T'ing-hsiang, 31, 32, 33, 36, 38, 50–51, 64, 67, 87, 116, 117, 151, 172
T'ang, 6, 10, 139, 200
Tartars, 10
Tatnall, Commodore, 94
Te-ming. *See* Chang, Te-yi
Teng, T'ing-tseng, 13
Tengchow, 69
Territorial jurisdiction, concept of lacking, 139–140
Thiers, 171
Ti, 7
T'i-chih, 51, 91, 109, 111, 113, 156, 199
Tien-k'o, 13
Tientsin, 17, 18, 24, 37, 43, 45, 46, 51, 52, 53, 74, 92, 93, 105, 107, 113, 114
Tientsin Massacre, 171, 172, 203
Tientsin, Treaty of, 18, 76, 82, 103, 108, 121, 152; major issues in, 46; signing and provisions of, 68–70, 71, 89, 99; views of, 94, 109–110; revision of, 141, 163
Ting, Jih-ch'ang, 174, 175
Treaty: Chinese idea of, 142; negotiations for, 35, 36. *See also* under names of treaties
Tributary relations, 4, 8, 112
Trojans, 132
Tsar, the, 29, 30, 169
Ts'en, Yü-ying, 177, 182
Tseng, Kuo-fan, 117, 152, 165, 180, 203
Tseng, Marquis, Chi-tse, 142, 143–144, 189–190, 196, 198, 202, 207, 209
Tso, Tsung-t'ang, 152, 160, 165, 173
Tsungli Yamen, 114, 121, 194, 201; establishment of, 80, 107–108; and translation of international law, 125, 127–128; actions of, 133, 155, 163, 168, 171, 176, 190; policies of, 143–144, 172, 192, 193; interest in missions abroad, 160–162
T'u-li-shen, 15
Tuan, Ch'eng-shih, 72
Tuan, Ching-chuan, 58
Tuan-hua, imperial clansman, 38
T'ung-chih, 144, 145, 169, 175, 208
Tung, Hsün, 128, 134, 135, 154
T'ung-wen kuan, 136, 138, 192, 205
Tungchow, 101, 102
Turgut khan, 15
Turkey, 3
Tzu-kung, 149
Tz'u-hsi, Empress Dowager, 182, 189, 204–205, 206

Ueno, Kagenori, 206

"Universal Commonwealth," 6
Universal empire, 208, 210
University of Indiana, 126

Vattel, 123, 124, 127
Verbiest, Ferdinandus, 50
Victoria, Queen of England, 169, 184

Wade, Thomas, 34, 152, 157, 170, 173, 199; and Ch'i-ying, 40–42; and Tientsin negotiations, 54–55, 67; memorandum of, 156–158, 158–160, 162; attitude toward Chinese, 170; and Margary Affair, 176–179; and mission of apology, 184, 200
Wan, Ch'ing-li, 63
Wan-kuo kung-fa, 129
Wan-kuo lü-li, 129
Wan-nien ho-yüeh, 142
Wang, An-shih, 201
Wang, K'ai-t'ai, 174
Wang, K'ai-yün, 183, 202
Wang, Mao-ying, 58, 63
Wang, Sung-sen, 193
Ward, John E., 100, 106, 126
Warring States period, 12, 13, 149
Wei, Yüan, 123
Wen-hsiang, 108, 127, 128, 168
Western Region, 9, 149
Westphalia, Treaty of, 3
Wheaton, Henry, 125, 126, 127, 129, 130, 153
Williams, S. W., 136–137
Wo-jen, 165
Woolsey, Theodore D., 138
Wu, Ch'ung-yao, 71
Wu, Emperor, 8, 200
Wu, Empress, 10, 11
Wu-erh-kun-t'ai, 31
Wu-sun tribe, 11

Xenophobia, Chinese, 115–116

Yanagihara, Sakimitsu, 172
Yang, 7
Yang, Ch'en, 192
Yang, Ju, 194
Yang, T'ing-hsi, 205
Yang-wu, 203, 204, 205, 206
Yangtze River, 6
Yeh, Ming-ch'en, 21, 23, 42, 50, 68, 80, 114, 142
Yellow River Valley, 6
Yen, Ching-ming, 202
Yen-kuan, 200

Yin, Ch'ao-yung, 57–58
Yin-han, opposition to treaty with Japan, 172
Yin, Keng-yün, 57, 61–64, 115
Yü-ch'ien, Grand Secretary, 23, 24, 50
Yüan, 13
Yüan, Shih-k'ai, 192
Yüan, Teh-hui, 124–125

Yüan-li, 129
Yung-cheng, Emperor, 112, 151
Yung Hung, 185
Yung-lo, 10
Yung Wing. *See* Yung Hung
Yunnan, 176, 177

Zayton, 139

BIBLIOGRAPHY

GLOSSARY

BIBLIOGRAPHY

Alcock, Sir Rutherford. "Chinese Statesmen and State Papers,"
Fraser's Magazine, 83:328-342, 503-514, 613-628
(New Series 3, 1871).

Allgood, G. China War 1860: Letters and Journal. London, 1901;
107 pp.

Anonymous. "The Life and Work of the Late Dr. W. A. P. Martin,"
The Chinese Recorder, 48.2:116-123 (Feb. 1917).

Asano Risaburo 浅野利三 . Bunkashikan kokusai shisō hattatsu
shi 文化史觀國際思想發達史 (A history of the
development of international ideas from the standpoint of
cultural history). 2nd ed.; Tokyo, 1928; 471 pp.

Baker, Elizabeth F. Henry Wheaton, 1775-1848. Philadelphia,
1937; 425 pp.

Banno Masataka 坂野正高 . "Ahen sensō go ni okeru saikeikoku
taigū no mondai" 阿片戰爭後に於ける 最惠國待
遇の問題 (The problem of the most-favored-nation
treatment after the Opium War); Tōyō bunka kenkyū 東洋文
化研究 , 6:19-41 (Oct. 1947).

------- "Gaikō kōshō ni okeru Shinmatsu kanjin no kōdō yōshiki--
1854 nen no jōyaku kaisei kōshō o chūshin to suru ichikōsatsu"
外交交渉に於ける 清末官人の行動樣式 --
一八五四年の條約改正交渉を中心とする
一考察 (Behaviors of Mandarins as diplomats late in
the Ch'ing dynasty--with special reference to treaty revision
negotiations in 1854); Kokusaihō gaikō zasshi 國際法外

交雑誌· (The journal of international law and diplomacy), 48.4:18-56 (Oct. 1949).

------- 'Sōrigamon setsuritsu no heikei" 總理衙門設立之背景 (Determining factors in the instituting of the Tsungli Yamen); Kokusaihō gaikō zasshi, 51.4:30-72 (Aug. 1952); ibid., 51.5:62-97 (Oct. 1952); ibid., 52.3:89-108 (June 1953).

------- "Tenshin jōyaku (1858-nen) chōin go ni okeru Shinkoku gaisei kikō no dōyō" 天津條約一八五八年調印後における為清國外政機構の動揺 (Institutional development in the Chinese conduct of foreign affairs after the signing of the Tientsin Treaties in 1858), Part I; Kokusaihō gaikō zasshi, 55.6:595-616 (Mar. 1957).

Bernard, Henri S.J. "Notes on the Introduction of the Natural Sciences into the Chinese Empire," The Yenching Journal of Social Studies, 3.2:220-241 (Aug. 1941).

Biggerstaff, Knight. "The Change in the Attitude of the Chinese Government toward the Sending of Diplomatic Representatives, 1860-1880." Ph.D. thesis (Harvard University, 1934).

------- "The T'ung-wen Kuan," CSPSR, 18.3:307-340 (Oct. 1934).

------- "The Ch'ung-hou Mission to France, 1870-71," Nankai Social and Economic Quarterly, 8.3:633-647 (Oct. 1935).

------- "The Establishment of Permanent Chinese Diplomatic Missions Abroad," CSPSR, 20.1:1-41 (Apr. 1936).

------- "The Official Chinese Attitude toward the Burlingame Mission," American Historical Review, 41.4:682-702 (July 1936).

------- "The First Chinese Mission of Investigation Sent to Europe," Pacific Historical Review, 6.4:307-320 (Dec. 1937).

------- "A Translation of Anson Burlingame's Instructions from the Chinese Foreign Office," Far Eastern Quarterly, 1.3:277-279

(May 1942).

Bland, J. O. P. and E. Backhouse. China under the Empress
    Dowager. London, 1910; 525 pp.

Boggs, Mary Edna. "William Alexander Parsons Martin, Missionary
    to China, 1850-1916." M. A. thesis (Presbyterian College
    of Christian Education, 1948); 62 pp. ≠ appendix, 64 pp.

Bonner-Smith, D. and E. W. R. Lumby, eds. The Second China War
    1856-1860 (Publications of the Navy Records Society, XCV).
    Greenwich, England, 1954; 413 pp.

Boulger, Demetrius C. The Life of Sir Halliday Macartney.
    London, 1908; 505 pp.

Bowring, Sir John. Autobiographical Recollections of Sir John
    Bowring. London: 1877, 401 pp.

BPP, see British Government Documents.

Brierly, J. L. The Law of Nations. Oxford, 1949; 306 pp.

British Government Documents

--- BPP: British Parliamentary Papers

    1857-1858, No. 60 (2322), Correspondence between Lord
        Elgin and the Chinese High Commissioner Yeh.

    1859, No. 33 (2571), Correspondence Relative to the Earl of
        Elgin's Special Missions to China and Japan, 1857-1859.

    1860, No. 68 (94), Correspondence Respecting Affairs in
        China.

    1860, No. 69 (2695), Convention between Her Majesty and
        the Emperor of the French Relative to Joint Captures in
        China.

    1860, No. 69 (2618), Correspondence Respecting Affairs in
        China.

1860, No. 69 (2587), Correspondence with Mr. Bruce, Her Majesty's Envoy Extraordinary and Minister Plenipotentiary in China.

1860, No. 69 (2606), Further Correspondence with Mr. Bruce.

1860, No. 69 (2641), Further Correspondence with Mr. Bruce.

1860, No. 69 (2677), Further Correspondence with Mr. Bruce.

1861, No. 66 (2754), Correspondence Respecting Affairs in China, 1859-60.

1861, No. 66 (2755), Treaties between Her Majesty and the Emperor of China; with Rules for Trade, and Tariff of Duties.

1861, No. 66 (2777), Further Correspondence Respecting Affairs in China (Expedition up the Yangtze Kiang).

1864, No. 63 (3345), Extract of a Despatch from Sir F. Bruce Respecting Maintenance of Treaty Rights in China.

1867-1868, No. 73 (3996), Memorials Addressed by Chambers of Commerce in China to the British Minister at Peking on the Subject of the Revision of the Treaty of Tientsin.

1868-1869, No. 64 (4097), Correspondence Respecting the Relations between Great Britain and China.

1870, No. 69 (c. 23), Despatch from Sir Rutherford Alcock Respecting a Supplementary Convention to the Treaty of Tientsin, signed by him, 23rd Oct. 1869.

1870, No. 69 (c. 59), Memorials Respecting the China Treaty Revision Convention.

--- China. Correspondence (Presented to both Houses of Parliament by command of Her Majesty). 7 vols.; London: Harrison and Sons, 1857-1884.

--- Hansard's Parliamentary Debates, Vols. 144-167 (1857-1862).

Britton, R.S. "Chinese Interstate Intercourse before 700 B.C.,"
The American Journal of International Law, 29:616-635
(1938).

Brown, Arthur J. "Rev. W.A.P. Martin, D.D., of China," The
Missionary Review of the World, 40.3:195-202 (Mar. 1917).

Buksgevden (Buxhöwden), Baron A. Russkii Kitai: Ocherki
diplomaticheskikh snoshenii Rossii s Kitaem--Pekinskii
dogovor 1860 g. (Russia's China: An account of the diplomatic
relations between Russia and China--the Treaty of Peking,
1860). Port Arthur, 1902; 239 pp.

Burns, Norma J. "W.A.P. Martin and the Westernization of China."
M.A. thesis (Indiana University, Mar. 1954).

Cady, John F. The Roots of French Imperialism in Eastern Asia.
Cornell University Press, 1954; 322 pp.

Chan, Y.W. "China's Anomalous Position in International Law,"
CSPSR, 7.4:182-198 (Oct. 1923).

Chang Chung-fu 張忠綏 . "Ya-p'ien-chan ch'ien Ch'ing-t'ing
pan-li wai-chiao chih chi-kuan yü shou-hsü" 鴉片戰前
清廷辦理外交之機關與手續 (The office and
procedure for dealing with diplomatic affairs of the Ch'ing
dynasty before the Opium War); Wai-chiao yüeh-pao 外交月
報(Foreign affairs; Peking), 2.2:1-7 (1933).

-------"Tzu Ya-p'ien chan-cheng chih Ying-Fa lien-chün ch'i-chung
Ch'ing-t'ing pan-li wai-chiao chih chi-kuan yü shou-hsü" 自
鴉片戰爭至英法聯軍期中清廷辦理外交
之機關與手續 (The office and procedure
for dealing with diplomatic affairs of the Ch'ing dynasty during
the period between the first and second Anglo- Chinese wars);

v

Wai-chiao yüeh-pao, 2.5:43-51 (1933).

-------"Tsung-li ko-kuo shih-wu ya-men chih yüan-ch'i" 總理各國事務衙門之緣起 (The origin of the Tsungli Yamen); Wai-chiao yüeh-pao, 3.1:1-11 (1933).

-------"Chung-kuo wai-chiao shih-pai ti cheng-chieh" 中國外交失敗的癥結 (The causes of the failures of Chinese diplomacy); Wai-chiao yüeh-pao, 6.5:1-7 (1935).

Chang Hsi-t'ung. "The Earliest Phase of the Introduction of Western Political Science into China (1820-52)," The Yenching Journal of Social Studies, 5.1:1-29 (July 1950).

Chang Hung 張洪. Shih-Mien lu 使緬錄 (My mission to Burma). 1 chüan; 1833.

Chang-ku ts'ung-pien 掌故叢編 (Collected historical documents). 10 sets; Peiping: Palace Museum.

Chang Li-sheng 張厲生. Chung-kuo chih min-tsu ssu-hsiang yü min-tsu ch'i-chieh 中國之民族思想與民族氣節 (Chinese nationalistic thought and nationalistic integrity). Chungking, 1940; 269 pp.

Chang P'ei-lun 張佩綸. Chien-yü chi 澗于集 (Collection of Chang P'ei-lun). 6 chüan; 1918.

Chang Te-i 張德彝. Sui-shih jih-chi 隨史日記 (Diary of an attaché); in Hsiao-fang-hu-chai yü-ti ts'ung-ch'ao 小方壺齋輿地叢鈔 (A collection of geographical writings in the Hsiao-fang-hu-chai), Series 11, pp. 146-158b.

Chang Yin-huan 張蔭桓. San-chou jih-chi 三洲日記 (My diary in three continents). 8 chüan; Peking, 1896.

Ch'en Ch'i-yüan 陳其元. Yung-hsien-chai pi-chi 庸閒齋筆記 (Notes of Ch'en Ch'i-yüan). 8 chüan; 1874.

Ch'en Chih 陳熾. Yung-shu 庸書 (The book of utility). 4 chüan; Preface, 1896.

Ch'en Ch'iu 陳鍫. "Wu-hsü cheng-pien shih fan-pien-fa jen-wu chih cheng-chih ssu-hsiang" 戊戌政變法人物之政治思想 (Political thought of anti-reformers during the coup d'état of 1898); Yen-ching hsüeh-pao 燕京學報 (Yenching journal of Chinese studies), 25:59-106 (June 1939).

-------"Huang En-t'ung yü Ya-p'ien chan-hou wai-chiao" 黃思彤與鴉片戰後外交 (Huang En-t'ung and Chinese diplomacy after the Opium War); Shih-hsüeh nien-pao 史學年報 (Historical annual; Peking), 3.2:111-141 (Dec. 1940).

Ch'en Fang-chih 陳芳芝. "Ch'ing-tai pien-chih shu-lüeh" 清代邊制述略 (A brief account of the border institutions in the Ch'ing period); Yen-ching hsüeh-pao 燕京學報, 34:133-164 (June 1947).

Ch'en Fu-kuang 陳復光. Yu-Ch'ing i-tai chih Chung-O kuan-hsi 有清一代之中俄關係 (Sino-Russian relations during the Ch'ing period exclusively). Kunming, 1947; 464 pp.

Ch'en Kung-lu 陳恭祿. Chung-kuo chin-tai shih 中國近代史 (Chinese modern history). Shanghai, 1935; 860 pp.

Ch'en T'ao 陳弢. T'ung-chih chung-hsing ching-wai tsou-i yüeh-pien 同治中興京外奏議約編 (A concise compilation of memorials from people outside the capital during the T'ung-chih Restoration). 8 chüan; 1875.

Ch'en T'i-ch'iang 陳体強. Chung-kuo wai-chiao hsing-cheng 中國外交行政 (China's administration of foreign affairs). Chungking, 1943; 382 pp.

Ch'en Wen-chin 陳文進. "Ch'ing-tai chih Tsung-li Ya-men chi ch'i ching-fei, 1861-1884" 清代之總理衙門及其經費 1861-1884 (The Tsungli Yamen and its expenditures, 1861-1884); Chung-kuo chin-tai ching-chi-shih yen-chiu chi-k'an 中國近代經濟史研究集刊 (Studies in modern economic history of China), 1.1:49-59 (Nov. 1932).

-------"Ch'ing-chi ch'u-shih ko-kuo shih-ling ching-fei, 1875-1911" 清季出使各國使領經費 , 1875-1911 (The expenditures of the Chinese legations in foreign countries at the end of the Tsing dynasty); Studies in Modern Economic History of China, 1.2:270-310 (May 1933).

Cheng Ho-sheng 鄭鶴聲. Chin-shih Chung-Hsi shih-jih tui-chao-piao 近世中西史日對照表 (Comparative tables of Sino-Western historical dates in modern times). Shanghai, 1936; 880 pp.

Chiang-shang-ch'ien-sou 江上蹇叟 (Hsia Hsieh 夏燮). Chung-Hsi chi-shih 中西紀事 (A record of Sino-Western events). 24 chüan; 1868.

Chiang T'ing-fu, see T. F. Tsiang.

Chih-kang 志·剛. Ch'u-shih T'ai-Hsi chi 初使泰西記(The first embassy to the West). 4 chüan; 1890.

Chin An-ch'ing 金安清 , ed. "Wo-chan tse-k'o lun" 我戰則克論 (Fighting will give us victory); Ch'ang-yüan ts'ung-shu 暢園叢書 (Collected works of Ch'ang-yüan), Neng-i pien 能一編 (1894).

Chin Liang 金梁. Chin-shih jen-wu chih 近世人物志 (Men of modern times). 1934; 366 pp.

-------Ssu-ch'ao i-wen 四朝佚聞 (Episodes of four reigns). 1 chüan; 1936.

Ch'in-ting Li-fan-pu tse-li 欽定理藩部則例 (Official
     regulations of the Court of Colonial Affairs). 64 chüan; 1908.

Ch'in-ting Ta-Ch'ing hui-tien 欽定大清會典 (Collected
     statutes of the great Ch'ing empire). 100 chüan; 1899.

Chinese Social and Political Science Review, see CSPSR.

Ch'ing-chi wai-chiao shih-liao, see WCSL.

Ch'ing-kung shih-lüeh 清宮史略 (Historical sketches of the
     Ch'ing palaces). 1 chüan.

Ch'ing-shih kao, see CSK.

Ch'ing-tai wai-chiao shih-liao 清代外交史料 (Historical
     materials concerning foreign relations in the Ch'ing period).
     Peking: Palace Museum, 1932-1933.

Ch'iu, Alfred K'ai-ming. "Chinese Historical Documents of the
     Ch'ing Dynasty, 1644-1911," Pacific Historical Review,
     1:324-336 (1932).

Chou Chia-mei 周家楣. Ch'i-pu-fu-chai ch'üan-chi 期不負齋
     全集 (Complete work of the Ch'i-pu-fu studio). 14 vols.;
     1895.

Ch'ou-pan i-wu shih-mo, see IWSM.

Chu K'o-ching 朱克敬, ed. Wan-kuo tsung-shuo 萬國總說
     (A general description of all nations). 3 vols.; 1884.

-------Jou-yüan hsin-shu 柔遠新書 (A new book on foreign
     affairs). 4 vols.; 1884.

Clyde, Paul H., ed. United States Policy toward China, Diplomatic
     and Public Documents, 1839-1939. Durham, North Carolina,
     1940; 321 pp.

Cooke, George W. China: Being "The Times" Special
     Correspondent from China in the Years 1857-58. London,
     1858; 457 pp.

Cordier, Henri. Histoire des relations de la Chine avec les
　　Puissances Occidentales, 1860-1900. 2 vols.; Paris,
　　1901-1902.

-------L'expédition de chine de 1857-58, Histoire Diplomatique,
　　Notes et Documents. Paris, 1905; 478 pp.

-------L'expédition de chine de 1860, Histoire Diplomatique, Notes
　　et Documents. Paris, 1906; 460 pp.

Costin, W. C. Great Britain and China 1833-1860. Oxford, 1937;
　　362 pp.

Cranston, Earl. "Shanghai in the Taiping Period," Pacific
　　Historical Review, 5:146-160 (1936).

Creel, Herrlee G. Sinism, a Study of the Evolution of the Chinese
　　World View. Chicago, 1929; 127 pp.

CSK: Ch'ing-shih kao 清史槁 (Draft history of the Ch'ing). Peking,
　　1928; 529 chüan.

CSL: Ta-Ch'ing li–ch'ao shih-lu 大清歷朝實錄 (Veritable
　　records of successive reigns of the Ch'ing dynasty). Tokyo,
　　1937-1938. Hsien-feng period, chüan 200-356; T'ung-chih
　　period, chüan 1-374; Kuang-hsü period, chüan 1-200.

CSPSR: The Chinese Social and Political Science Review. Peiping,
　　quarterly; 1916-1937.

Dennett, Tyler. Americans in Eastern Asia. New York, 1941;
　　725 pp.

Eisele, Leona W. A Digest of the Krasnyi Arkhiv, Part II.
　　Ann Arbor, 1955; 251 pp.

En-hua Yung-ch'un 恩華詠春 . Pa-ch'i i-wen pien-mu 八旗藝
　　文編目 (Catalog of works by members of the Eight

Banners). 2 vols.

Escarra, Jean. La Chine et le Droit International. Paris, 1931;
420 419 pp.

Fairbank, John K. "The Provisional System at Shanghai in 1853-54, "
CSPSR, pt. 1, 18.4:455-504 (Jan. 1935); ibid. , pt. 2,
19.1:65-124 (Apr. 1935).

-------"The Mechanics of Imperialism in China, " Amerasia,
1:295-300 (1937).

-------"The Manchu Appeasement Policy of 1843, " Journal of the
American Oriental Society, 59.4:469-484 (Dec. 1939).

-------"Chinese Diplomacy and the Treaty of Nanking, 1842, "
The Journal of Modern History, 12.1:1-30 (Mar. 1940).

-------"Tributary Trade and China's Relations with the West, "
Far Eastern Quarterly, 1.2:129-149 (Feb. 1942).

-------"The Manchu-Chinese Dyarchy in the 1840's and '50's, "
The Far Eastern Quarterly, 12.3:265-278 (May 1953).

-------Trade and Diplomacy on the China Coast, The Opening of the
Treaty Ports, 1842-1854. 2 vols.; Cambridge, Mass. , 1953.

-------"China's Response to the West: Problems and Suggestions, "
Cahiers d'histoire Mondiale, 3.2:381-406 (1956).

-------"Synarchy under the Treaties, " in Fairbank, ed. , Chinese
Thought and Institutions. Chicago, 1957; pp. 204-231.

Fairbank, J. K. and Banno Masataka. Japanese Studies of Modern
China, A Bibliographical Guide to Historical and Social
Science Research on the 19th and 20th Centuries. Rutland,
Vermont, and Tokyo, 1955; 331 pp.

Fairbank, J. K. and S. Y. Teng. "On the Ch'ing Tributary System, "
HJAS, 6.2:135-246 (June 1941).

-------China's Response to the West. 2 vols.; Cambridge, Mass.,
    1954.

Fan Wen-lan 范文瀾 . Chung-kuo chin-tai shih 中國近代史
    (Chinese modern history). Peking, 1949; Vol. I, 543 pp.

Fang Pao 方苞 . "Chou-kuan chi-chu"周官集註(Collected
    commentaries on the Officials of Chou); in K'ang-hsi-t'ang
    ch'üan-chi 抗希堂全集　 (Complete works of K'ang-hsi-
    t'ang), ts'e 29-36; 1746.

Feng Kuei-fen 馮桂芬. Chiao pin -lu k'ang-i 校邠廬抗議
    (Protests from the Chiao-p'in Studio). 10 chüan; 1884.

Foster, John W. American Diplomacy in the Orient. Boston, 1903;
    498 pp.

Foulke, Roland R. A Treatise on International Law. 2 vols.;
    Philadelphia, 1920.

Fox, Grace. British Admirals and Chinese Pirates 1832-69.
    London, 1940; 227 pp.

Gilbert, Rodney. The Unequal Treaties: China and the Foreigner.
    London, 1929; 248 pp.

Gladstone, W. E. Speeches of the Right Hon. W. E. Gladstone,
    1844-1857. London.

Grant, General Sir Hope. Incidents in the China War of 1860.
    London and Edinburgh, 1875; 263 pp.

Gros (Baron). Livre Jaune: Négociations entre la France et la
    Chine en 1860. Paris, 1864; 248 pp.

Gumpach, J. Von. The Burlingame Mission. Shanghai, 1872;
    891 pp.

Hall, William E. A Treatise on International Law. Oxford, 1904;

764 pp.

Hart, Robert. "Note on Chinese Matters," in appendix to
Frederick W. Williams, Anson Burlingame and the First
Chinese Missions to Foreign Powers. New York, 1912.

HJAS: Harvard Journal of Asiatic Studies. Biannually; Cambridge,
Mass.

Hodgkin, Henry T. China in the Family of Nations. London, 1923;
267 pp.

Hozumi Nobushige 穗積重遠. Hōsō yawa 法窗夜話 (Nightly
discourse on law). 10th ed.; Tokyo, 1932; 385 pp.

Hsia Nai 夏鼐. "Ya-p'ien chan-cheng chung ti T'ien-tsin t'an-p'an"
鴉片戰爭中的天津談判 (The Tientsin negotiations
during the Opium War); Wai-chiao yüeh-pao 外交月報
(Foreign affairs), 4.4:43-56 (Apr. 15, 1934); ibid., 4.5:95-
123 (May 15, 1934).

Hsiao I-shan 蕭一山. Ch'ing-tai t'ung-shih 清代通史 (A
general history of the Ch'ing period). 4 vols.; Peking,
1927-1928.

-------Ch'ing-shih 清史 (History of the Ch'ing period). Taipei,
1952; 221 pp.

Hsiao Kung-ch'üan 蕭公權. Chung-kuo cheng-chih ssu-hsiang
shih 中國政治思想史 (A history of Chinese political
thought). 2 vols.; Shanghai, 1947.

Hsü Ching-ch'eng 許景澄. Hsü-wen-su-kung i-kao 許文肅公
遺稿 (Manuscripts of Hsü Ching-ch'eng, posthumous
publication). 12 chüan.

-------Hsü-wen-su-kung wai-chi 許文肅公外集 (Collected
works of Hsü Ching-ch'eng). 5 chüan. Series I, Fu-lu

附錄 (Appendix), 1 chüan; Series II, Shu-cha 書札 (Letters),
2 chüan; Series III, Jih-chi 日記 (Diary), 1 chüan.

Hsüeh Fu-ch'eng 薛福成 . Yung-an ch'üan-chi 庸盦全集
(Collected works of Hsüeh Fu-ch'eng). 21 chüan; Shanghai,
1897. Series I, Yung-an wen-pien 庸盦文編 (Literary
works), 4 chüan, with Hsü-pien 續編 (Supplements), 2 chüan,
and Wai-pien 外編 (Extra supplements), 4 chüan; Series II,
Hai-wai wen-pien 海外文編 (Overseas literary works),
4 chüan; Series III, Ch'ou-yang ch'u-i 籌洋芻議 (Discussions on foreign affairs), 1 chüan; Series IV, Ch'u-shih
Ying-Fa-I-Pi ssu-kuo jih-chi 出使英法義比四國日記
(Diary of my mission to four countries: England, France,
Italy and Belgium), 6 chüan.

-------Ch'u-shih kung-tu 出使公牘 (Official correspondence
of envoys). 10 chüan; 1897.

-------"Shu Han-yang Yeh-hsiang Kuang-chou chih pien" 書漢陽
葉相廣州之變 (On Viceroy Yeh of Han-yang and
the Canton Incident); in Tso Shun-sheng 左舜生 , Chung-
kuo chin-pai-nien shih tzu-liao 中國近百年史資料
(Materials relating to Chinese history of the last hundred
years), I, 51-63. Shanghai, 1928.

-------"Shu K'o-erh-ch'in chung-ch'in-wang Ta-ku chih-pai" 書
科爾沁忠親王大沽之敗 (On the defeat
of Prince Seng-ko-lin-ch'in at Taku); in Tso Shun-sheng,
Chung-kuo chin-pai-nien shih tzu-liao, I, 67-74.

Hu Sheng 胡繩. Ti-kuo chu-i yü Chung-kuo cheng-chih 帝國主
義與中國政治 (Imperialism and Chinese politics).
Peking, 1952; 222 pp.

Hua Kang 華岡 . Chung-kuo min-tsu chieh-fang yün-tung shih
中國民族解放運動史 (A history of the Chinese
people's liberation movement). Shanghai, 1951; 607 pp.

Huang Hung-shou 黃鴻壽 . Ch'ing-shih chi-shih pen-mo 清史
紀事本末 (A complete account of historical events in
the Ch'ing period). 80 chüan; Shanghai, 1925.

Huang Yen-yü. "Viceroy Yeh Ming-ch'en and the Canton Episode
(1856-1861)," HJAS, 6.1:37-127 (Mar. 1941).

Hummel, Arthur W., ed. Eminent Chinese of the Ch'ing Period
(1644-1912). 2 vols.; Washington, 1943.

Inaba Kunsan 稻葉君山 . Shincho zenshi 清朝全史 (Complete
history of the Ch'ing dynasty), trans. Tan Tao 但燾 .
Vol. 2, Shanghai, 1924.

IWSM: Ch'ou-pan i-wu shih-mo 籌辦夷務始末 (The complete
account of the management of barbarian affairs). Peiping,
1930. Hsien-feng period, 80 chüan; T'ung-chih period,
100 chüan.

Jones, F. C. Extraterritoriality in Japan and the Diplomatic Relations
Resulting in its Abolition, 1853-1899. New Haven, 1931;
237 pp.

Jones, J. Mervyn. "The Retroactive Effects of the Ratification of
Treaties," American Journal of International Law, 29:51-65
(1935).

Kantorovich, Anatolii. Amerika v bor'be za Kitai (America in
the struggle for China). Moscow, 1935; 639 pp.

Kearny, T. "The Tsiang Documents, Elipoo, Keying, Pottinger and
Kearny and the Most-favored-nation and Open Door Policy in

China in 1842-44--An American View, " CSPSR, 16.1:75-104.

Kellen, William V. Henry Wheaton, An Appreciation. Boston, 1902; 52 pp.

Kiernan, E. V. G. British Diplomacy in China, 1880-1885. London, 1939; 327 pp.

Ko Shih-chün 葛士濬 . Huang-ch'ao ching-shih-wen hsü-pien 皇朝經世文續編 (A supplementary compilation of noted writings of our imperial dynasty). 120 chüan; 1888.

Kuo Pin-chia 郭斌佳. "Hsien-feng-ch'ao Chung-kuo wai-chiao kai-kuan" 咸豐朝中國外交概觀(A general view on Chinese diplomacy during the Hsien-feng period); She-hui ko-hsüeh chi-k'an 社會科學季刊 (Quarterly journal of social science), 5.1:81-126 (Feb. 1935).

Kuo Sung-t'ao 郭嵩燾 . Yang-chih shu-wu ch'üan-chi 養知書屋全集 (Complete works of the knowledge-cultivating study). 30 chüan; 1892. Series I, Tsou-kao 奏稿 (Memorials), 12 chüan; Series II, Wen-chi 文集 (Literary works), 28 chüan.

-------Yü-ch'ih lao-jen tzu-hsü 玉池老人自叙 (Autobiography of Kuo Sung-t'ao). 1 chüan; 1893.

-------Sui-pien cheng-shih 綏邊徵實 (An inquiry into the reality of managing the border affairs). 1898.

-------Shih-Hsi chi-ch'eng 使西紀程 (A record of my mission to the West); in Hsiao-fang-hu-chai yü-ti ts'ung-ch'ao, Series 11, pp. 146-158b.

Kuo T'ing-i 郭廷以 . Chin-tai Chung-kuo shih 近代中國史 (Modern Chinese history). 2 vols; Changsha, 1940-1941.

LaFargue, T. E. China's First Hundred. Pullman, Washington, 1942; 176 pp.

Lane-Poole, Stanley and Frederick V. Dickins. The Life of Sir
Harry Parkes. 2 vols.; London, 1894.

Lay, Horatio N. Our Interests in China. London, 1864; 71 pp.

-------Note on the Opium Question, and Brief Survey of Our
Relations with China. London, 1893; 23 pp.

Legge, James. The Chinese Classics. 5 vols.; London, 1861-1872.

Lei Hai-tsung 雷海宗 . "Wu-ping ti wen-hua" 無兵的文化
(A civilization without soldiers); She-hui ko-hsüeh 社會科
學 (The social sciences; Peking), 1.4:1005-1030 (July 1936).

-------"Ku-tai Chung-kuo ti wai-chiao" 古代中國的外交
(Ancient Chinese diplomacy); She-hui ko-hsüeh, 3.1:1-12
(Apr. 1941).

Li Hung-chang 李鴻章 . Li-wen-chung-kung ch'üan-chi 李文忠·
公全集 (Complete works of Li Hung-chang). 165 chüan;
Shanghai, 1921. Series I, Tsou-kao 奏稿 (Memorials),
80 chüan; Series II, P'eng-liao han-kao 朋僚函稿
(Letters to friends and colleagues), 20 chüan; Series III,
I-shu han-kao 譯署函稿 (Letters to the Tsungli Yamen),
20 chüan; Series IV, Ts'an-ch'ih chiao-t'ang han-kao 竄池
敎堂函稿 (Letters relating to the Ts'an-ch'ih
church), 1 chüan; Series V, Hai-chün han-kao 海軍函稿
(Letters to the Admiralty), 4 chüan; Series VI, Tien-kao
電稿 (Telegrams), 40 chüan.

Li Shu-ch'ang 黎庶昌 . Feng-shih Lun-tun chi 奉使倫敦記
(My mission to London); in Hsiao-fang-hu chai yü-ti ts'ung-
ch'ao, Series 11.

Li Tz'u-ming 李慈銘 . Yüeh-man-t'ang jih-chi 越縵堂日記
(Diary in the Yüeh-man Study). 51 ts'e.

Liang Ch'i-ch'ao 梁啟超 . Chung-kuo ssu-shih-nien ta-shih-chi
中國四十年大事記 (Major events in China during

the last forty years); in Yin-ping-shih ho-chi 飲冰室合集 (Collected works in the ice-drinker's study), Monographs , ts'e 3.

Lin, T.C. "The Amur Frontier Question between China and Russia, 1850-1860, " Pacific Historical Review, 3:1-27 (1934).

-------"Manchuria Trade and Tribute in the Ming Dynasty: A Study of Chinese Theories and Methods of Control over Border Peoples, " Nankai Social and Economic Quarterly, 9.4:855-892 (Jan. 1937).

Liu Ch'ang-yu 劉長佑 . Liu-wu-shen-kung i-shu 劉武慎公遺書 (Writings of Liu Ch'ang-yu). 28 chüan; 1894.

Liu Chin-tsao 劉錦藻. Huang-ch'ao hsü-wen-hsien t'ung-k'ao 皇朝續文獻通考 (Supplementary encyclopedia of the imperial Ch'ing dynasty). 320 chüan; 1905.

Liu Hsi-hung 劉錫鴻. Ying-yao jih-chi 英軺日記 (Diary of Liu Hsi-hung); in Hsiao-fang-hu-chai yü-ti ts'ung-ch'ao, Series 11, pp. 160-209b.

-------Liu-kuang-lu i-kao 劉光祿遺稿 (Writings of Liu Hsi-hung). 2 chüan.

Liu, Pinghou C. "Chinese Foreign Affairs--Organization and Control. " Ph.D. thesis (New York University, 1936); 264 pp.

Liu Shu-ping 劉樹屏 . Wai-chiao kang-yao 外交綱要 (Essentials of diplomacy). Peking, 1915.

Liu Ting-sheng 柳定生 . "Kuo Sung-t'ao chuan" 郭嵩燾傳 (Biography of Kuo Sung-t'ao); Shih-ti tsa-chih 史地雜誌 (History and geography; Hangchou), 1.1:35-41 (May 1937).

Lo Meng-ts'e 羅夢册 . Chung-kuo lun 中國論 (On China). Chungking, 1943; 116 pp.

Lo Tun-yung 羅惇曧 . "Pin-tui sui-pi" 賓退隨筆 (Random notes after the guests are gone); Yung-yen 庸言 (The justice;

Tientsin), 2.5:1-16 (May 1914).

Loch, Henry B. Personal Narrative of Occurrences during Lord Elgin's Second Embassy to China in 1860. 3rd ed.; London, 1900; 185 pp.

Lu Ch'in-ch'ih 陸欽墀. "Ying-Fa lien-chün chan-chü Kwang-chou shih-mo" 英法聯軍佔據廣州始末 (A complete account of the occupation of Canton by the Anglo-French armies); Shih-hsüeh nien-pao 史學年報 (Historical annual), 2.5:265-304 (Dec. 1938).

Ma Chien-chung 馬建中. Shih-k'o-chai chi-yen 適可齋記言 (Views of Ma Chien-chung). 4 chüan; 1897.

Mai Chung-hua 麥仲華, ed. Huang-ch'ao ching-shih-wen hsin-pien 皇朝經世文新編 (A new compilation of noted writings of our imperial dynasty). 32 chüan; 1901.

Mancall, Mark. "Major-General Ignatiev's Mission to Peking, 1859-1860," Papers on China, 10:55-96. Harvard University, Center for East Asian Studies, 1956.

Martens, F.F. Le conflict entre la Russie et la Chine. Bruxelles, 1880; 75 pp.

-------Rossiia i Kitai (Russia and China). 1881; 83 pp.

Martin, W.A.P. (Ting Wei-liang), trans. Wan-kuo kung-fa 萬國公法 (Public law of all nations). 4 vols.; Peking, 1864.

-------"Traces of International Law in Ancient China," The Chinese Recorder, Vol. 14, No. 5 (Sept.-Oct. 1883).

-------A Cycle of Cathay. 2nd ed.; New York, 1897; 464 pp.

-------The Lore of Cathay. New York, 1901; 480 pp.

Marx, Francis. "Another Chapter on the Amoor," Fraser's Magazine, 63.375:318-328 (Mar. 1861).

Mason, Mary G. Western Concepts of China and the Chinese, 1840-1876. New York, 1939; 288 pp.

McCune, George. "The Exchange of Envoys between Korea and Japan during the Tokugawa Period," The Far Eastern Quarterly, 5:308-325 (May 1946).

Meadows, Thomas. The Chinese and Their Rebellions. London, 1856; 656 pp.

Meng Sen 孟森 . "Ch'ing Hsien-feng shih-nien yang-ping ju-ching chih jih-chi i-p'ien" 清咸豐十年洋兵入京之日記 一篇 (A diary concerning the entry of foreign soldiers into Peking in 1860); Shih-hsüeh chi-k'an 史學集刊 (Historical journal; Peking), 2:179-193 (Oct. 1936).

Miao Ch'üan-sun 繆荃孫 . Hsü pei-chuan chi 續碑傳集 (Supplementary collection of tombstone biographies). 86 chüan.

Michie, Alexander. The Englishman in China during the Victorian Era. 2 vols.; London, 1900.

Miyazaki Ichisada 宮崎市定 . "Shinagawa shiryō yori mitaru Ei-Futsu rengōgun no Pekin shinnyū jiken--tokuni shusenron to waheiron" 支那側史料より見たる英法聯軍の北京侵入事件 -- 特に主戰論と和平論 (The incident of the intrusion into Peking of the Anglo-French allied force as viewed from the Chinese sources, with special reference to the arguments for war and peace); Tōa kenkyū shohō 東西研究所報 , No. 24:852-884 (Oct. 1943).

Moges, Marquis de. Recollections of Baron Gros's Embassy to China and Japan in 1857-1858 (the authorized translation of Gros's Souvenirs d'une Ambassade en Chine et en Japon en 1857 et 1858). Paris, 1860; London, 1860; 368 pp.

Morison, J. L. The Eighth Earl of Elgin. Hodder and Stoughton,
　　　Ltd. , 1928; 318 pp.

Morse, Hosea Ballou. The International Relations of the Chinese
　　　Empire. 3 vols.; London, 1910-1918.

Mutrécy, Charles de. Journal de la Campagne de Chine 1859-60-61.
　　　2 vols.; Paris, 1862.

Nieh Tsung-ch'i 聶宗岐 . "Sung-Liao chiao-p'ing k'ao" 宋遼交
　　　聘考 (Embassies between Liao and Sung); Yen-ching
　　　hsüeh-pao, No. 27:1-52 (June 1940).

Nye, Gideon Jr. The Gage of the Two Civilizations: Shall
　　　Christendom Waver? Macao, 1860; 325 pp. ⊬ appendices.

Ōhira Zengo 大平善梧 . "Nihōn no kokusai ho no juyō" 日本の
　　　國際法の受容 (The reception of international
　　　law by Japan); Shōgaku Tōkyū 商學討究 , 4. 3:299-314
　　　(Dec. 1953).

Oliphant, Laurence. Narrative of the Earl of Elgin's Mission to
　　　China and Japan in the Years 1857, '58, '59. 2 vols.;
　　　London, 1859.

Oppenheim, L. International Law, ed. H. Lauterpacht. 7th ed.;
　　　2 vols.; London, 1948-1952.

Osatake Takeru 尾佐竹猛 . Kinsei Nippon no kokusai kannen no
　　　hattatsu 近世日本の國際觀念之發達 (The
　　　development of international ideas in modern Japan).
　　　Tokyo, 1932; 149 pp.

Pasvolsky, Leo. Russia in the Far East. New York, 1922; 181 pp.

Pauthier, G. Histoire des relations politiques de la Chine avec les
　　　puissances occidentales. Paris, 1859; 238 pp.

Pei-yang yang-wu chü 北洋洋務局 , ed. Yüeh-chang ch'eng-an
hui-lan 約章成案滙覽 (A comprehensive guide to
treaties, regulations, and precedents), Part II. 42 chüan.

Pelcovits, Nathan A. Old China Hands and the Foreign Office.
New York, 1948; 349 pp.

Popov, A. "Tsarskaya diplomatiya v epokhu Taipinskogo vosstaniya"
(Tsarist diplomacy during the Taiping rebellion); Krasnyi
Arkhiv (Red archives), 21:182-199 (1927).

Record of Occurrences in China, Old Series, No. 1:138-144 (June
1858). Royal Asiatic Society, North China Branch.

Reed, William B. "Private Diary," July 5, 1857-April 13, 1859. MS.
2 vols.; Library of Congress, Washington, D.C.

-------"The China Question," North American Review, 90:125-180
(1860).

Rennie, D.F. Peking and the Pekingese during the First Year of the
British Embassy at Peking, 1861-62. 2 vols.; London, 1865.

Reports of the Annual Conference (Association for the Reform and
Codification of the Law of Nations).

Rubinchek, Leonid S. A Digest of the Krasnyi Arkhiv, Part I.
Cleveland, 1947; 394 pp.

Russian Government Documents

-------Krasnyi Arkhiv (Red archives), Vol. 21 (1927).

-------Russkii Arkhiv (Russian archives), No. 3 (1878).

San hsing-shih shu-tu 三星使書牘 (Correspondence of the three
envoys). 4th ed.; 6 chüan; Shanghai, 1910.

Sargent, A.J. Anglo-Chinese Commerce and Diplomacy. Oxford,
1907; 332 pp.

Schwarzenberger, Georg. "The Rule of Law and the Disintegration of the International Society," The American Journal of International Law, 33.1:56-77 (Jan. 1939).

Shao Hsün-cheng 邵循正 . Chung-Fa Yüeh-nan kuan-hsi shih-mo 中法越南關係始末 (A complete account of Chinese-French relations concerning Annam). Peking, 1935; 215 pp.

Shen Chao-lin 沈兆霖. Shen-wen-chung-kung chi 沈文忠公集 (Collection of Shen Chao-lin). 10 chüan; 1869.

Shen Wei-tai. China's Foreign Policy 1839-1860. New York, 1932; 197 pp.

Shigematsu Toshiaki 重松俊章 . "Kanjin no gaikō shisō ni tsuite: 漢人外交思想に就て (On the Chinese idea of diplomacy); Rekishi chiri 歴史地理 (History and geography), 29.2: 155-167 (Feb. 1917); ibid., 29.3:259-268 (Mar. 1917).

Shih-liao hsün-k'an 史料旬刊 (Historical materials published every ten days), No. 1-39 (1930-1931). Peking: Palace Museum.

Shih-liao ts'ung-k'an ch'u-pien 史料叢刊初篇 (Miscellaneous historical materials, first series), compiler Lo Chen-yü 羅振玉 . 10 chüan; 1924.

Shinobu Jumpei. "Vicissitudes of International Law in the Modern History of Japan," Kokusaihō gaiko zasshi, 50.2:1-39 (Tokyo, May 1951).

Shumakher, Petr. "K istorie priobrateniya Amura, snosheniya s Kitaiem s 1848 po 1860 god" (Toward a history of appropriating the Amur--relations with China from 1848 to 1860); Russkii Arkhiv (Russian archives), 3:257-342 (1878).

Sullivan, Joseph Lewis. "Count N. N. Muraviev-Amursky."
Ph. D. thesis (Harvard University, 1955); 381 pp.

Swinhoe, Robert. Narrative of the North China Campaign of 1860,
London, 1860; 391 pp.

Swisher, Earl. "The Management of the American Barbarians:
A Study in the Relations between the United States and China
from 1840-1860." Ph. D. thesis (Harvard University, 1941);
427 pp.

-------China's Management of the American Barbarians, A Study
of Sino-American Relations, 1841-1861, with Documents.
New Haven, Conn., 1953; 844 pp.

Ta-Ch'ing lieh-ch'ao shih-lu, see CSL.

Tabohashi Kiyoshi 田保橋潔. "Shin Dōchichō gaikoku kōshi no
kinken" 清同治朝外國公使の覲見　(The audience
of foreign ministers in the T'ung-chih period of the Ch'ing);
Seikyū gakusō 青丘學叢, No. 6:1-31　(Nov. 1931).

-------"Nisshi shinkankei no seritsu--bakumatsu ishin ki ni okeru"
日支新關係の成立――幕末維新期に於ける (The
establishment of a new relationship between Japan and China
in the late Tokugawa and Restoration periods); Shigaku zasshi
史學雜誌 (Historical review), 44.2:27-63 (Feb. 1933);
ibid., 44.3:42-66 (Mar. 1933).

Tang, Edgar C. "The Censorial Institution in China, 1644-1911."
Ph. D. thesis (Harvard University, 1932); 183 pp.

Temperley, Harold and Lillian M. Penson. A Century of Diplomatic
Blue Books, 1814-1914. Cambridge, England, 1938; 600 pp.

Teng Ch'u-min 鄧初民. "Ch'ing-mo ti wai-chiao" 清末的外
交 (Late Ch'ing diplomacy); Wai-chiao chi-k'an 外交

李刊　　　(International affairs), 2.2:13-17 (Chungking, Dec. 1942).

Teng, S.Y. and J.K. Fairbank.　China's Response to the West. 2 vols.; Cambridge, Mass., 1954.

THHL:　Tung-hua hsü-lu 東華續錄 (Tung-hua supplementary records).　T'ung-chih period, 100 chüan; Kuang-hsü period, 39 chüan.

THL:　Tung-hua lu 東華錄　(Tung-hua complete records), Hsien-feng period, chüan 41-69.

Ting Pao-chen 丁寶楨.　Ting-wen-ch'eng-kung tsou-kao 丁文誠公奏稿 (Memorials of Ting Pao-chen).　26 chüan; Chengtu, 1896.

Ting Wei-liang, see W.A.P. Martin.

Ting Yün-shu 丁運樞, Ch'en Shih-hsün 陳世勲, and Ko Yü-ch'i 葛毓琦, eds.　Chang-kung hsiang-li chün-wu chi-lüeh 張公襄理軍務紀略　(A brief account of Squire Chang's contributions to military affairs).　6 chüan; 1906.

Treaties, Conventions, etc. between China and Foreign States.　2 vols.; Shanghai: Statistical Department of the Inspectorate General of Customs, 1917.

Tseng Chi-tse (Marquis Tseng).　"China: The Sleep and the Awakening, " The Chinese Recorder, 18:146-153 (1 887).

------- Tseng-hui-min-kung i-chi 曾惠敏公遺集　(Collected works of Tseng Chi-tse).　15 chüan (1893). Series I, Tsou-kao 奏稿 (Memorials), 6 chüan; Series II, Wen-chi 文集 (Literary works), 5 chüan; Series III, Shih-chi 詩集 (Poetry), 2 chüan; Series IV, Shih-Hsi jih-chi 使西日記 (Diary of my mission to the West), 2 chüan.

Tseng Kuo-fan 曾國藩 . Tseng-wen-cheng-kung ch'üan-chi 曾文
正公全集 (Complete works of Tseng Kuo-fan).
156 chüan; 1876.

Tseng Yu-hao. Modern Chinese Legal and Political Philosophy .
Shanghai, 1930; 320 pp.

Tsiang, T. F. (Chiang T'ing-fu) 蔣廷黻 . Chin-tai Chung-kuo
wai-chiao-shih tzu-liao chi-yao 近代中國外交史資料
輯要 (A collection of essential sources of Chinese
modern diplomatic history). Shanghai, 1931; Vol. 1, 413 pp.

-------"Kuo-chi kung-fa shu-ju Chung-kuo chih ch'i-yüan" 國際
公法輸入中國之起源 (The origin of the intro-
duction of international law into China); Cheng-chih hsüeh-pao
政治學報 (Journal of political science), June 1932.
Peking: National Tsing-hua University.

-------"Tsui-chin san-pai-nien Tung-pei wai-chiao-shih" 最近三百
年東北外交史 (Diplomatic history of Manchuria
in the last three hundred years); The Tsing Hua Journal 清華
學報 , 8.1:1-70 (1932).

-------"Chung-kuo yü chin-tai shih-chieh ti ta-pien-chu" 中國與
近代世界的大變局 (China and the great changes
of the modern world); The Tsing Hua Journal, 9.4:783-828
(Oct. 1934).

-------Chung-kuo chin-tai shih 中國近代史 (Chinese modern
history). Changsha, 1939; 128 pp.

-------"Notes and Suggestions: Origins of the Tsungli Yamen, "
CSPSR, 15.1:92-97 (Apr. 1931).

-------"Bismarck and the Introduction of International Law into
China, " CSPSR, 15.1:98-101 (Apr. 1931).

-------"The Secret Plan of 1858," CSPSR, 15.2:291-299 (July 1931).

-------"The Extension of Equal Commerical Privileges to Other
      Nations than the British after the Treaty of Nanking,"
      CSPSR, 15.3:422-444 (Oct. 1931).

-------"Sino-Japanese Diplomatic Relations, 1870-94," CSPSR,
      17.1:1-106 (Apr. 1933).

-------"China and European Expansion," Politica, 2.5:1-18
      (Mar. 1936).

Tso Hsi-chiu 左錫九 , ed. Hai-fang yao-lan 海防要覽 (Essential
      writings on maritime defense). 2 vols.; 1884.

Tso Tsung-t'ang 左宗棠 . Tso-wen-cheng-kung ch'üan-chi 左文
      正公全集 (Complete works of Tso Tsung-t'ang).
      100 chüan; 1888.

Tsui-chin chih wu-shih-nien 最近之五十年 (The past fifty
      years, 1872-1922). Pub. by the Shen-pao 申報 , Shanghai,
      1923, in commemoration of its Golden Jubilee.

Tung Hsün 董恂. Ti-fen shu-wu shih-wen kao 狄芬書屋詩文
      稿 (Poetic and literary manuscripts of Tung Hsün). 6 ts'e;
      1858.

Tung-hua hsü-lu, see THHL.

Tung-hua lu, see THL.

Tung, L. China and Some Phases of International Law. Shanghai,
      1940; 210 pp.

T'ung I 童嶷. "I-Man-Jung-Ti yü tung-nan-hsi-pei" 夷蠻戎狄
      與東南西北 (The I, Man, Jung, and Ti [barbarians] and
      East, South, West, and North); Yü-kung 禹貢 , 7.10:11-17
      (July 16, 1937).

Ueda Toshio 植田捷雄 . "Shina no kaikoku to kokusaihō"

支那の開國と國際法 (The opening of China and international law); Tōyō bunka kenkyu 東洋文化研究, 1.1:31-48 (Oct. 1944).

-------Tōyō gaikōshi gaisetsu 東洋外交史概説 (A survey of Far Eastern diplomatic history). Tokyo, 1948; 266 pp.

-------"Nippo no kaikoku to Chugoku" 日本の開國と中國 (The influence of the situation in China upon the opening of Japan); Kokusaihō gaikō zasshi, 49.5:88-102 (Nov. 1950).

United States Government Documents, unpublished. National Archives, Washington.

China Archives, 1844-1861. 20 vols.

China. Dispatches, Vols. 15-53, 1857-1880.

China. Embassy, Miscellaneous Correspondence, 1856-1875. 5 boxes of MS.

China. Instructions, Department of State, Vol. 1, Apr. 24, 1843-Aug. 31, 1867; Vol. 2, Sept. 13, 1867-Dec. 27, 1878.

China. Legation Archives, Consulate Records, Shanghai, Vol. 34, 1861-1863; Vol. 35, 1864; Vol. 36, 1865-1866.

China Letters Received, Department of State, 1841-1861.

China. Notes, Department of State, Vol. 1, Apr. 1, 1868-Dec. 30, 1885.

China, Notes to, Department of State, Vol. 1, June 3, 1868-Jan. 1899.

United States Government Documents, published.

---United States Congressional Documents

House Documents, 39th Congress, 1st Session (1865-1866), Vol. 1, Pt. 2, No. 1245.

House Executive Documents, 33rd Congress, 1st Session, No. 123; 38th Congress, 1st Session (1863-1864), Vol. 2, No. 1181; 38th Congress, 2nd Session (1864-1865), Vol. 3,

No. 1218.

Senate Executive Documents, 32nd Congress, 1st Session, No.
   38; 35th Congress (1857-1858), 1st Session, No. 47; 35th
   Congress, 2nd Session, No. 22; 36th Congress (1859-1860),
   1st Session, Vol. 10, No. 30.

---USFR: Foreign Relations of the United States, 1860-1880.

USFR, see U.S. Government Documents.

Vattel, E. The Law of Nations. New York, 1796; 563 pp.

Wade, T. "On China," The China Review, 1.1:38-44 (July-Aug.
   1872); ibid., 1.2:118-124 (Sept.-Oct. 1872).

Walrond, Theodore. Letters and Journals of James, Eighth Earl
   of Elgin. London, 1872; 467 pp.

Walsh, Warren B. "The Beginnings of the Burlingame Mission,"
   Far Eastern Quarterly, 4.3:274-277 (May 1945).

-------"A Bandit Threat to the Burlingame Mission," Far Eastern
   Quarterly, 5.4:455-460 (Aug. 1946).

Wang Chih-ch'un 王之春 . Ko-kuo t'ung-shang shih-mo chi 各國
   通商始末記 (A complete account of trading with the
   various nations); also known as Kuo-ch'ao jou-yüan chi 國朝
   柔遠記 (An account of the imperial dynasty's benevolence
   toward men from afar). 20 chüan; 1895.

Wang K'ai-yün 王闓運 . Hsiang-i-lou jih-chi 湘綺樓日記
   (Diary in the Hsiang-i Chamber). 32 ts'e; 1927.

Wang Mao-yin 王茂蔭 . Wang-shih-lang tsou-i 王侍郎奏議
   (Memorials of Vice-President Wang). 11 chüan; 1887.

Wang, S.T. The Margary Affair and the Chefoo Agreement.
   Oxford, 1940; 138 pp.

Wang T'ing-hsi 王廷熙 and Wang Shu-min 王樹敏, eds. Huang-
   ch'ao Tao-Hsien-T'ung-Kuang tsou-i, 皇朝道咸同光奏議

xxix

(Memorials of the Tao-kuang, Hsien-feng T'ung-chih, and Kuang-hsü periods of our imperial dynasty). 64 chüan; Shanghai, 1902.

Wang Tsao-shih 王造時. "San-ch'ien-nien lai i-ta pien-chü" 三千年來一大變局 (A great change in the three-thousand-year history of China); in Hsin-yüeh yüeh-k'an 新月月刊 (New moon monthly), 3.10:1-17.

Wang T'un-ling 王桐齡. "Han-T'ang chih ho-ch'in cheng-ts'e" 漢唐之和親政策 (The policy of diplomacy by marriage during the Han and T'ang periods); Shih-hsüeh nien-pao, No. 1 (Peking, July 10, 1929).

WCSL: Ch'ing-chi wai-chiao shih-liao 清季外交史料 (Historical materials concerning foreign relations in the late Ch'ing period, 1875-1911). Peiping, 1932-1935; Kuang-hsü period, 30 chüan.

Wei Yüan 魏源. Hai-kuo t'u-chih 海國圖志 (An illustrated gazetteer of the maritime countries). 100 chüan; 1852.

Wen Chin. The Chinese Crisis from within. London, 1901; 354 pp.

Wen-hsiang 文祥. Wen-wen-chung-kung shih-lüeh 文文忠公事略 (A brief account of Wen-hsiang's life). 4 chüan; 1882.

Wen-hsien ts'ung-pien 文獻叢編 (Collectanea from the Historical Records Office). 37 sets.

Wheaton, Henry. Elements of International Law. 6th ed.; Boston, 1855; 728 pp.

Williams, Frederick W., ed. "The Journal of S. Wells Williams, LL.D.," Journal of the North-China Branch of the Royal Asiatic Society, 42:1-232 (1911).

-------Anson Burlingame and the First Chinese Mission to Foreign Powers. New York, 1912; 370 pp.

-------"The Mid-Victorian Attitude of Foreigners in China,"

Journal of Race Development, 8.4:411-430 (Apr. 1928).

Williams, S. Wells. "Narrative of the American Embassy to Peking,"
Journal of the North-China Branch of the Royal Asiatic
Society, No. 3:315-349 (Dec. 1859).

Wilson, George G. "The Family of Nations Idea and Japan," The
Journal of Race Development, 2.3:246-255 (Jan. 1912).

Wo-jen 倭仁. Wo-wen-tuan-kung i-shu 倭文端公遺書
(Works of Wo-jen). 11 chüan; Peking, 1862.

Wodehouse, H.E., trans. "Mr. Wade on China," part 1, The China
Review (Hongkong), 1.1:38-44 (July-Aug. 1872); part 2, ibid.
1.2:118-124 (Sept. -Oct. 1872).

Wright, Mary C. The Last Stand of Chinese Conservatism, The
T'ung-chih Restoration, 1862-1874. Stanford, 1957; 426 pp.

Wright, Stanley F. China's Struggle for Tariff Autonomy 1843-1938.
Shanghai, 1938; 775 pp.

-------Hart and the Chinese Customs. Belfast, 1950; 949 pp.

Wrong, George M. The Earl of Elgin. London, 1905; 294 pp.

Wu Ch'eng-chang 吳成章. Wai-chiao-pu yen-ko chi-lüeh 外交
部沿革記略 (A brief account of the development of the
Ministry of Foreign Affairs). 2 vols.; Ministry of Foreign
Affairs, 1913.

Wu Hsiang-hsiang 吳相湘. Wan-Ch'ing kung-t'ing shih-chi 晚
清宮廷實紀 (Veritable accounts of the palaces in the
late Ch'ing). Taipei, 1952; 258 pp.

Wu Hung-chu. "China's Attitude towards Foreign Nations and
Nationals Historically Considered," CSPSR, 10.1:13-45.

Wu Ju-lun 吳汝綸. T'ung-ch'eng Wu-hsien-sheng jih-chi 桐城
吳先生日記 (The diary of Mr. Wu of T'ung-ch'eng).
16 chüan; 1928.

Wu K'o-tu 吳可讀. Hsi-hsüeh-t'ang wen-chi 攜雪堂文集
(Literary collection of Wu K'o-tu). 4 chüan; 1900.

-------"Ying-Fa lien-chün shih-tai chih Pei-ching ching-hsiang" 英
法聯軍時代之北京景象 (Situations in Peking
during the time of the Anglo-French campaign); in Tso Shun-
sheng 左舜生, Chung-kuo chin-pai-nien shih tzu-liao
hsü-pien, pp. 125-132.

Yang Hung-lieh 楊鴻烈. "Chi Kuo Sung-t'ao ch'u-shih Ying-Fa"
記郭嵩燾出使英法 (On Kuo Sung-t'ao's mission to
England and France); Part I, Ku-chin 古今, No. 11: 11-15
(Nov. 16, 1942); Part II, ibid., No. 12:29-32 (Dec. 1, 1942).

-------"Chung-kuo she-chih chu-I shih-kuan ti ching-kuo" 中國設
置駐義使館的經過 (The establishment of the
Chinese legation in Italy); Ku-chin, No. 25:11-15 (June
16, 1943); ibid., No. 26:19-23 (July 1, 1943).

Yano Jinichi 矢野仁一 Kindai Shina ron 近代支那論 (On
modern China). Tokyo, 1927; 373 pp.

-------Kindai Shina shi 近代支那史 (Modern Chinese history). Tokyo,
1928; 561 pp.

-------Kinsei Shina gaiko shi 近世支那外交史 (Modern
Chinese diplomatic history). Tokyo, 1935; 946 ≠ 24 pp.

Yin Chao-yung 殷兆鏞. Yin P'u-ching shih-lang tzu-ting nien-p'u
殷譜經侍郎自定年譜 (Vice-President Yin Chao-
yung's chronological autobiography). 2 vols.

Yin Keng-yün 尹耕雲. Hsin-pai-shih-chai chi 心百石齋集
(Collection of the Hsin-pai-shih Study). 4 chüan; 1885.

Yu Ch'ang-ho 余長河. "Kuo Sung-t'ao yü Chung-kuo wai-chiao"
郭嵩燾與中國外交 (Kuo Sung-t'ao and Chinese
diplomacy); I-ching 逸經, No. 31:21-24 (1937).

Chang Ch'ien 張騫

Chang I 張儀

Chang Kuo-liang 張國樑

Chang P'ei-lun 張佩綸

Chang Ssu-kuei 張斯桂

Chang Te-i 張德彞

Chao Te-che 趙德轍

Chen-tsung 真宗

Ch'en Ch'i-chang 陳其璋

Ch'en Chih-ho 陳之鶴

Ch'en Ch'in 陳欽

Ch'en Lan-pin 陳蘭彬

Ch'en Su 陳濬

chi-mi 羈縻

Ch'i-shan 琦善

Ch'i-ying (Kiying, Keying) 耆英

Chiang Tun-fu 蔣敦復

Ch'iang 羌

Ch'ien Pao-ching 錢寶青

ch'in-ch'ai ta-ch'en 欽差大臣

Ching 荊

Ching-ch'ung fu 景崇府

ching-t'ien fa-tsu 敬天法祖

Ch'ing-ch'ang 慶常

Chou Tsu-p'ei 周祖培

Chu-ko Liang 諸葛亮

Chung-hsing Shuo 中行說

Ch'ung 蟲

Ch'ung-hou 崇厚

Ch'ung-lun (Tsunglun) 崇綸

Chü-wai p'ang-kuan lun 局外旁
      觀論

Ch'üan 犬

Fang Chün-shih 方濬師

Feng-i 馮儀

Heng-fu 恒福

Ho Chin-shou 何金壽

Ho Hsiu 何休

Ho Jih-chang 何日璋

Ho Kuei-ch'ing 何桂清

Hsiao Hsing-jen 小行人

Hsiao Wang-chih 蕭望之

Hsien-liang Monastery 賢良寺

Hsin-i lüeh-lun 新議略論

Hsiung-nu 匈奴

Hsü Chi-yü 徐繼畬

Hsü Ch'ien-shen 許鈐身

Hsü Ching-ch'eng 許景澄

Hsü P'eng-shou 許彭壽

Hsüeh Fu-ch'eng 薛福成

Hsüeh Huan 薛煥

Hua-sha-na 花沙納

Huang Hui-ho 黃惠和

Huang Tsung-han 黃宗漢

Hui-t'ung kuan 會同館

Hui-t'ung ssu-i kuan 會同四夷館

I-hsin, Prince Kung 恭親王奕訢
I-i chih-i 以夷制夷
I-kuan ling-ch'eng 譯官令丞
I-li (Kuldja) 伊黎
I-li-pu 伊里布
I-shan 奕山
Indosscythians 月氏

jen 仁
jen-ch'en wu wai-chiao 人臣無外交
Jui-lin 瑞麟

K'an-feng chuan-to 看風轉舵
k'ao-cheng 考証
Kuan-wen 官文
Kuei-liang 桂良
Kuo Sung-t'ao 郭嵩燾
Kung, Prince 恭親王
Kung Chao-yuan 龔照瑗
kyorin 交鄰

Lao Ch'ung-kuang 勞崇光
li 禮
Li Ch'ang-hua 李常華
Li-fan-yüan 理藩院
Li Feng-pao 李鳳苞
Li Hsien 李賢

Li Hung-chang 李鴻章
Li Han-chang 李瀚章
Li K'ai-fang 李開芳
Li-pu 吏部
Li Tsung-hsi 李宗羲
Liang Ch'en 梁誠
Liao 遼
Lin Feng-hsiang 林鳳翔
Lin Tse-hsü 林則徐
Liu Ching 劉敬
Liu Hsi-hung 劉錫鴻
Liu K'un-i 劉坤一

Ma Hsin-i 馬新貽
Man 蠻
Mao Hung-t'u 毛鴻圖
Mien-yü, Prince Hui 惠親王綿愉

Ming-shan 明善
Mitsukuri Rinsho 箕竹麟祥
Mu-chang-a 穆彰阿

Newchwang 牛莊
Nishi Amane 西周

Okubo Toshimichi 大久保利通

Pan Ch'ao 班超
P'an Shih-ch'eng 潘仕成
Pei-t'ang 北塘
Pei-yang ta-ch'en 北洋大臣

P'eng Yün-chang 彭蘊章
Piao 表
Pin-ch'un 斌椿

sadae 事大
Seng-ko-lin-ch'in 僧格林沁
Shang Yang 商鞅
Shen Pao-chen 沈葆楨
Shih-Hsi chi-ch'eng 使西紀程
Shih Tsan-ch'ing 石贊清
Shu 舒
Soeshima Taneomi 副島種臣
Ssu-i-kuan 四夷 (譯) 館
Su, Prince 肅親王
Su Ch'in 蘇秦
Su Shih 蘇軾
Su-shun 肅順

Ta-Ch'ing hui-tien 大清會典
Ta Hsing-jen 大行人
Ta hung-lu 大鴻臚
ta-t'ung 大同
T'an T'ing-hsiang 譚廷襄
T'an-yüan 澶淵
Tengchow 登州
Ti 狄
t'i-chih 體制
Tien-k'o 典客
Ting Pao-chen 丁寶楨
Tsai-yüan, Prince I 怡親王載垣

Ts'en Yü-ying 岑毓英
Tseng Chi-tse 曾紀澤
Tso Tsung-t'ang 左宗棠
Tuan Ch'eng-shih 段誠實
Tuan Ch'ing-ch'uan 段晴川
Tungchow (T'ung-chou) 通州
Tung Hsün 董恂

Wan Ch'ing-li 萬青藜
Wang An-shih 王安石
Wang Feng-tsao 王鳳藻
Wang K'ai-t'ai 王凱泰
Wang K'ai-yün 王闓運
Wang Mao-yin 王茂蔭
Wang Sung-sen 王松森
Wei Yüan 魏源
Wen-hsiang 文祥
Wo-jen 倭仁
Wu Ch'ung-yao 伍崇曜
Wu-erh-kun-tai 烏爾棍泰
Wu-sun 烏孫

Yanagihara Sakimitsu 柳原前光
Yang Ju 楊儒
yang-wu 洋務
Yang T'ing-hsi 楊廷熙
Yang Ch'en 楊晨
Yin Chao-yung 殷兆鏞
Yin Keng-yün 尹耕雲

Ying-han 英翰　　　Yü-ch'ien 裕謙
Yung Hung 容閎　　Yüan Teh-hui 袁德輝
Yung-cheng 雍正